Marketing Graffiti

Radical and unique in its approach and presentation, *Marketing Graffiti* turns the traditional marketing introduction on its head by helping students to understand the part they already play as 'consumers' in the marketing process.

Most marketing textbooks tackle the subject as a business function, i.e. how to 'do' marketing in companies and other organizations. *Marketing Graffiti* shows how marketing is not just a business function but a part of our culture, and one in which we are all active as part-time marketers.

By rejecting managerially driven structures in this way, Saren's approach makes marketing immediate and instantly recognizable as a process and a phenomenon in which we are already complicit. It helps readers to become aware of what they already know.

Critically examining a wide range of products, businesses, technologies, information, services, advertisements, packaging and branding, Saren utilizes everyday images and phenomena to draw out the conceptual foundations of marketing from a social science and cultural studies perspective as something that we all experience in everyday life.

This new edition of the first critical marketing textbook discusses the role new technologies (such as social media) play in marketing culture and how this can potentially place more power in the clicks of the consumer. It includes new, updated or expanded sections on market exclusion, the role of the consumer in innovation, space and place, pricing, consumer communities, collaborative consumption and social media marketing. Leading experts in these fields of research and marketing practice also contribute additional sections on these topics.

This essential marketing guide is supported by a range of teaching support materials including the latest journal and online references, guides to further reading, teaching slides and test bank questions.

Michael Saren is Professor of Marketing at the University of Leicester, UK. He has an honorary fellowship of the UK Academy of Marketing, a PhD from the University of Bath and a visiting professorship at Birmingham University. He was a founding editor of the journal *Marketing Theory*.

Marketing Graffiti

The Writing On the Wall

Second Edition

Michael Saren

Routledge
Taylor & Francis Group

LONDON AND NEW YORK

Second edition published 2018
by Routledge
2 Park Square, Milton Park, Abingdon, Oxon OX14 4RN

and by Routledge
711 Third Avenue, New York, NY 10017

*Routledge is an imprint of the Taylor & Francis Group, an
informa business*

[First edition published by Butterworth-Heinemann 2006]

British Library Cataloguing-in-Publication Data
A catalogue record for this book is available from the British
Library

Library of Congress Cataloging-in-Publication Data
Names: Saren, Michael, author.
Title: Marketing graffiti : the writing on the wall / Michael
    Saren.
Description: Abingdon, Oxon ; New York, NY :
    Routledge, 2018. | Earlier editon published in 2006 as:
    Marketing graffiti : the view from the street. | Includes
    bibliographical references and index.
Identifiers: LCCN 2017014352 (print) | LCCN 2017031054
    (ebook) | ISBN 9781315795300 (eBook) |
    ISBN 9781138013322 (hardback : alk. paper) |
    ISBN 9781138013339 (pbk. : alk. paper)
Subjects: LCSH: Marketing.
Classification: LCC HF5415 (ebook) | LCC HF5415 .S2748 2018
    (print) | DDC 658.8—dc23
LC record available at https://lccn.loc.gov/2017014352

ISBN: 978-1-138-01332-2 (hbk)
ISBN: 978-1-138-01333-9 (pbk)
ISBN: 978-1-315-79530-0 (ebk)

Typeset in Frutiger
by Apex CoVantage, LLC

Visit the companion website:
www.routledge.com/cw/Saren

CONTENTS

List of figures

List of Tables

List of contributors

Dr Mairead Brady
Trinity College Dublin, Ireland
Information technology sections

Professor Christina Goulding
University of Birmingham, UK
Why consume?

Annmarie Hanlon
University of Derby, UK
Social media marketing

Professor Gerard Hastings
University of Stirling, UK
Building social relationships

Professor Christopher Moore
Glasgow Caledonian University, UK
Fast fashion branding

Professor Jaqueline Pels
Universidad Torcuato Di Tella,
Argentina
*A network perspective to business
relationships*

Professor Emmanuella Plakoyiannaki
University of Leeds, UK
*Organizational processes and
capabilities*

Dr Cláudia Simões
Open University, UK
Corporate identity and branding

Dr Georgia Stavraki
University of Surrey, UK
*Organizational processes and
capabilities*

Professor Julie Tinson
University of Stirling, UK
The role of communications

writing on walls

As consumers in a marketing culture we are also part-time marketers. We all write on walls too, metaphorically at any rate.

The book is organized in six main chapters. You can read them in any order.

This book is the first access point to your knowledge of today's marketing values. You can begin at any chapter and follow the key links between sections. Essential further reading and any links are indicated after each section, with full references at the end of the chapter.

About this book

In theory, marketing ought to be all about consumers, but most marketing books discuss the subject as a business discipline, from a managerial point of view. It can't just be about consumers though. There are also important wider effects of marketing on society and the environment which have to be considered. Yet most textbooks still approach the subject in a how-to-do-it fashion; i.e. how to organize and manage marketing in companies and other organizations. But marketing is not just about being a marketing manager, and it occurs in many places other than businesses and organizations.

In today's world marketing is all encompassing. Everything is marketed – the church, politics, science, history, celebrities, careers, sport, art, fiction, fact. Marketing involves promotion, selling and consumption. However, marketing is more than just an economic activity. It drives the consumer society, a culture of consumption, for which it is often criticized. Marketing affects everybody – as consumers we cannot escape the market, even those of us who try to live simply.

Consumers are not just passive recipients of what marketers do. We all re-interpret marketing messages; display brand logos; present ourselves through what we consume; make choices; complain; window shop; view celebrities; compete with other consumers. This book explains marketing *as consumers experience it*, as active participants in it as well as the target subjects of it.

Marketing may appear to affect more and more of the world nowadays, but its powerful effects are not new. Over the centuries, trade, exchange, what we now call marketing, influenced how and why empires were built, technologies were applied, property law developed, transport routes were constructed, the shopping architecture of cities evolved, languages were adopted and spread. It was in order to calculate market exchange that Europeans imported mathematical symbols from Babylon and India.

Since then markets have developed to cover the whole world. This has had social as well as economic consequences. One of the consequences of consumer culture has been the rise of consumerism and a shift away from values of community and citizenship towards those of materialism and competition. Individuals' participation in markets as legitimate consumers is an essential aspect of social cohesion and social relations.

But the marketplace is not a level playing field and free markets are rarely completely 'free'. In most markets, power relations between buyers and sellers and other intermediaries are far from equal and some people are better equipped to thrive in this competitive global market context than others.

The prevailing managerial and consumer cultural view of marketing has extended its reach into just about every aspect of business, public, civil, charitable and even military and scientific activity in modern societies. It could, some experts have argued it should, be applied to just about everything (see McKenna, R. (1991) Marketing is everything. *Harvard Business Review*, Jan/Feb; and Kotler, P. (1972) A generic concept of marketing, *Journal of Marketing*, **36**, April: 46–54.).

This book agrees that marketing today can be applied to everything. But this doesn't mean that it *should* be applied everywhere. It is not a straightforward matter of organizing marketing as an integrated system of core activities, nor is it just about the managerial aspects of marketing decisions and behaviour, nor just about selling and advertising or distribution and retailing – and certainly not marketing as the *control* of consumers. On the contrary, ideally marketing should be about informing, supplying and enabling consumers, helping them consume better (which could mean less), creating their own value (sometimes for themselves) and using their market power for wider ends in society than simply consumption.

This is the approach to marketing which this book aims to explain.

The contents

Topics in this book reflect the view of marketing as a social and cultural phenomenon, not just a business function. Therefore, this book does not adopt the managerial approach, unlike most textbooks. Rather, it seeks to explain how consumers, organizations, society can and do use marketing, for example in areas of social marketing and the construction of consumer 'identity'. The subject is considered from a relational perspective as a social science – that is, how people and organizations relate to each other in and through marketing.

It takes a critical perspective on the values of marketing, not only 'market value'. Beyond a critique of unethical marketing practices, it questions and analyses established traditional marketing theories and the assumptions behind them.

The structure is not organized according to the core marketing functions used in companies – advertising, distribution, strategy, sales, product development, etc. It does, though, introduce how companies and managers think and go about marketing in their businesses, but not in the terms found in traditional textbooks. This book does not explain these using the old concepts and the gendered, militarized language of traditional marketing – strategy and tactics, campaigns and offensives, intelligence and planning, control and implementation, targeting, market penetration, winning customers, beating competitors.

Instead, the content covers how marketing creates solutions; how marketers build relations with customers, other companies, society; how they build brands, use mass and social media; how marketing moves space and time.

This book is not written from a single authorial perspective. It includes expert contributions on specific topics from experienced academics and practitioners, who cover a range of views about the subject. These contributions are written in different styles and presented here in different ways, allowing for variety and reflecting the bricolage subject that is marketing.

For readers

This is not only an introductory textbook aimed at readers who are studying marketing. It is written also for advanced undergraduate and postgraduate students who want an alternative type of text taking a different approach. Many teachers of marketing have been clamouring for a new type of non-managerial text, beyond the '4Ps'. Hopefully the structure and contents here will enable and encourage marketing to be taught in many different ways.

This book will hopefully not put off the general reader. It is a short introductory book which covers the latest ideas. We are all consumers affected by marketing. If you are curious to understand how, and perhaps keen to change some of it, this book provides a starting point for some answers.

How to use this book

If you are studying marketing for the first time, this book provides a short overview of the subject from a broad perspective. It provides a topical introduction to the range of activities and effects that marketing involves nowadays. It aims to be easy to read, allowing you the reader to start with whichever topic interests you and follow through the cross-referenced links to related issues. Hopefully, whichever way you read it, you will get a flavour of the subject and can check out topics in greater depth using the suggestions for further reading.

Advanced students of the subject, already familiar with marketing theories and concepts, will find this book provides an alternative approach to the widely used texts, sets the subject in its wider contexts and covers the latest thinking, drawing on relevant ideas from associated literature beyond conventional marketing.

Those readers who work in almost any organization, or for themselves, will find in these pages some useful ideas about marketing, from a more wide-ranging perspective. Some of you may want to put this relational, critical approach to the subject into practice. This requires a fundamental reappraisal of what constitutes marketing activity, which cannot be reduced and simplified into a set of point-by-point managerial prescriptions. For those readers interested in taking the implications for business and society further, the book provides a guide to the reading and rethinking required.

For teachers of marketing who are looking for an alternative way of introducing the subject to new students or developing new approaches for advanced classes, *Marketing Graffiti* can be used as an alternative and/or supplementary text. Your course can be built around the variable structure and links in the book, using your own further reading in addition to that suggested here.

marketing contexts

Marketing does not take place in isolation. This chapter outlines the wide range of contexts which affect and are affected by marketing activities. Many of these, such as society, culture and the media, are outside the organizations undertaking the marketing work. Others are inside the organization, which raises key issues about where marketing takes place and who does it. Another question is what are markets? We will see that they can be viewed in different ways, and the perspective that is chosen fundamentally affects how marketing operations are analysed and conducted. This section also reviews the values, ethics and history of marketing itself which lie behind the activities that today are undertaken in its name.

Views of markets

This section is about the alternative perspectives or *ways of looking at markets* taken by authors in marketing. In order to study and understand what marketing is about, it is important to be clear what a market actually is. And this is not as straightforward as it might appear because there are many views of what characterizes a market – differences between academic subjects such as economics and psychology, differences between management disciplines such as marketing and strategy, and even, as we shall see, different views of markets within marketing. These issues are separate from the different views people have as to whether markets are *good or bad things*, which are discussed in the section on Marketing values.

In this section five views of markets are outlined:

- Markets as exchange
- Markets as competition
- Markets as collaboration
- Markets as information
- Markets as practice.

Markets as exchange

Any market must have certain core elements, namely a buyer, a seller and *some form of exchange between the two*. What is exchanged can be a product, a service, knowledge, meaning, time saved, an agreement or a promise. As in the case of a gift or a free offer, there even need not be money exchanged in return – although many would argue that *something* must be returned, if only satisfaction or obligation (see Consuming Experience).

There is also no need for the consumer to meet the buyer, even to know who they are. Internet markets are obvious examples, though more generally you do know who has exchanged or who makes a book you are reading. For example, you may have bought this book in a bookstore or perhaps on the internet, but the author has no direct contact with you, nor necessarily does the publisher. Your purchase was the result of a series of exchanges, a long supply chain (see Moving Space), from woodcutter, to paper manufacturer, to printer, to publisher, to bookseller, to you.

If there is an exchange between buyer and seller, both parties must expect to gain something. If there were no anticipation of mutual benefit, then there would be no incentive for each to conduct the exchange. The benefit may not actually occur – e.g. when the product fails to satisfy the customer (if you don't like this book) or the buyer fails to pay the buyer (if you stole this book) – but each party must believe that they will benefit from the market exchange.

Things a market requires:

- *A buyer*
- *A seller*
- *An exchange*
- *Information and knowledge*
- *Something which is exchanged*
- *Potential for mutual benefit.*

Things a market does not require:

- *Money*
- *Direct contact.*

So, one way to view markets is as a transaction or exchange.

Exchange theory assumes that human beings are need-directed with a natural tendency to try and improve their material circumstances. It has its foundations in psychology and economics (Housten & Grassenheimer, 1987). At the consumer behavioural level, then, in order to encourage consumers' readiness to spend their money with a particular firm, marketers must provide them with something beneficial in exchange. Exchange involves the transfer of tangible or intangible items between two or more social actors (Bagozzi, 1978).

Many authors view it this way. In his influential text *Marketing: Theory and Practice*, Baker (1995) also takes a marketing-as-exchange position, calling for efforts to improve our understanding of the manner in which the marketing system works 'which underlies the need to develop a workable theory of exchange'.

Markets as competition

Another way to view markets is in terms of competition. All markets must have a degree of competition involved. This view has three types or dimensions of competition:

1 *Sellers competing with each other for markets, i.e. for sales or buyers.* This form of competition can be seen in most industries, with the exception of monopolies where there is only one firm selling in the market. Even here, though, there is often a substitute from another industry which buyers can choose, e.g. customers can choose gas or electricity as power, and rail or bus transport. So even if there is only one supplier in each market, the availability of alternatives means that a monopoly firm in these cases still has to compete with other industries for buyers' choice.

2 *Buyers competing with each other for sellers' offerings on the market, i.e. for goods, services or other purchases.* You only have to attend an auction or watch buyers at cut price sales to observe competition of buyers against each other. Unless there is great over-supply relative to the strength of demand from customers, they will always effectively be in competition with each other for availability and lower prices; also sometimes buyers compete in the way they use and display their purchases (see Consuming Experience).

3 *Sellers competing with buyers, i.e. for best price or terms.* Even where there is only one seller and one buyer and one product and no alternative substitutes, there may be no competition in terms of types 1 or 2 above, but there still normally is an element of competition between the buyer and the seller. This occurs because each tries to maximize their benefits from the transaction, which in some markets takes the form of negotiation, bargaining or 'haggling' over the price and quantity bought. For example, if as a result of the negotiation a lower price results then the buyer benefits, and where a higher price results then the supplier gains.

Early marketing writers adapted theories of competitive advantage from economics and strategic management (Chamberlin, 1933; Alderson, 1957). The ability of a firm to create and maintain competitive advantage over rival firms is a central objective of its marketing strategy. The way in which this ability can be

achieved depends on various factors, including: unique (hard to imitate) capabilities of the firm (e.g. skills of employees, higher quality products); the conditions of the business environment (e.g. government regulation, technological advances); the number and intensity of rival firms in the industry (e.g. barriers to new firms entering); the conditions in the marketplace (e.g. customers' loyalty, retailers' power); as well as the overall competitive strategy followed by a firm (Porter, 1985).

So, according to this view, markets are *competitive arenas* where firms aim to achieve competitive advantage over their rivals. To some extent they are limited in their ability to achieve this because of the industry, technology and market conditions, but it is important to note the *proactive nature* of the firms' strategies, which can be achieved through strategic decision-making that is firmly based on knowledge superior to their rivals (Nonaka, 1994).

Markets as collaboration

Another view of markets highlights the fact that buyers and sellers not only compete, they also often collaborate. This emphasis has developed in the past 20 years largely due to the wider influence of the business thinking and culture of firms from the Far East and Asia. For example, Japanese business methods and ideas of collaboration, quality control, employee relations and procurement practices have all had an enormous impact on business methods and thinking in the West. Chinese culture and business also operates with the notion of *Guanxi* (see Marketing values).

So also in marketing, several authors agree with Gummesson (1997b) that 'collaboration in a market economy needs to be treated with the same attention and respect as competition'. Rindova and Fombrun (1999) argued that a firm's competitive advantage depends on three key elements:

1 The efforts of the firm
2 The conditions of the environment
3 'The nature of the firm–constituent interactions'.

This last point refers to collaboration by the firm with other 'constituencies', i.e. suppliers, buyers, distributors, consumers, media, sponsors. Rindova and Fombrun pointed out that competitive advantage can also be built on relationships and that 'relationships with constituents . . . are not just exchanges but sustained social interactions in which past impressions affect future behaviours', a view which is similar to the 'network theory' of competitive advantage (e.g. Håkansson & Snehota, 1995).

The types of collaboration in markets can be much broader than this, however. Three main types of collaborations can be identified, similar to those of competition:

1 Firms collaborate with other firms, even competitors – in alliances and joint ventures. For instance, airlines collaborate to provide global services (e.g. British Airways, Qantas, Iberia) and IT firms combine with suppliers and business partners to provide a 'platform' or whole offering for customers, e.g. Pentium, Intel, IBM.
2 Buyers also collaborate with each other. This can be a formal cooperation, such as customer cooperatives, buying clubs, user groups (e.g. services, gyms, health), enthusiast societies (e.g. car owners, football supporters). Alternatively, this can be an informal or social arrangement – information sharing, instruction, friends.
3 Buyers and sellers collaborate. The very act of buying requires information sharing, dialogue, agreement and trust between the buying and selling parties. Especially in business-to-business (B2B) and service markets, the buyer is often involved with the seller in producing or making together some key aspect of the delivery or transaction or use.

The idea of markets as collaboration links to the fields of relationship and network marketing (see Building Relations), which developed from studies of Business to Business (B2B) and services marketing where collaboration and relationships have been found to be *central* to success. Although one review identified at least 36 separate definitions of the field (Harker, 1998), all these relational approaches emphasize long-term collaboration (as opposed to competition and exchange) between market and social actors.

It is actually possible for *all* marketing activities, problems, systems and behaviour to be conceptualized and conducted by focusing on the collaborations involved to identify best practices, analyse behaviour and provide solutions (see Creating Solutions). For example, network theory has been applied extensively to industrial marketing by the North European IMP group (see Mattsson, 1985; Ford, 1990). This has enabled them to explain the behaviour of marketing systems in terms of networks of relationships and collaboration using sophisticated sociometric methods, exchange theory and even chaos theory.

Payne (1995) pointed out that firms operate in several different types of markets (see Figure 1.1).

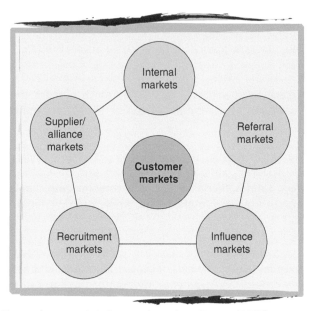

Figure 1.1 Six markets model. *Source*: based on Payne (1995)

Markets as information

When a sale takes place, it is not only products, services and money that are exchanged – so too is information. Indeed, certain information must be known by both parties beforehand *in order for a sale to occur*. For example, sellers need to know how to reach buyers and how to communicate with them; buyers have to know where and how to buy, how to use the product and its price. So markets can be viewed as a process by which information and knowledge is produced, communicated and exchanged (see Moving Space: Moving information – the role of IT). Adverts, prices, availability, delivery, place of purchase and how to best use products are all types of *information that are useful for customers*.

Sellers also need information in order to engage in a market. Because satisfying consumers is the central focus of marketing (see Marketing values), marketers need information about consumers, their wants and needs, and what will satisfy them. Consumer information aids marketing decision-making, therefore pricing decisions, promotion decisions, product decisions, distribution decisions, etc. should all be aimed at satisfying the consumer. This requires more than details about what they buy, where, etc.; knowledge about their needs, future preferences and, preferably, what affects them is needed. For example, the use of loyalty cards in retail stores is not just to encourage repeat visits by customers (i.e. 'loyalty'), but also to produce on a daily basis lots of useful information about buyers' purchasing habits (see Creating Solutions: Information for innovative solutions).

Even the collection and use of this type of information about consumers is not sufficient for making marketing decisions. Lots of other types of information are needed to aid marketers' decision-making too, such as costs, production, competitors, industry - information about the whole context of the market (see Internal and external contexts). Information itself is not enough either. Marketers must have the ability to integrate and frame all the information within the context of their experience, expertise and judgement (see Moving Space: Moving information – the role of IT).

> *Another way of viewing markets is as an information production, processing and communication system. Lots of information of various types mentioned above flows all the time between all the participants in the marketing process. Every purchase, every movement of goods, every advert, every shop display produces and communicates market information.*

Markets as practice

The view of 'marketing as practice' focuses on how marketing activities and processes influence the operation and format of markets. It goes further by regarding marketing practices as playing a key role in the 'construction' of markets themselves. The nature and type of activities that managers, distributors, retailers and customers perform affect the operations and outcomes in their 'enacted marketplaces'. This approach means that markets should not be viewed as pre-existing institutions or entities that are separate from these participants – they are actually 'brought into being' and shaped by the activities of marketing managers, retailers and consumers themselves. Underlying their activities, it is the way these participants see things – i.e. their own understanding and the definition of the market they adopt – that affects the nature, type, place, time and frequency of exchanges that take place. This is how practices, or more fundamentally the assumptions behind practices, 'create' markets.

> *The 'markets as practice' view rejects Williamson's dictum that: 'In the beginning there were markets' (1979: 22). On the contrary, it is activities and practices of participants that occur first and that 'bring markets into being'.*

For example, where, when and how a supplier offers their products for sale affects where, when and how customers go to view and buy them, or not. The way the resulting exchanges take place shapes the type and nature of 'market' that arises from these activities. Behind these activities is the choice of approach that the supplier takes for offering their products to potential customers in the first place – this 'choice' is usually subsumed within what is commonly called the marketing 'strategy'. Araujo, Finch and Kjellberg (2010) argue that this type of marketing decision and practice by suppliers influences the operation of their markets. They show that the particular definition and understanding of the market that managers adopt itself affects their operations and the outcomes in their chosen 'enacted marketplace'.

So rather than regarding marketing practices as operating within pre-defined markets, Araujo *et al.* argue that marketing practices should be seen as playing a 'performative' role in the creation of market and consumption phenomena. This notion of 'performativity' incorporates issues such as how theoretical and other assumptions permeate market participants' language and behaviour and raises the wider question of how we understand the relationship between marketing theories and practices themselves (Kjellberg and Helgesson, 2007).

FURTHER READING

Markets as exchange

Bagozzi, R.P. (1978) Marketing as exchange: a theory of transactions in the marketplace. *American Behavioral Scientist*, **21** (March/April), 535–556.

Baker, M. (1995) *Marketing: Theory and Practice*. Macmillan Press: London.

Market competition

Day, G.S. & Nedungadi, P. (1994) Managerial representations of competitive advantage. *Journal of Marketing*, **58** (2), 31–44.

Porter, M. (1985) *Competitive Advantage: Creating and Sustaining Superior Performance*. Free Press: New York.

Rindova, V.P. & Fombrun, C.J. (1999) Constructing competitive advantage: the role of firm–constituent interactions. *Strategic Management Journal*, **20** (8), 691–710.

Market collaboration

Ford, I. D. (ed.) (1990) *Understanding Business Markets: Interaction, Relationships and Networks*. Academic Press: New York.

Gummesson, E. (1997) In search of marketing equilibrium: relationship marketing versus hypercompetition. *Journal of Marketing Management*, **13** (5), 421–430.

Market information

Glazer, R. (1991) Marketing in an information intensive environment: strategic implications of knowledge as an asset. *Journal of Marketing*, **55**, 1–19.

Menon, A. & Varadarajan, P. (1992) A model of marketing knowledge used in firms. *Journal of Marketing*, **56** (October), 53–71.

Perkins, W. & Rao, R. (1990) The role of experience in information use and decision making by marketing managers. *Journal of Marketing Research*, **27** (February), 1–10.

Markets as practice

Araujo, L., Finch, J. & Kjellberg, H. (eds.) (2010) *Reconnecting Marketing to Markets*. Oxford: Oxford University Press.

Araujo, L., Kjellberg, H. & Spencer, R. (2008) Market practices and forms: introduction to the special issue. *Marketing Theory*, **8** (1), 5–14.

Kjellberg, H. & Helgesson, C. (2007) On the nature of markets and their practices. *Marketing Theory*, **7** (2), 137–162.

Internal and external contexts

The role of marketing can be regarded as managing the boundary between the organization and its external contexts, and all marketing activities take place within the wider contexts of organizations, industries, cultures and countries. Also, our knowledge of markets and marketing has developed over many decades into theories and ideas from associated areas of knowledge such as economics, psychology and sociology. Another key context which affects marketing is its history – where it came from and how it has developed. These are the contexts of marketing.

The organizational or internal context

Marketing activities take place within the wider contexts of organizations, industries, cultures and countries, so the marketing endeavour is often viewed as a *boundary-spanning* role between the organization and its environment. Of course, the most immediate environment for marketing is the organization in which it takes place, but marketing is considered to extend beyond the marketing department or marketing function.

The most immediate context for marketing activities is the organization in which it takes place. Marketing is sometimes defined as 'what the marketing department of a firm does'. This is not a satisfactory definition for at least three main reasons:

1 Although most organizations nowadays have a function or department labelled 'Marketing', sometimes still it is little more than a sales unit which delivers advertising, personal selling and promotional activities. Such organizations have been labelled 'sales orientated'. As we explain in this book, marketing in today's world is concerned with creating and delivering 'solutions' for customers (see Creating Solutions), whoever they may be, not just selling things to them.

2 In order to aspire to be fully 'marketing orientated', *all the activities of the organization* must be centred on the customer. This means that marketing activities must be undertaken by *all functions* and personnel, not only those in the department called 'Marketing'. This is what Evert Gummesson (1997a) meant when he said everybody in the organization is a 'part-time marketer'.

3 In order to provide something of value to their customers or users outside, the activities and departments involved *inside* the organization each must deliver their part of the process to the other internal units and functions involved. For instance, the research department must develop the new system for IT, who must ask the purchasing staff to order all the necessary components and material from suppliers; they must then integrate these into existing IT systems for the manufacturing team, who must make the products to order for sales, and the service division must back up sales, etc. In this way, each internal activity can be viewed as having an output and thus a customer *inside* the organization. This is the notion of internal marketing (see Varey & Lewis, 1999) where all departments, not just those labelled 'Marketing', are users of others' output and have 'customers' in other functions.

The marketing concept must be operationalized in order to organize all the activities of the company to meet the needs of all its various customers. According to leading researchers such as Kohli and Jaworski (1990) and Narver and Slater (1990), the further concept of market orientation (MO) is necessary in order to operationalize marketing's ideal approach to the market. It is suggested that market orientation '. . . consists of three behavioural components – customer orientation, competition orientation, and interfunctional coordination, and two decision criteria, long-term focus and profitability' (Narver & Slater, 1990: 24; see Figure 1.2).

The MO approach has provided a managerial checklist and framework to implement the original marketing concept, but there are several issues which have

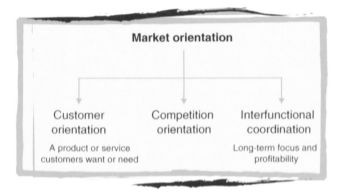

Figure 1.2 Market orientation

curtailed its potential. First, MO studies generally assume that the market orientation construct is generic, i.e. its components are not expected to be affected by the industry type, environmental level or the business strategy pursued by the firm. There is reason to believe that these capabilities are not generic, however, but that the importance and relevance of the firm's capabilities or competences vary according to the strategy pursued by the firm (Miles & Snow, 1978).

Many authors describe marketing as the business function that resides at the boundary and manages the interface between the firm and its outside world. The role of marketing is to integrate activities inside the firm in order to focus those outwards, especially to customers. One complication with any description of the marketing context, however, is that the distinction between the organization and its environment is not as clear-cut as this 'internal' versus 'external' explanation suggests. In fact, many companies contract out to other firms and agencies large parts of their marketing and other business activities. For example, market research, advertising and technical research are very often contracted to outside agencies, even by large firms. This is done to save the cost of permanently employing lots of specialists and to allow more flexibility of costs and operation. Internally, firms are more likely to retain control of overall marketing and key operations – that is, activities such as marketing strategy and planning, sales management, in-store promotions, costing and pricing. In practice, many marketing activities for firms usually span the internal–external divide, making the boundary itself between inside and outside the firm even more unclear (see Webster, 1992).

Nevertheless, bearing this qualification in mind, it is more helpful to think about and discuss the external aspects of the organization's context separately here in order to then lead on to consider how these boundaries can best be managed by marketing.

The environmental or external context

The basic idea behind the external marketing context is that the marketing activities of a company take place between – and are crucially determined by – other organizations and people in the immediate *micro-environment* – suppliers, buyers, competitors, etc. The company has some influence over these immediate influences through its marketing activities, e.g. by lowering its price it may encourage buyers to purchase more but also may encourage competitors to reduce their price. At a further distance, other factors in the external *macro-environment* are also powerful influences, such as technology, cultural norms, economic conditions, etc. (see Figure 1.3). These forces in the macro-environment affect marketing more indirectly by influencing conditions such as

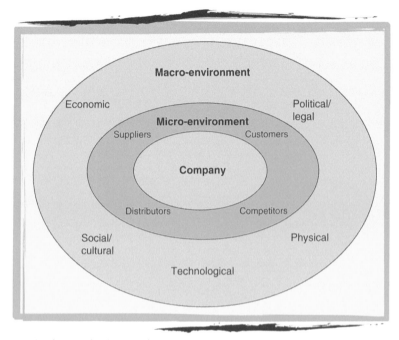

Figure 1.3 **The marketing environment**

the disposable income and thus spending power of customers, the opportunities for new products, the reach and effects of advertising, etc. The organization has little influence over the macro-environment, which is determined much more by the state of the general economy, social forces, technological advances, government policies, etc.

One criticism of this conventional view of the marketing environment depicted in Figure 1.3 is that, as the diagram shows, the company is at the centre. This reflects a company-centric, not customer-centric view of the environment. Critics would argue that according to the traditional marketing concept (see Marketing values), the depiction of the marketing environment should be centred on the consumer, not the seller. Thus a better way of viewing the marketing environment, and a more marketing-orientated one, would be if it turned the 'onion' inside out, putting consumers at the centre and competing companies at the periphery. In Figure 1.4, therefore, the firm's environment shows the consumer at the centre, with sellers fighting for their trade from the outside and also competing for distribution channels to customers, for retail space, for advertising placements, etc.

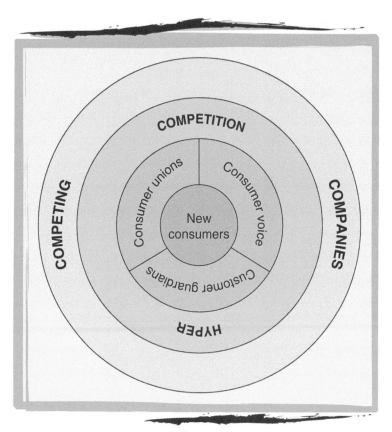

Figure 1.4 Consumers at the centre of the environment

The external context or environment is not entirely all-encompassing for marketing, however, but selective and partial. Companies cannot possibly affect or even engage with *all* of it. Most firms are not even aware of all the macro forces and trends in technology, society, economy and public policy that may affect them. There are many examples where managers complain that an important external event occurred 'out of the blue'. Marketers will have their own individual view about which particular external elements are important for their business and will also select a small subset of these to monitor, investigate or exploit. This is what is called *environmental scanning*, which is systematic information gathering to monitor important trends in the environment.

For example, oil and gas companies undertake regular scanning of oil prices, availability, costs, etc. and forecast future possible scenarios. They also constantly monitor key long-term macro-environmental factors such as government stability and national policies in selected countries where they might have or seek exploration licences. Other factors that are assessed include new technologies, regulation of automobiles, transport investments, road infrastructure capacity, and taxation of emissions. In other words, managers in such companies *selectively* monitor and forecast only a few of all the possible factors that might be relevant to their company's markets now or in the future. They cannot explore everything in the environment, nor can they engage in all markets everywhere. The parts which managers consider relevant are determined by the way they look at their business, the outside world and their strategy for operating in it. That part of the macro-environment that sellers choose to engage with is called the *enacted environment*.

A question of scale

Companies are not all able to engage with the marketing environment at the same level. Depending on their locations, size and resources, they choose to operate in markets at an appropriate level of the environment for their capabilities and strategy. This relates to the issue of the potential scales or levels of the environment in which marketing operations occur. The marketing environment can be regarded as consisting of several interrelated layers, according to Möller (1994). These range from the individual level as the smallest scale to the whole society at the macro-level. Möller aims to construct a 'comprehensive representation of the complex and multi-layered domain of marketing'. At each layer which makes up this holistic picture markets can exist comprising exchange between:

- individuals as customers and sellers
- groups of individuals – such as family buying, company sales teams and buying centres
- management teams or units as decision makers
- marketing departments and their interactions with other companies, departments or functions like purchasing, finance, engineering
- organizations or firms as buyers and sellers
- interorganizational buying and selling operations, such as with partnerships, consortia or other intermediaries
- institutional systems and their dynamics (e.g. distribution channels)
- markets, industries and cultures and their dynamics (forming the context or environment of marketing and consuming behaviours).

These layers are not entirely distinct. They are obviously interrelated in practice if an individual is buying from a large firm. From each market actor's point of view, however, they are choosing to engage with a particular layer of the marketing environment; in this case, the individual engages at the firm level, whereas the large firm selling engages at the level of individuals. In their totality, however, these layers comprise the potential complex multi-level marketing environment. It is important to understand on what level or layer a company is focusing and what kind of assumptions its managers make about that part of the marketing environment. Actions and behaviours of actors and organizations at each level permit different marketing strategies to be pursued which are appropriate for the type of participants and the nature of exchange at that level.

Managing marketing boundaries

The way in which firms engage with their environment depends on the way in which their managers and employees view the macro-environment and their assumptions and criteria for deciding between and dealing with key elements, such as different markets, levels, regions, customers, products, suppliers, etc. In marketing, there are four main approaches to managing marketing's boundaries. These are:

1 Functionalist
2 Managerialist
3 Collaborative
4 Relational.

The following sections outline the theoretical bases and historical background of these approaches.

1   Functionalist approach

The functionalist approach studies marketing behaviour as a system and tries to establish ways of making it work better, more efficiently. It is associated with the great marketing theory pioneer Wroe Alderson, writing in the 1950s and 1960s (see Alderson, 1957). Academic study and development of marketing as a separate discipline is essentially a twentieth century occurrence. It corresponds to the increasing distance of the producer from the final consumers, over whom manufacturers have thus lost control and influence, with distributors, agents and retailers filling the gap.

Figure 1.5 illustrates this shift in market structure and power over the period of the second half of the twentieth century. The rise of marketing was seen by Alderson and others as the solution to this problem for manufacturers. In other words, marketing started to be used by producers of agricultural and manufactured products in order to attempt to wrest knowledge, contact, control and influence over consumers back from the various middlemen in the elongated

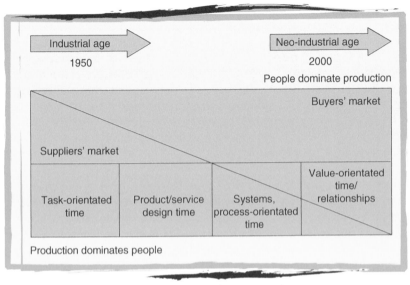

Figure 1.5 Shift from suppliers' market to buyers' market

distribution channels. The early editions of the main marketing publication, *The Journal of Marketing*, from 1936 contained papers that used the term 'marketing' to mean primarily aspects of distribution as the flow of goods and services from the place of production to the point of consumption. Functionalist marketing utilizes the techniques, tools and language of systems analysis to acquire the means for producers to directly reach and communicate with customers, who came to be regarded by marketing as the espoused central focus of all business systems.

2 Managerialist approach

The next approach shifts the focus from a functionalist, systems approach for analysing markets to one which focuses on managerial and buyer behaviour. The managerial and buyer behaviour view of the 1960s and 1970s studied individual firms and consumers to discover how to control their market behaviour in order to maximize profit (firms) and satisfaction (consumers). The buyer behaviourist view regarded the consumer as a conditioned organism, open to reconditioning and treated as a 'behaving machine', performing cognitive functions within a black box (see Shankar & Horton, 1999). Managerial marketing attempts to influence the behaviour of this 'buyer machine' through manipulating the so-called marketing mix or 4Ps of product, place, promotion and price.

The task for marketers is to develop an optimal marketing mix solution to compete for the preferences of a chosen target segment of consumers, households or organizational buyers. In order to achieve this, they utilize the techniques, tools and language of market research to acquire the means to understand and analyse buyer preferences, choose a target market, differentiate and position the product in relation to the product alternatives, and estimate the customers' reactions in terms of attitudes, buying intentions or sales. The title of Philip Kotler's (1967) classic textbook *Marketing Management: Analysis, Planning, Implementation and Control* epitomizes the managerialist approach to managing the marketing boundaries.

There are several problems with this approach. It prioritizes management interest and values and the role of managers is the main focus, not that of consumers, employees and other boundary actors; in fact, they often represent a minority interest. As the image illustrates, managerialist marketing is mainly concerned with how managers and their firms think they are perceived in the market, i.e. how *they* think *they* look to customers when *they* look in the metaphorical mirror.

Where are we going?

How do we look?

What do customers think of us?

How do we stand against competitors?

How can we improve our performance?

Marketing management through the looking glass

As such, this approach is highly normative and firm-centric, and it assumes that managing complex marketing boundaries can be enacted through a 'how to' step-by-step guide, rather than by analysing and problematizing the boundary relations and management issues in the first place. Above all, however, although it espouses business as the most important form of boundary relationship and organization, managerialism is surprisingly silent about the organization of marketing activities. It does not contain any theory-based prescriptions for organizing marketing activities. The marketing mix is offered as a decision set or output of marketing, not its organization. A further limitation concerns the absence of attention to strategic issues. Although it covers tactical mix decisions, the managerialist view is silent about which specific markets the firm should be in and how to compete in these markets.

The importance of these limitations makes all the more surprising the belief that it can also be applied to any other form of non-business activity, such as a health service or university education. The recent extension of the application of the managerial view of marketing into almost every aspect of activity in modern societies – public, civil, charitable, social and even military and scientific – does nevertheless demonstrate that this is indeed what has occurred (see McKenna, 1991).

3   Collaborative approach

Another view of marketing's boundary management role highlights the fact that buyers and sellers do not only compete with each other for the best deal, they must also often collaborate. This emphasis has developed in the past 20 years largely due to the wider influence of the business thinking and culture of firms from the Far East and Asia. For example, Japanese business methods and ideas of collaboration, quality control, employee relations and procurement practices have all had an enormous impact on business methods and thinking in the West. Chinese culture and business also operates with the notion of *Guanxi*, which is an alternative culture-based value system to the Western market basis of legal frameworks, property rights and contracts. In the West, the concept of trust is nevertheless critical for any marketing collaboration or partnership to work.

As Morgan and Hunt (1994) emphasize:

commitment and trust are 'key' because they encourage marketers to (1) work at preserving relationship investments by cooperating with exchange partners, (2) resist attractive short-term alternatives in favour of the expected long-term benefits of staying with the existing partners, and (3) view potentially high risk actions as being prudent because of the belief that their partners will not act opportunistically. When commitment and trust – not just one or the other – are present they produce outcomes that promote efficiency, productivity and effectiveness.

Proponents of this approach to managing marketing boundaries agree with Evert Gummesson (1997a) that 'collaboration in a market economy needs to be treated with the same attention and respect as competition'. Three main types of collaborations can be identified, similar to those of competition:

1   Firms collaborate with other firms, even competitors – in alliances and joint ventures. For instance, airlines collaborate to provide global services (e.g. British Airways, Qantas, Iberia) and IT firms combine with suppliers and business partners to provide a 'platform' or whole offering for customers, e.g. Pentium, Intel, IBM. Figure 1.6 illustrates how in the automobile industry various organizations collaborate in supply chains in order to provide a unified offer to customers. Indeed, as the diagram shows, they actually collaborate with customers who themselves become involved in value creation as part of the collaborative network constructed around the leading brand of Ford, Nissan or Volkswagen.

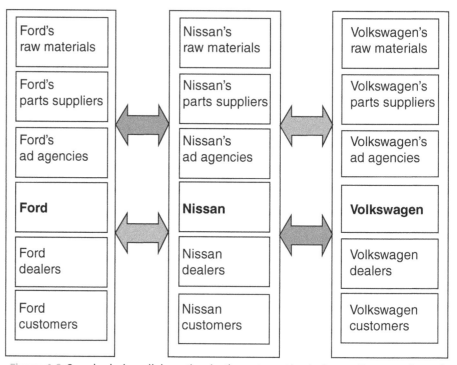

Figure 1.6 Supply chain collaboration in the automotive industry. *Source*: adapted from Morgan & Hunt (1994)

2 Buyers also collaborate with each other. This can be a formal cooperation, such as customer cooperatives, buying clubs, user groups (e.g. services, gyms, health), enthusiast societies (e.g. car owners, football supporters). Alternatively, this can be an informal or social arrangement – information sharing, instruction, friends.

3 Buyers and sellers collaborate. The very act of buying requires information sharing, dialogue, agreement and trust between the buying and selling parties. Especially in business-to-business (B2B) and service markets, the buyer is often involved with the seller in producing or making together some key aspect of the delivery or transaction or use.

The idea of market as collaboration links to the fields of relationship and network marketing (see Building Relations), which developed from studies of marketing in B2B and services where collaboration and relationships have been found to be *central* to success. All these relational approaches emphasize long-term collaboration (as opposed to competition and exchange) between market and social actors.

It is actually possible for *all* marketing activities, problems, systems and behaviour to be conceptualized and conducted by focusing on the collaborations involved to identify best practices, analyse behaviour and provide solutions (see Creating Solutions). For example, network theory has been applied extensively to industrial marketing by the north European IMP group (see Ford, 1990). This has enabled them to explain the behaviour of marketing systems in terms of networks of relationships and collaboration using sophisticated sociometric methods, exchange theory and even chaos theory.

4   Relational approach

The move towards the relational approach to managing marketing boundaries began to become popular in the early 1990s when some academic researchers and marketing practitioners began to criticize the managerialist marketing mix approach for its essentially product-orientation, as opposed to customer orientation, and for its short-term transactional view of marketing exchange, as opposed to a longer-term relational perspective (see Grönroos, 1994). Their focus on relationships obviously relates directly to the management of organization–environment boundaries and encompasses all marketing relationships, including some which can be beyond and independent of markets and commodity exchange such as those with stakeholders, employees and the general public (see Webster, 1992; Payne, 1995).

The relational approach to marketing has arisen for a number of reasons: fragmentation of mass markets through information and communication technologies, the ability to collect and analyse more data about individual customers, higher levels of product quality forcing companies to seek competitive advantage in other ways, more-demanding customers and rapidly changing customer buying patterns. The relational approach developed from a combination of ideas in business-to-business marketing, information technology-enabled developments in database and direct marketing, and the wider application of some key characteristics from services marketing (see Möller & Halinen, 2000).

Consequently, by utilizing these developments in technologies and relationship-marketing thinking, companies have sought new ways of establishing relationships with customers and, ultimately, ways of maintaining these relationships in order to retain customers that they attract. This requires a fundamental shift in marketing from a focus on transactions (i.e. sales) to relationships (i.e. retention) as companies move from short-term transaction-orientated marketing activities to that of long-term relationship building. The key differences between these approaches are shown in Table 1.1.

The difference in the relational approach to marketing's boundary management is its explicit focus on marketer–supplier relationships and the dynamics of these

Table 1.1 Transactional versus relationship marketing approaches

Transactional marketing	Relationship marketing
Focus on single sales	Focus on customer retention
Orientation to product feature	Orientation to customer value
Short timescale	Long timescale
Little emphasis on customer service	High emphasis on customer service
Moderate customer contact	High customer contact
Quality is primarily a concern of production	Quality is the concern of all
Limited customer commitment	High customer commitment

Source: adapted from Payne (2000)

relationships. It also emphasizes that both the seller and customer can be active participants in these relationships, as opposed to the managerial view which sees the marketer as the active agent and the customer as essentially reactive

or passive. The key task for marketing now becomes that of managing these relationships with customers and others, not just the management of products, channels, organizations or an internal 'mix' of marketing variables.

The assumptions that managers make about the conceptualization of the marketing environment and their organization's relationship with it will be the main element that determines which of these four approaches is adopted for managing the firm's marketing boundaries.

Marketing history

Marketing has been around a long time – and for most of the time it has had a pretty poor reputation. In classical Greece, commerce and moneymaking were not activities in which reputable free men should become involved. The early original Christian church in Constantinople believed that 'no Christian can be a merchant'; indeed, Christ cast them out of the temple. By the end of the Middle Ages, however, trade and commerce had acquired wealth and status for leading public figures, and the merchant guilds in particular played a major role in the rise of city-states such as Venice. A key element in the rise of the mercantilist class – and with it the early form of what we would now call marketing – was the legal establishment of free trade and property rights, which permitted citizens to confront one another on equal terms in the marketplace (Black, 1984).

Academic study and development of marketing as a separate discipline is essentially a twentieth century occurrence. It corresponds to the rise of US business schools and in them the first courses on marketing, which occurred at the end of the nineteenth century. The first of these was Wharton at the University of Pennsylvania in 1881 (Lazer & Shaw, 1988).

Early histories of marketing were written by Hotchkiss (1938, cited in Enright, 2002) and later by Bartels (1962). Hotchkiss took the long view, setting out three periods in the development of marketing, from the fifth to the twentieth centuries. Bartels, by contrast, sees it as an entirely twentieth century phenomenon. Both these seminal authors, however, regard the operation and channels of distribution as central to, if not the same as, marketing and particularly the increasing distance of the producer from the final consumers, over whom manufacturers have thus lost control and influence, with distributors, agents and retailers filling the gap.

> There has recently been much more attention to studying marketing from a historical viewpoint, which is defined as the description, analysis or explanation of events through time (see Savitt, 1980). These largely cover: (i) the history of marketing thought and theories; (ii) the history of individuals and organizations critical to the development of marketing, e.g. scholars, companies, regulations, agencies, institutions, professional associations; and (iii) the history of core marketing activities and functions, advertising, retailing, merchandising, branding, product innovation. (See also Kerin, 1996.)

The rise of marketing was seen by both Bartels and Hotchkiss, in their different ways, as the solution to this problem for manufacturers. In other words, marketing started to be used by producers in order to attempt to wrest knowledge, contact, control and influence over consumers, back from the various middlemen in the elongated distribution channels. And this was done by developing market research, public relations, consumer motivation research, advertising, and direct sales methods – all of which first began to be employed by businesses in the USA in the 1930s and 1940s.

Later, in the 1950s and 1960s, a lot of marketing utilized the techniques, tools and language of psychology as it attempted to acquire the means to understand customer behaviour, the customer being the espoused central focus of business. The buyer behaviourist view regarded the consumer as a conditioned organism, open to reconditioning and treated as a 'behaving machine', performing cognitive functions within a black box (Shankar & Horton, 1999).

The early editions of the main marketing publication, the *Journal of Marketing*, from 1936 contained papers that also used the term 'marketing' to mean primarily aspects of distribution as the flow of goods and services from the place of production to the point of consumption. The ways in which marketing ideas and theories developed have been plotted and categorized into various 'schools of thought' (Sheth & Gardener, 1988; Crosier, 1975). The key development in marketing thinking at this time, however, was the move from the functionalist approach to analysing markets to one which focused on managerial and buyer behaviour (see subsection on Managing marketing boundaries). The functionalist approach was associated with Wroe Alderson, writing in the 1950s and 1960s (Alderson, 1957). Managerial marketing is most closely associated with Philip Kotler (1967) and the buyer behaviour approach is typified by Engel, Kollat and Blackwell (1968).

Historical analysis of the antecedents and development of the Western market-based economies following World War II shows that the mass consumer society of the 1950s did not develop in a vacuum, but emerged from changing societal and industrial requirements and the growth in production capabilities that were an outcome of the war itself (Strasser, 1989). In the same way that mass manufacturing techniques were applied to the production of consumer goods after the war, marketing incorporated all the pre-war techniques of propaganda, persuasion and control, which had been refined and applied to political warfare (Schwarzkopf, 2011).

One reason for the shift in the 1950s and 1960s towards a managerial approach to marketing using scientific methods was overtly and consciously ideological. Faria and Wensley (2005: 12) argue that 'the concept of marketing' was then of strategic importance for US business and government because 'it had the power to suppress the idea that a society without a free market and monopolized by the State could be more beneficial for their citizens'. As research by authors such as Wooliscroft (2004) has shown, there was also pressure from the major research foundations, such as Ford, Rockefeller and Carnegie, on the major US business schools in the post-World War II period. They consciously directed their funding to encourage scientific methods and management-orientated research and teaching for ideological reasons, in order to propagate US business and capitalism in the face of the political, military and economic threat from the Soviet Union at this time.

Marketing as a science

> Marketing would appear to be primarily an area for application of find-
> ings from the sciences (primarily the behavioural sciences) and not a
> science in itself. Should then the attempt to make it a science be aban-
> doned as a wild-goose chase?
>
> (Buzzell, 1963: 34)

The above quote from Robert Buzzell's 1963 *Harvard Business Review* article, 'Is
marketing a science?', expressed the question over which marketing theorists
have been locked in debate (in one form or another) ever since. Those who had
first raised the need for better theory in marketing tended to recommend a scientific approach to its development and evaluation as a social science. Those who
responded from a managerial perspective regarded marketing as a vocation, an
application of scientific principles, like engineering or medicine. Managers certainly don't regard marketing as scientific:

> The businessman's [sic] practical wisdom is of a completely different
> character than scientific knowledge. While it does not ignore general-
> ities, it recognizes the low probability that given combinations of phe-
> nomena can or will be repeated . . . In place of scientific knowledge,
> then, the businessman collects lore.
>
> (Ramond, 1962, quoted in Buzzell, 1963: 34)

Few would disagree with this today, but the paucity of managers' use of marketing models and theories is not a sufficient reason for abandoning the possibility of the development of scientific theories in marketing. To do so requires
detailed attention to exactly what constitutes a scientific approach to theory.
Buzzell (1963) argued that marketing is not a science because it does not meet
his definition. In order to qualify as a distinct science in its own right, marketing

would have to meet some rather stringent requirements. For example, it is generally agreed that a science is:

> . . . a classified and systematized body of knowledge, organized around one or more central theories and a number of general principles, usually expressed in quantitative terms, knowledge which permits the prediction and, under some circumstances, the control of future events. Few believe that marketing now meets these criteria.
>
> (Buzzell, 1963: 33)

Shelby Hunt, the leading proponent of the 'marketing is science' school, argued that these definitions are over restrictive, and proposed that: 'Theories are systematically related sets of statements, including some law-like generalizations, that are empirically testable. The purpose of theory is to increase scientific understanding through a systematized structure capable of both explaining and predicting phenomena' (Hunt, 1971: 65). By 1983 Hunt was able to assert that 'marketing theorists agree on the nature of theory' and to cite that both advocates and critics 'basically concur as to the general characteristics of theory' (Hunt, 1983: 10).

Similarly, Roger Kerin argues that by 1965 marketing literature had become more scientific, particularly in terms of quantitative analysis being an integral element. 'Marketing phenomena, originally addressed by intuition and judgement, were increasingly studied with fundamental tenets of the scientific method' (Kerin, 1996: 5) The debate about whether it is possible to have scientific theories in marketing then moved on from the 'definition' issue to the question of what marketing theory should be like.

Marketing theory and the spirit of the times

For the reasons highlighted earlier (see subsection on Marketing history), marketing theories are not immune from the spirit of the times. On the positive side the fast-moving capabilities of marketing discussed previously enable it to develop new theories relatively quickly and adapt more easily to changes in the economic and social environment. On the other hand, it is arguable that this tendency has encouraged marketing theorists to follow the latest trends sometimes uncritically in topics like celebrity culture, virtual technology and neuropsychology, where the theoretical implications may be less profound than their current emphasis in the business, media or social scene. This might not be a problem if it only leads to a few false avenues for theory to pursue. As we have seen, however, attention to theory is very limited in marketing and there is a finite amount of research resources to devote to it; there are therefore opportunity costs to consider in following fashion. Most obviously, the danger is that

Reading the marketing textbooks of the 1950s and 1960s, replete with reference to the housewife doing the grocery shopping and the husband making car and financial decisions, all in two-parent families, it is not hard to see that those textbooks and their attendant theory are historically bound. Firms' goals and behaviour change across time as what is legally and socially acceptable corporate behaviour changes.
Wooliscroft, 2011: 500

theorists are constantly changing their focus of attention and too little theory remains to be developed and nurtured within the discipline.

Looking at the recent history of marketing theories, we can see how they are developed, enhanced and superseded sometimes in fairly short order according to the dictates of the latest intellectual fashion. Industrial marketing became B2B; business-to-consumer (B2C) separates managerial aspects from consumer research; and now both are superseded by consumer-to-consumer (C2C) and peer-to-peer (P2P) marketing. Even the 4Ps did not remain four for long, expanding quickly to five, seven or nine Ps. Bagozzi' s (1978) emphasis on social and economic theories of exchange as central to marketing discipline has gone out of fashion as the attention of marketing researchers has shifted to theories of networks, value creation, relationships, marketplace institutions, sustainability and consumer culture.

Reibstein, Day and Wind (2009) argue that in recent years the domain of academic marketing has been shrinking. This is often due to marketing frameworks, concepts and methods being pre-empted by other academic disciplines, usually where the topic overlaps with other areas, and to marketers' lack of progress in researching these topics and developing theory when they fell out of fashion or were superseded by new issues. They cite the example of the strategy field which has incorporated key marketing concepts such as product–market selection, segmentation, positioning, innovation, diffusion processes and value propositions (e.g. Christensen & Raynor, 2003; Kim & Mauborgne, 2005; Porter, 1985). Sometimes academic marketing has left voids that other management disciplines have filled, such as work on product quality and variety, product design and integrated customer solutions which is now predominantly in the operations management area (e.g. Ulrich & Eppinger, 2007).

During the 1970s and 1980s, the by-then-dominant ideological, managerial and mechanistic view of marketing extended its reach into just about every aspect of activity in modern societies. It could, so its 'widening' adherents argue (see McKenna, 1991; Kotler, 1972), be applied to just about everything – actually, not 'just about', but literally everything!

This book agrees that marketing today can be applied to everything. But this doesn't mean that it *should* be applied everywhere. It is not a straightforward matter of organizing marketing as an integrated system, as functionalists would have it, nor is it just about the managerial aspects of marketing decisions and behaviour, nor just about selling and advertising or distribution and retailing – and certainly not marketing as the *control* of consumers. On the contrary, marketing should be about liberating consumers, helping them consume better (which could mean less), creating their own value (sometimes for themselves) and using their market power for wider ends in society than simply consumption. These aspects of the purpose and values of marketing are considered in the next section on Marketing values.

FURTHER READING

Concept of internal marketing

Varey, R.J. & Lewis, B.R. (eds.) (2000) *Internal Marketing: Directions for Management*. Routledge: London.

Internal vs external marketing boundaries

Webster, F. Jr (1992) The changing role of marketing in the corporation. *Journal of Marketing*, **56** (4), 1–17.

External environment and scanning

Daft, R.L., Sormunen, J. & Parks, D. (1988) Chief executive scanning, environmental characteristics and company performance: an empirical study. *Strategic Management Journal*, **9**, 123–139.

Review of marketing history

Enright, M. (2002) Marketing and conflicting dates for its emergence. *Journal of Marketing Management*, **18** (5/6), 445–462.

Shaw, E.H. & Jones, D.G.B. (2005) A history of schools of marketing thought. *Marketing Theory*, **5** (3), 239–281.

Marketing theory

Baker, M.J. & Saren, M. (2016) *Marketing Theory: A Student Text*, 3rd edition. Sage: London.

Maclaran, P., Saren, M. & Tadajewski, M. (eds.) (2008) *Marketing Theory, Volumes I, II & III – Sage Library in Marketing Series*. Sage: London.

Wooliscroft, B. (2011) Marketing theory as history. *Marketing Theory*, **11** (4), 499–501.

marketing values

Market value

The primary value in traditional marketing seems to be 'market value', i.e. creation of economic value to sellers and buyers. The very purpose of marketing according to some authorities is value creation (e.g. Doyle, 2000; Srivastava *et al.*, 1999). But the key questions remain – *what* is this value, *how* is it created and for *whom*?

More than half a century ago, Wroe Alderson (1957) recognized that unless a firm creates and delivers value to customers, it has no real purpose, nor can it meet its business objectives. The creation and delivery of value to customers requires both an operational and a marketing component and, critically, the integration of the two. It is primarily from works on strategy, management, economics, consumer behaviour, engineering, operations research, accountancy and finance that the business concepts and measures of value have been developed.

> *Creating value for customers is the key source of competitive advantage in the 21st century.*
> Woodruff, 1997

Marketing managers need to think in terms of different value propositions and how they can be created and delivered. According to Martinez (1999), these value propositions can then be analysed from three different perspectives – the customer perspective 'what customers get', the marketing perspective 'what marketing needs to do', and the operational perspective 'what the company needs to do'.

Before explaining the nature of value propositions, it is necessary to take one step back and see where this idea comes from. The traditional 'performative' or 'utilitarian' views of value (i.e. value analysis, value engineering, etc.) look at ways of maximizing the functionality of a product or service process, while eliminating waste. This view is still seen today in engineering operations management disciplines, with authors such as Womack and Jones (1994) encouraging companies to focus on the whole rather than the parts, thus allowing companies to distinguish value from waste. Similarly, Fawcett and Fawcett (1995) showed that a firm's ability to add value does not arise typically from any single functional expertise, but is attributed to the greater coordinated effort.

> *The nature and types of consumer value constitute the essential foundation and fundamental basis for both academic study and the managerial practice of marketing.*
> Holbrook, 1999

Many different definitions of value

- *Porter (1985) – a firm is profitable if the value it commands exceeds the costs involved in creating the product.*
- *Merrifield (1991) defines value as the increase in value that occurs at each stage of the manufacturing process and that value resides in the concentration of resources focused on selected business areas.*

> - Condra (1985) interprets value as a fair return in goods, services or money for something exchanged that are judged worth equal or more than something similar (competitors' product).
> - Treacy & Wiersema (1997) define value as resulting from the fulfilment of customers' expectations, through which the organization achieves the economic benefit.
> - Miles & Snow (1978) – value comes from choosing customers and narrowing the operational focus to best serve that market segment; customer satisfaction and loyalty don't, by themselves, create unmatched value.

One problem from a marketing perspective is that the definitions of value shown in the box are mainly focused on the *producers' point of view* (organizational benefits), without giving much consideration to the customers' point of view. Marketing research shows that customers do not perceive product value in solely functional, product or any one-dimensional terms. For example, Wilson and Jantrania (1994) separated product-related aspects of value creation from vendor-related types and distinguished economic from non-economic components of value (see Figure 1.7).

Consumer-based studies successfully identify various perceptions of types of value, but for managers these illustrate nothing about the means by which they are created or the strategic dimensions of the process. It is from the strategic management literature that the seminal contribution on the strategic value-creation process has been developed, based largely on the works of Michael Porter and the concept of the value chain (1980). This permitted marketers to think beyond categories of perceived value to the strategic means and processes for delivering to or enabling the customer.

	Economic	Non-economic
Intrinsic (Product)	• Performance • Reliability • Technology • Price	• Brand name • Styling • Packaging • Appearance
Extrinsic (Vendor)	• Operator training • Maintenance training • Warranty • Parts • Identifiable post-purchase costs	• Reputation • Reliability • Responsiveness • Dyad relations • Service

Figure 1.7 Components of product value. *Source*: Wilson & Jantrania (1994)

This brief summary of viewpoints provides a snapshot of contemporary know-ledge about customer value. By all accounts this is quite fragmented knowledge (Woodruff, 1997; Tzokas & Saren, 1999). In order to overcome this, we turn to the concept of value propositions and attempt to integrate the value-creation process with market offerings.

Value propositions

Treacy and Wiersema (1997) define the value proposition as 'an implicit promise a company makes to customers to deliver a particular combination of values'. The subsequent application of this concept has changed the focus of operations of many businesses, i.e. companies such as IBM have shifted the traditional, inter-nally focused functions to customer-orientated, market-driven processes, look-ing towards a form of value delivery. In doing so, these companies have to make some fundamental decisions on segmentation and target customers' profiles (see Walters & Lancaster, 1999).

Treacy and Wiersema (1997) identified firms offering three kinds of value propositions:

1 **Operational excellence.** *These companies provide middle of the mar-ket products at the best price with the least inconvenience. Low price and hassle-free service.*
2 **Product leadership.** *These organizations offer products that push per-formance boundaries. The proposition to customers is an offer of the best product in the best time. Moreover, product leaders do not build their propositions with just one innovation; they continue to innovate year after year, product after product.*
3 **Customer intimacy.** *These organizations focus on delivering not what the market wants, but what specific customers want. Customer-intimate companies do not pursue one-time transactions; they cultivate relationships. They specialize in satisfying unique needs. Their prop-osition to the customer is: 'We have the best solution for you and we provide all the support you need to achieve optimum results.'*

Treacy and Wiersema's (1997) three value propositions (see box) integrate the operational delivery aspects of value with marketing issues, linked together through customers. However, based on empirical evidence, Martinez (1999) has found their categories to be limited in scope and flexibility. Firms using this analy-sis may miss some characteristics and competencies critical to their businesses. For example, Intel and Nike are both considered product leaders, i.e. proposition 2 in the box. On one hand, Intel is considered to be a product leader because it creates new products, new designs, technology and innovations year after year. Intel's capabilities reside in the research and development of microprocessors. On the other hand, Nike is also considered to be a product leader largely because of the successful management of its brand, image and marketing. Although Nike also conducts product development and has produced some breakthrough products, its success results more from its brand management and marketing skills.

So, here we have an example of two very different companies, with very different operations, marketing and product strategies, yet when viewed using Treacy and Wiersema's model they share the same value proposition – that of product leaders. Martinez (1999) highlights that product leaders can come in two distinct forms. First, a 'hard' form represented by new designs, innovations, product development, etc., and secondly a 'soft' form, where the focus is on brand management, corporate image and marketing communications.

The value chain concept

Of the many changes that took place in management thinking towards the end of the twentieth century, perhaps the most significant has been the emphasis placed upon the search for strategies that will provide superior value in the eyes of the customer. One concept in particular that Michael Porter has brought to a wider audience is the 'value chain'.

Value-chain activities can be categorized into two types – primary activities (inbound logistics, operations, outbound logistics, marketing and sales, and service) and support activities (infrastructure, human resource management, technology development and procurement). These support activities are integrating functions that cut across the various primary activities within the firm. A firm can deliver more value to its customers by performing these activities more efficiently than its competitors or by performing the activities in a unique way that creates greater differentiation.

The value chain concept identifies each step in the 'chain' and enables an analysis of how each contributes to creating customer value. Also, when the organization identifies an activity which is not contributing as much as possible to value in relation to its cost-effectiveness, then it enables managers to consider various internal or external solutions, e.g. contracting it out to be performed by another firm (see Creating Solutions). Some, such as Normann and Ramirez (1994), argue that there is a danger in paying too much attention to the disaggregating or breaking down of value activities in the value chain. Indeed, they *should not* be treated as separate activities to be managed but rather as an integrated and seamless process flow.

> *Competitive advantage cannot be understood by looking at a firm as a whole. It stems from the many discrete activities a firm performs in designing, producing, marketing, delivering, and supporting its product. Each of these activities can contribute to a firm's relative cost position and create a basis for differentiation . . . The value chain disaggregates a firm into its strategically relevant activities in order to understand the behaviour of costs and the existing and potential sources of differentiation. A firm gains competitive advantage by performing these strategically important activities more cheaply or better than its competitors.*
>
> Porter, 1985

Organizations to which critical tasks are outsourced must not be seen as subcontractors but rather as true partners in an *extended value chain* (see Figure 1.8).

Figure 1.8 The extended value chain. *Source*: Porter (1985)

This raises the potential of a role for the consumer in value creating, as opposed
to the internal value focus of these 'production-orientated' models, like that of
Porter. Instead, in marketing we should examine in more depth the consumer's
role in terms of 'the value chain' and other models. According to Porter's (1980)
original value chain model, firms create additional margin as goods and services
are exchanged along the supply (or value) chain. Each firm adds margin through
value-adding activities and ultimately the buyer determines the value of the
final output as 'the amount buyers are willing to pay for what a firm provides
them'. Therefore, until the customer 'speaks' in the market, the value of the
output is only an assumption.

The customer's voice in value

*Until the customer 'speaks' in the marketplace by offering a given price,
the market value of the final product is only an assumption. If we take an
example of a product which ultimately 'fails' in the marketplace (i.e. the
customer will not buy or only pays an insufficient price beneath cost), the
value added by each firm in the supply chain (e.g. suppliers of raw materials, processing, parts, assembly, manufacture, distributors, retailers) will
have been based on the assumption of a successful final value judgement
of the product in the market. Firms' calculated margins throughout the
exchange and supply processes will have been based on this assumption.
But, because this is not realized, their so-called value-adding activities
did not actually add value. Therefore, value creation can only be judged
ex-post and the calculation of 'margins' during the production and delivery process is merely hypothetical and may or may not be realized. It
is the consumer that has the crucial deciding role in determining final
value. Firms' role in the system is to create potential value that may or
may not be realized by the customer (Tzokas & Saren, 1997).*

This is the fundamental problem with the 'traditional' view of value, which ignores the true role of the customer according to Evert Gummesson (1997a):

> Production is viewed as value creation or value added by the supplier, whereas consumption is value depletion caused by the customer. If the consumer is the focal point of marketing, however, value creation is only possible when a product or service is consumed. An unsold product has no value, and a service provider without customers cannot produce anything.

Beyond 'speaking' in the marketplace, the role of the consumer in the 'system's' value-creation process is nevertheless far from clear. In marketing theory you would expect the customer to occupy a central position, but competitive models have assumed that value is something that is produced by the firm and delivered to the customer. According to this view, value is created by organizational processes within firms and is progressively built up through exchange and collaboration between them *within the supply chain*. Piercy (1998) developed this view of the value creation by distinguishing 'value defining, value developing and value delivering' organizational processes that ultimately create customer value (see Figure 1.9).

Other scholars, such as Normann and Ramirez (1994), take a contrary view of the value-creation process whereby value is co-created through *interaction* between the firm and the customer, not in value chains, but in value *'constellations'*. So consumers can play a key role in value creation too, not just firms, and the role

In today's fast-changing environment, strategy is no longer a matter of positioning a fixed set of activities along that old industrial model, the value chain. Successful companies increasingly do not just add value, they reinvent it. The key strategic task is to reconfigure roles and relationships among a constellation of actors – suppliers, partners, and customers – in order to mobilize the creation of value by new combinations of players. . . . As a result, a company's strategic task becomes the ongoing reconfiguration and integration of its competencies and customers.
Normann & Ramirez, 1994

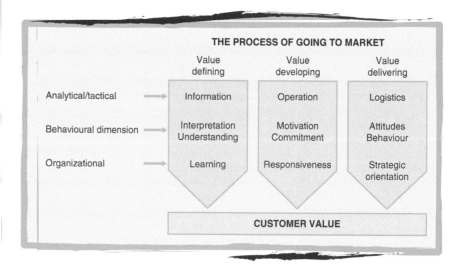

Figure 1.9 The dimensions of organizational processes. *Source*: Piercy (1998)

of consumption – i.e. the activities, behaviours and motivations that consumers undertake when making decisions and forming perceptions about products and services – is not just to 'use up' or 'deplete' value, but is also one of value creation (see Consuming Experience).

The values of marketing

Elaine Fear argues that the world is now so unpredictable and unstable that the old certainties no longer serve as a guide. The dominance of ever-faster-changing markets (which have 'won the struggle for our national soul') means for management that competitiveness comes from better understanding and adapting to the 'chaos' of the business environment (see Internal and external contexts).

> *The market has won the struggle for our national soul.*
> Elaine Fear, in Lloyd-Reason & Wall, 2000

The three 'drivers' that Riddlerstralle and Nordstrom (1999) regard as moving things forward in this 'unknown' future world are: technology, institutions and values. They argue that all three of these have important and wide-ranging impacts at different levels on individuals, companies and society. By 'values', however, they don't mean *market* values. Much more broadly than this, they cite differences internationally in *cultural* values. In China, for instance, markets are founded on the concept of *Guanxi* or trust – an alternative value system to the Western market basis of legal frameworks, property rights and contracts. Obviously in different countries their cultural values affect consumers' demand for particular products, such as furnishing, food or clothing.

But one core 'value' underpinning the concept of marketing is the belief in choice: the right of consumers to have the freedom to choose from a selection of options in what they buy, from where and from whom; and also the corollary for sellers is the free choice of what to sell, where and to whom. So choice means lots of supplies and products on the market and the implicit assumption that more choice is always 'better' – i.e. 'more' is a value in itself. Thus, marketing values don't just lead to more choice, they also arguably lead to *abundance and excess* and the necessary provision of *more* than consumers need or want. Battaille (1988) argues that all human systems lead to excess and waste. Thus, in this respect marketing values are merely reflecting the human condition, which always creates more than is needed and therefore produces waste. Riddlerstralle and Nordstrom (1999) provide some fascinating examples of abundant choice (see box below).

There is another related, yet competing, value that results from free markets and consumer choice. This is that the customer is *the* chooser, the one in control, and the term often used is the 'sovereign'. This royal metaphor goes back a long way and it is deeply rooted in ideas of exchange, customer service and free market choice. As early as Shakespeare's *Merchant of Venice*, Antonio is described as a 'royal merchant'. Adam Smith (1961), who was after all a moral philosopher, described the consumer as 'sovereign' in the marketplace. The royal title was also applied by Horkheimer (1967) to describe the 'courting' and 'majesty' of the customer in the pre-nineteenth century era.

> In 1996 there were 1778 new business books published on the American market and 20000 new grocery product launches; Sony launched 5000 new products and in 1998 there were 30000 new US record albums. Norway, with a population of 4.5 million, has 200 newspapers, 100 weekly magazines and 20 TV channels to choose from.
>
> (Riddlerstralle & Nordstrom, 1999)

The majesty of the customer . . . hardly plays any part any longer for the individual in relation to the advertising apparatus, the standardization of commodities and other economic realities.
Horkheimer, 1967, quoted in Schipper, 2002

Is the customer really king?

Far from today's customer being 'king', Horkheimer (1967) observed marketing now has such a powerful control apparatus ('technologies of governance') of the 'free' market that it results in consumers becoming so dependent on the knowledge of experts, technologies and systems that their freedom, 'inner as well as empirical', has been lost.

In the surplus society the customer is more than king: the customer is the mother of all dictators.
Riddlerstralle & Nordstrom, 1999

> Underlying values can be identified by examining the words, the language that is used by proponents and writers on the subject.
>
> (Fairclough, 1995; Stern, 1990)

Marketing has certainly generated an extensive apparatus of technologies and techniques aimed at developing brand loyalty and customer 'lock-in'. Hence the enormous amount of recent attention in marketing practice and literature to customer retention, loyalty programmes, customer relationship management and consumer 'lifetime value' (see Building Relations). This does not refer to value for the customers themselves, but value for the *firm*.

Hirschman (1993) goes one step further in her discussion of the language employed to discuss the consumer in many marketing texts, which, she argues, are littered with metaphors of war and combat. Market segments are 'targeted' for 'penetration'. Market share must be 'fought for' and 'won'. Customers must be 'influenced' lest they 'defect' to the opposition. Thus, consumers are worked upon until they are 'captive', although unaware of this captivity.

Some argue that this is nothing new. Marketing has always been concerned with the influence, if not manipulation, of consumer demand. What is different about the techniques of the new 'customer relationship management' is that the objective has shifted from sale closure to customer retention and loyalty; IT-enabled techniques are employed not only to stimulate desires and needs, but more fundamentally to develop psychological loyalty, lock-in and dependence on the brand (see Building Relations).

> - *Is the consumer really sovereign nowadays?*
> - *How much choice do customers really have?*
> - *Do these terms really reflect today's marketing values?*

What are marketing's values?

Desmond (1998) traced marketing's ethics from the early twentieth century when the first marketing scholars were educated in the tradition of German historicism and the social dynamics of the free market. He showed that this view of marketing as satisfying human needs through exchange is not 'value free'; it inherently contains so-called 'utilitarian' values, which, simply put, prescribe the ideal outcome as 'the greatest happiness for the greatest number'.

Ethics is the branch of moral philosophy that deals with moral judgements, standards and rules of conduct, and involves perceptions regarding right and wrong. It requires an individual to behave according to the rules of moral philosophy. The early theories studied ethics from a normative perspective, meaning that they were concerned with '*constructing and justifying the moral standards and codes that one ought to follow*' (Hunt & Vitell, 1986). More recently, positivist studies of ethics attempted to describe and explain how individuals actually behave in ethical situations.

Gaski (1999: 316) defined ethics from the dictionary as 'standards of conduct and moral judgement or the system of morals of a particular . . . group'. He conducted a survey to identify the normative ethical frameworks from a comprehensive review of the previous 25 years of marketing literature – i.e. what it says market-ers *should and should not do*. Finding that there were surprisingly few distinct ethical recommendations, he concluded that most so-called ethical guidelines for marketers are mere restatements of other principles of bland legalistic def-initions or statements of economic self-interest; there is a 'total redundancy and superfluity of marketing ethics . . . a vacant construct, representing nothing beyond what is already contained elsewhere' (Gaski, 1999).

These findings, and their assumptions, have been heavily criticized by Smith (2001). While accepting that marketers should obviously act in obedience of law and their own and their company's self-interest, he argues that meeting these obligations is usually a necessary, *but not a sufficient*, condition for proper busi-ness conduct. He points out that there are circumstances where meeting ethical standards demands more of them than this because 'managers may face situa-tions where ethics, the law and self-interest are inconsistent' (Smith, 2001).

> *Clearly, there is scope for content in marketing ethics that goes beyond the law and self-interest.*
> Smith, 2001

Laczniak and Murphy (2008) take a different ethical perspective than the norma-tive framework by examining distributive justice in marketing by employing Rawls' (1999) notion of fairness to ask the question: whose conception of fair-ness should be used to settle competing marketing claims? The model which has been applied most extensively is the Hunt–Vitell (1986) 'general theory' of mar-keting ethics in which both *deontological* (ethical rules) and *teleological* (end results) arguments were used to ground their theory. Applications of this theory have examined sales professionals (Singhapakdi & Vitell, 1991) and international managers (Singhapakdi *et al.*, 1999).

Thus, there are serious issues concerning marketing's ethics that have been raised by those writers who have studied the values of marketing from a theoretical point of view. However, the research results, or lack of them, from those who have examined marketing practices are even more disturbing.

Marketing ethics research

> *Marketing has become the soul of the corporation.*
> Deleuze, 1992

One area of this research has investigated the types of ethical problems that managers face in the course of their everyday work. Empirical research on eth-ical beliefs in business organizations began with a well-known study of atti-tudes of *Harvard Business Review* readers towards business ethics, conducted by Baumhart in 1961. This lists the ethical problems that business managers wanted to eliminate, including the following list: gifts, gratuities, bribes, 'call girls', price discrimination and unfair pricing, dishonest advertising, unfair competitive prac-tices, cheating customers, unfair credit practices, overselling, price collusion by competitors, dishonesty in making or keeping a contract, unfairness to employ-ees, and prejudice in hiring. Five of the eight most important ethical problems have to do with marketing activities. Brenner and Molander (1977) conducted a follow-up study and found the same set of undesirable practices. Findings such as these prompted Murphy and Laczniak (1981) to conclude that 'the function within business firms most often charged with ethical abuse is marketing'.

A famous study by Chonko and Hunt (1985) looked at both the nature and extent of marketing management ethical problems and examined the effectiveness of top management actions and codes of ethics in promoting ethical behaviour. They found that the major ethical issues facing marketing managers were bribery, fairness, honesty, price, product, personnel, confidentiality, advertising, manipulation of data and purchasing.

Social values in marketing

One school of socialization theory says that individuals progress from basic moral imperatives ('don't do this, do that') to applying systematic criteria to analyse moral dilemmas, and eventually further develop to using more complex, equivocal and multidimensional bases in their moral reasoning (Goslin, 1969). So the development of marketing values can also be seen to progress along a similar path in its ethical and social reasoning. Having been around as a professional discipline and as an academic subject for well over half a century, it can be argued that the moral and ethical basis of marketing theory and practice is moving towards more complex modes of analysis and understanding. Even in traditional marketing textbooks such as that of Kotler et al. (2001), alternative and wider values are taken into account, beyond the utilitarian, free market, managerial and consumer choice bases for decisions. Kotler's societal marketing concept 'calls upon marketers to build social and ethical considerations into their marketing practices' (Kotler et al., 2001).

Marketers are concerned with human behaviour. As the most basic motive they need to understand why customers, competitors and stakeholders behave as they do so that they can engage with and ultimately generate profits from this behaviour. The need for profits ensures that marketers study human behaviour assiduously and energetically, and their successful acquisition funds the resulting stream of marketing and academic research. As a result, the commercial marketing profession and its activities can essentially be seen as an enormous laboratory dedicated to understanding why people do as they do.

This understanding has the potential to bring enormous public benefits. A US review concluded that more than 50 per cent of morbidity and premature death is directly attributable to lifestyle factors (Hastings & Saren, 2003). Major killers like Aids, lung cancer and obesity are primarily caused by consumers' own behaviour and lifestyle choices. Furthermore, many other social ills such as crime, racism and road accidents can, at least partly, be seen as problems of human behaviour. So marketing's understanding can be applied to social issues. The ideas and techniques used by Philip Morris to sell cigarettes to smokers can be used to unsell them, as well as encourage healthier pursuits such as exercise or safer sex (see Building Relations: Building social relationships).

There is nothing unusual in the way Kotler et al. (2001) entitle the discussion of the product and other concepts as 'Marketing Management Philosophies', yet there are no references to philosophy.
Lawson & Wooliscroft, 2004

Despite the potential to bring about these benefits – and indeed its enormous contribution to economic growth – marketing, as David Jobber (2001) reminds us, has a bad name. In common parlance it is often used as a byword for deception and exploitation, and many see it as an engine driving forward materialism and excess consumption. More specifically, individual industries come under periodic criticism from both governmental and non-governmental organizations. The litigation currently focusing on the tobacco industry, and dark suggestions that the food industry is next in line, provide extreme examples of this criticism.

In essence, these attacks on marketing are recognizing that it exerts a powerful influence on society and that this influence can be negative as well as positive. Social marketing bridges this gap between the corporate sector and public welfare. It understands both worlds. As a result it has enormous potential. Andreasen (2003) provides an excellent review of the origins and future potential of social marketing (see Building Relations: Building social relationships).

Sustainable and ecological values

Sustainable marketing is more than just about making products 'green' or 'environmentally friendly'. It requires a completely different way of thinking about the role of marketing and how it deals with change.

There is widespread criticism of the traditional, managerial, anthropocentric and consumerist marketing which, it is argued, must be fatally implicated in the waste, destruction and excess that many environmentalists see as the consequence of the modern market and consumption system. The traditional language of marketing employs the grammar of the mechanistic world, where matter is regarded as inert and mute, passive and exploitable (Kajzer & Saren, 2000). It speaks the language of material possession, individuality and newness, of the assumption of unlimited growth and the accumulation of waste (Sherry, 2000). The key to success is growth in sales and material output, and the primary purpose of marketing is to design strategic plans and sales forecasts to support this goal. Traditional marketing theory is predicated on the central role of the product in the exchange process and the notion of the '*product concept*' as a distinct entity and object of exchange. This has led to fragmentation of elements in the environment and treating resources as if they consisted of separate parts, to be exploited by different interest groups (Capra, 1983).

The biological business metaphor

There are several new business concepts, such as *biological business* (Clippinger, 1999), *living companies* (de Geus, 1999) and *living strategies* (Gratton, 2000). What they all have in common is the use of biological knowledge in order to create more flexible, more adaptable practices. However, many of the business theories using organism metaphors seem to be grounded in the need to make the life of the company *'sustainable'*, long term and competitive, and to master human behaviour, but simultaneously ironically fail to fully include the considerations of the natural environment.

There are also 'new marketing' books, such as Fuller's *Sustainable Marketing: Managerial–Ecological Issues* (1999), that introduce notions of sustainability into marketing. Like many such authors, however, Fuller takes a very managerial approach to ecological issues. He argues that sustainability is 'a logical extension of contemporary marketing . . . Sustainable Marketing is structured around the traditional "4Ps" of marketing and explains how marketing mix decisions can and do influence environmental outcomes.' Fuller appears to think that the issues of sustainability in marketing are essentially managerial. Managers can 'bolt on', as it were, a 'green extension' to the basic marketing concept and the traditional 4Ps approach to marketing and, *voila*, marketing is sustainable!

However, reading works by other advocates of sustainable marketing – such as Kilbourne *et al.* (1997) – there is a clear sense that nothing short of a *revolutionary reassessment* of basic marketing ideas, techniques, orientation and practice is required to achieve the undeniably radical goal of sustainability. The roles of people, society and technologies all have to fundamentally change.

Firms will have to be increasingly flexible and creative in finding new ways of doing business that are consistent with an uncertain world and the need for a commitment towards sustainable development. In some ways, change may be seen as a measure of sustainability and organizations in the future will need to embrace change and uncertainty as a vital management function (Welford, 2000). Thus, a fully sustainable view of marketing is that it not only has to take into account eco-management of resources in meeting customers' and firms' needs, but also pay greater attention to organizational–environmental configurations that are dynamic, flexible and provide space for dealing with uncertainty. Sustainable marketing requires a critical re-examination of the concept of the marketing and environment interface, and the components that make it up (see Internal and external contexts).

In light of current environmental problems and marketing's contribution to them, there is a need for marketing to account for the wider context of its relationship with the natural environment of which it is part. One way to reconsider this is by examining the nature and characteristics of living ecological systems, from disciplines such as ecology and biology (Mayr, 1997), popular science

Placing marketing in an ecological context means that it may no longer be viewed as a transaction 'meeting' customers' needs and wants, but as part of a much greater and more complex process. If ecological aspects of life could be taken into account they would give a new dimension to the formulation of marketing strategies.
Kajzer & Saren, 2000

If the metaphor of the machine inspired managers in the industrial age, the image of living systems may inspire a truly sustainable post industrial marketing.
Senge & Carstedt, 2001

(Capra, 1983), environmental management (Welford, 2000), environmental philosophy (Ferry, 1995) and design (Tsui, 1999).

The essential requirement of a more 'sustainable' approach to marketing concerns not only efficient resource management but also learning to think in new ways, generating a new, more adaptable, marketing mindset that thrives in uncertain and complex conditions – a new dynamic approach to reconceptualizing and reorienting marketing activities that alters the way we look at products, brands, consumption, consumers and relationships; is built upon ecological principles, cyclical patterns of information; and is highly flexible and easily changed.

FURTHER READING

Marketing value

Doyle, P. (2000). *Value-based Marketing: Marketing Strategies for Corporate Growth and Shareholder Value.* Wiley: Chichester.

Holbrook, M. (ed.) (1999) *Consumer Value.* Routledge: New York.

Marketing ethics

Gaski, J. (1999) Does marketing ethics really have anything to say? A critical inventory of the literature. *European Journal of Marketing*, **18** (3), 315.

Hunt, S.D. & Vitell, S. (1986) A general theory of marketing ethics. *Journal of Macromarketing*, **6** (Spring), 5–16.

Marketing as practice

Geiger, S., Harrison, D., Kjellberg, H. & Mallard, A. (eds.) (2014) *Concerned Markets: When Political and Economic Orders and Values Meet.* Edward Elgar: Cheltenham, 46–71.

Helgesson, C.-F. & Kjellberg, H. (2013) Values and valuations in market practice. *Journal of Cultural Economy*, **6** (4): 361–369.

Zwick, D. & Cayla, J. (2011) *Inside Marketing: Practices, Ideologies, Devices.* Oxford University Press: Oxford.

Sustainable and ecological values

Fuller, D. (1999) *Sustainable Marketing: Managerial–Ecological Issues.* Sage: London.

Hastings, G. (2012) *The Marketing Matrix.* Sage: London.

Kilbourne, W. (1998) Green marketing: a theoretical perspective. *Journal of Marketing Management*, **14**, 641–655.

References

Alderson, W. (1957) *Marketing Behaviour and Executive Action*. Irwin: Homewood, IL.

Andreasen, A. (2003) The life trajectory of social marketing: some implications. *Marketing Theory*, **3** (3), 293–304.

Araujo, L., Finch, J. & Kjellberg, H. (eds.) (2010) *Reconnecting Marketing to Markets*. Oxford: Oxford University Press.

Bagozzi, R.P. (1978) Marketing as exchange: a theory of transactions in the marketplace. *American Behavioral Scientist*, **21** (March/April), 535–556.

Baker, M. (1995) *Marketing: Theory and Practice*. Macmillan Press: London.

Bartels, R. (1962) *The Development of Marketing Thought*. Irwin: Homewood, IL.

Battaille, G. (1988) *The Accursed Share* (R. Hurley, trans.). Zone Books: New York.

Baumhart, R.C. (1961) How ethical are businessmen? *Harvard Business Review*, **39** (July/August), 6–19.

Black, A. (1984) *Guilds and Civil Society in European Political Thought from the 12th Century to the Present*. Methuen: London.

Brenner, S.N. & Molander, E.A. (1977) Is the ethics of business changing? *Harvard Business Review*, **55** (January/February), 57–71.

Buzzell, R. (1963) Is marketing a science? *Harvard Business Review*, January/February, 32–48.

Capra, F. (1983) *The Turning Point*. HarperCollins: London.

Chamberlin, E. (1933) *The Theory of Monopolistic Competition*. Harvard University Press: Cambridge, MA.

Chonko, L.B. & Hunt, S.D. (1985) Ethics and marketing management: an empirical examination. *Journal of Business Research*, **13** (August), 339–359.

Christensen, C.M. & Raynor, M.E. (2003) *The Innovator's Solution: Creating and Sustaining Successful Growth*. Harvard Business School Press: Boston.

Clippinger, H.J. III (1999) *The Biology of Business: Decoding the Natural Laws of Enterprise*. Jossey-Bass: San Francisco.

Condra, L.L.W. (1985) *Value Added Management with Design of Experiments*. Chapman & Hall: London.

Crosier, K. (1975) What exactly is marketing? *Quarterly Review of Marketing*, Winter, 21–25.

Deleuze, G. (1992) Postscripts on the Societies of Control. *October*, 59.

Desmond, J. (1998) Marketing and moral indifference. In: *Ethics and Organisation* (M. Parker, ed.). Sage: London.

Doyle, P. (2000) *Value-based Marketing: Marketing Strategies for Corporate Growth and Shareholder Value*. Wiley: Chichester.

Engel, J.F., Kollat, D.T. & Blackwell, R.D. (1968) *Consumer Behaviour*. Holt, Rinehart & Winston: New York.

Enright, M. (2002) Marketing and conflicting dates for its emergence. *Journal of Marketing Management*, **18** (5/6), 445–462.

Fairclough, N. (1995) *Critical Discourse Analysis: The Critical Study of Language*. Longmans: London.

Faria, A. & Wensley, R. (2005) A critical perspective on marketing strategy. *Proceedings of 2005 ENANPAD Conference,* September, Brasilia-DF, Brazil.

Fawcett, S. E. & Fawcett, S. A. (1995) The firm as a value-added system: integrating logistics, operations and purchasing. *International Journal of Purchasing, Distribution and Logistics Management*, **25** (5), 24–42.

Ferry, L. (1995) *The New Ecological Order*. University of Chicago Press: Chicago.

Ford, I. D. (ed.) (1990) *Understanding Business Markets: Interaction, Relationships and Networks*. Academic Press: New York.

Fuller, D. (1999) *Sustainable Marketing: Managerial–Ecological Issues*. Sage: London.

Gaski, J. (1999) Does marketing ethics really have anything to say? A critical inventory of the literature. *European Journal of Marketing*, **18** (3), 315.

de Geus A. (1999) *The Living Company*. Nicholas Brealey: London.

Goslin, D. (1969) *Handbook of Socialisation Theory and Research*. Rand McNally: Chicago.

Gratton, L. (2000) *Living Strategy: Putting People at the Heart of Corporate Purpose*. Pearson Education: Harlow.

Grönroos, C. (1994) Quo vadis, marketing? Toward a relationship marketing paradigm. *Journal of Marketing Management*, **10**, 347–360.

Gummesson, E. (1997a) Relationship marketing as a paradigm shift: some conclusions from the 30R approach. *Management Decision*, **35** (3/4, April/March), 267–273.

Gummesson, E. (1997b) In search of marketing equilibrium: relationship marketing versus hypercompetition. *Journal of Marketing Management*, **13** (5), 421–430.

Håkansson, H. & Snehota, I. (1995) *Developing Relationships in Business Networks*. Routledge: New York.

Harker, M. (1998) Relationship marketing defined. Presented at UK Academy of Marketing Doctoral Colloquium, July, Sheffield Hallam University, UK.

Hastings, G. B. & Saren, M. (2003) The critical contribution of social marketing: theory and application. *Marketing Theory*, **3** (3), 305–322.

Hirschman, E. (1993) Ideology in consumer research, 1980 and 1990: a Marxist and feminist critique. *Journal of Consumer Research*, **19** (March), 537–555.

Holbrook, M. (ed.) (1999) *Consumer Value*. Routledge: New York.

Horkheimer, M. (1967). *Zur Kritik der instrumentellen Vernunft* (*Towards a Critique of Instrumental Reason*). Europäische Verlagsanstalt: Frankfurt-am-Main.

Housten, F. & Grassenheimer, J. (1987) Marketing and exchange. *Journal of Marketing*, **51**, 3–18.

Hunt, S.D. (1971) The morphology of theory and the general theory of marketing. *Journal of Marketing*, **35**, April, 65–68.

Hunt, S.D. (1983) General theories and the fundamental explananda of marketing. *Journal of Marketing*, **47**, Fall, 9–17.

Hunt, S.D. & Vitell, S. (1986) A general theory of marketing ethics. *Journal of Macromarketing*, **6** (Spring), 5–16.

Jobber, D. (2001) *Principles and Practice of Marketing*, 3rd edition. McGraw-Hill: London.

Kajzer, I. & Saren, M. (2000) The living product: a critical re-examination of the product concept. In: *The Business Strategy and Environment Conference Proceedings*, University of Leeds. ERP Environment, pp. 219–226.

Kerin, R. (1996) In pursuit of an ideal: the editorial and literary history of the *Journal of Marketing*. *Journal of Marketing*, **60** (1), 1–13.

Kilbourne, W., McDonagh, P. & Prothero, A. (1997) Sustainable consumption and the quality of life: a macroeconomic challenge to the dominant social paradigm. *Journal of Macromarketing*, **17**, 4–24.

Kim, W.C. & Mauborgne, R. (2005) *Blue Ocean Strategy: How to Create Uncontested Market Space and Make the Competition Irrelevant*. Harvard Business School Press: Boston.

Kjellberg, H. & Helgesson, C. (2007) On the nature of markets and their practices. *Marketing Theory*, **7** (2), 137–162.

Kohli, A.K. & Jaworski, B.J. (1990) Market orientation: the construct, research propositions, and managerial implications. *Journal of Marketing*, **54** (2), 1–18.

Kotler, P. (1967) *Marketing Management: Analysis, Planning, Implementation and Control*. Prentice Hall: Englewood Cliffs, NJ.

Kotler, P. (1972) A generic concept of marketing. *Journal of Marketing*, **36** (April), 46–54.

Kotler, P., Brown, L., Adam, S. & Armstrong, G. (2001) *Marketing*. Pearson: Frenchs Forest, NSW.

Laczniak, G.R. & Murphy, P.E. (2008) Distributive justice: pressing questions, emerging directions and the promise of a Rawlsian analysis. *Journal of Macromarketing*, **18** (March), 5–11.

Lawson, R. & Wooliscroft, B. (2004) Human nature and the marketing concept. *Marketing Theory*, **4** (4), 311–326.

Lazer, W. & Shaw, E. (1988) The development of collegiate business and marketing education in America: historical perspectives. In: *A Return to Broader Dimensions: Proceedings of the 1988 AMA Winter Educators Conference* (S. Shapiro & A.H. Walle, eds.). American Marketing Association: Chicago, pp. 147–152.

Lloyd-Reason, L. & Wall, S. (eds.) (2000) *Dimensions of Competitiveness: Issues and Policies*. Edward Elgar: Cheltenham.

McKenna, R. (1991) Marketing is everything. *Harvard Business Review*, **69** (1, January/February), 65–80.

Martinez, V. (1999) Sustainable added value. Unpublished master's thesis in Technology Management, Strathclyde University.

Mattsson, L. G. (1985) An application of the network approach to marketing. In: *Changing the Course of Marketing: Alternative Paradigms for Widening Marketing Theory* (N. Dholakia & J. Arndt, eds.). JAI Press: Greenwich, CT.

Mayr, E. (1997) *This is Biology: The Science of the Living World*. Harvard University Press: Cambridge, MA.

Merrifield, B. (1991) Value-added: the dominant factor in industrial competitiveness. *International Journal of Technology Management*, special publication on the role of technology in corporate policy, 226–235.

Miles, R. & Snow, C. (1978) *Organisational Strategy, Structure and Process*, international student edition. Stanford University Press: Stanford, CA.

Möller, K. (1994) Interorganizational marketing exchange: metatheoretical analysis of current research approaches. In: G. Laurent, G. Lilien & B. Pras (eds.), *Research Traditions in Marketing*. Kluwer: Boston, pp. 348–382.

Möller, K. & Halinen, A. (2000) Relationship marketing theory: its roots and directions. *Journal of Marketing Management*, **16** (1–3), 29–54.

Morgan, R. M. & Hunt, S. D. (1994) The commitment–trust theory of relationship marketing. *Journal of Marketing*, **58** (7), 20–38.

Murphy, E. P. & Laczniak, G. R. (1981) Marketing ethics: a review with implications for managers, educators and researchers. In: *Review of Marketing* (B. M. Enis & K. J. Roering, eds.). American Marketing Association: Chicago, pp. 251–266.

Narver, J. C. & Slater, S. F. (1990) The effect of a market orientation on business profitability. *Journal of Marketing*, **54** (4), 20–34.

Nonaka, I. (1994) A dynamic theory of organizational knowledge. *Organization Science*, **5** (1), 14–37.

Normann, R. & Ramirez, R. (1994) *Designing Interactive Strategy: From Value Chain to Value Constellation*. Wiley: Chichester.

Payne, A. (1995) *Advances in Relationship Marketing*. Kogan Page: London.

Payne, A. (2000) Relationship marketing: managing multiple markets. In: *Cranfield School of Management, Marketing Management: A Relationship Marketing Perspective*. Macmillan: Oxford.

Piercy, N. (1998) *Market-led Strategic Change: A Guide to Transforming the Process of Going to Market*, 2nd edition. Butterworth-Heinemann: Oxford.

Porter, M. (1980) *Competitive Strategy*. Free Press: New York.

Porter, M. (1985) *Competitive Advantage: Creating and Sustaining Superior Performance*. Free Press: New York.

Rawls, J. (1999) *A Theory of Justice*, revised edition. Harvard University Press: Cambridge, MA.

Reibstein, D. J., Day, G. & Wind, J. (2009) Guest editorial: Is marketing academia losing its way? *Journal of Marketing*, July, **73** (4), 1–3.

Riddlerstralle, J. & Nordstrom, K. (1999) *Funky Business*. ft.com/Pearson: London.

Rindova, V. P. & Fombrun, C. J. (1999) Constructing competitive advantage: the role of firm–constituent interactions. *Strategic Management Journal*, **20** (8), 691–710.

Savitt, R. (1980) Historical research in marketing. *Journal of Marketing*, **44** (Fall), 52–58.

Schipper, F. (2002) The relevance of Horkheimer's view of the customer. *European Journal of Marketing*, **36** (1/2), 23–36.

Schwarzkopf, S. (2011) The consumer as 'voter', 'judge' and 'jury': historical origins and political consequences of a marketing myth. *Journal of Macromarketing*, **31** (1), 8–18.

Senge, P. & Carstedt, G. (2001) Innovating our way to the next industrial revolution. *MIT Sloan Management Review*, Winter, 24–37.

Shankar, A. & Horton, B. (1999) Ambient media: advertising's new media opportunity? *International Journal of Advertising*, **18** (3): 305–321.

Sherry, J. F. (2000) Distraction, destruction, deliverance: the presence of mindscape in marketing's new millennium. *Marketing Intelligence and Planning*, **18** (6/7), 328–336.

Sheth, J. N. & Gardener, D. M. (1988) History of marketing thought: an update. In: *Marketing Theory: Philosophy of Science Perspectives* (R. Bush & S. D. Hunt, eds.). Amateur Marketing Association: Chicago.

Singhapakdi, A. & Vitell, S. J. (1991) Selected factors influencing marketers' deontological norms. *Journal of Academy Marketing Science*, **19**, 137–142.

Singhapakdi, A., Rawas, Y. A. M., Marta, J. K. & Ahmed, M. I. (1999) A cross-cultural study of consumer perceptions about marketing ethics. *Journal of Consumer Marketing*, **16** (3), 257–272.

Smith, A. (1961) *The Wealth of Nations*. Methuen: London.

Smith, N. C. (2001) Ethical guidelines for marketing practice: a reply to Gaski and some observations on the role of normative marketing ethics. *European Journal of Marketing*, **31** (1), 3–18.

Srivastava, R. K., Shrevani, T. K. & Fahey, L. (1999) Marketing, business processes and shareholder value: an organizationally embedded view of marketing activities and the discipline of marketing. *Journal of Marketing*, **63**, 168–179.

Stern, B. (1990) Literary criticism and the history of marketing thought: a new perspective on 'reading' marketing theory. *Journal of the Academy of Marketing Science*, **18**, 329–336.

Strasser, S. (1989) *Satisfaction Guaranteed: The Making of the American Mass Market*. Pantheon Books: New York.

Treacy, M. & Wiersema, F. (1997) *The Disciplines of the Market Leaders*. Addison-Wesley: Reading, MA.

Tsui, E. (1999) *Evolutionary Architecture: Nature as a Basis for Design*. Wiley: New York.

Tzokas, N. & Saren, M. (1997) Building relationship platforms in consumer markets: a value chain approach. *Journal of Strategic Marketing*, **5** (2), 105–120.

Ulrich, K.T. & Eppinger, S.D. (2007) *Product Design and Development*. McGraw-Hill: New York.

Varey, R.J. & Lewis, B.R. (1999) A broadened conception of internal marketing. *European Journal of Marketing*, **33** (9/10), 926–944.

Walters, D. & Lancaster, G. (1999) Value-based marketing and its usefulness to customers. *Management Decision*, **37** (9), 697–708.

Webster, F. Jr (1992) The changing role of marketing in the corporation. *Journal of Marketing*, **56** (4), 1–17.

Welford, R. (2000) *Corporate Environmental Management: Towards Sustainable Development*. Earthscan: London.

Williamson, O.E. (1979) "Transaction-cost economics: the governance of contractual relations". *Journal of Law and Economics*, **22**, 233–261.

Wilson, D.T. & Jantrania, S. (1994) Understanding the value of a relationship. *Asia–Australia Marketing Journal*, **2** (1), 55–66.

Womack, J.P. & Jones, D.T. (1994) From lean production to the lean enterprise. *Harvard Business Review*, March/April, 93–103.

Woodruff, R.B. (1997) Marketing in the 21st century customer value: the next source for competitive advantage. *Journal of the Academy of Marketing Science*, **25** (3), 256.

Wooliscroft, B. (2004) Paradigm dominance and the hegemonic process. PhD thesis, University of Otago, New Zealand.

Wooliscroft, B. (2011) Marketing theory as history. *Marketing Theory*, **11** (4), 499–501.

Building Relations

Few businesses, or people, can do everything by themselves. Therefore, a key element in marketing is building relationships. In particular, long-term 'interactions' between buyers and sellers are important in explaining marketing behaviour and the development of markets. This chapter covers the role of communications, networks and institutions in establishing market relations. It also explains how marketing techniques can be used for beneficial effects on social relations, as well as negative ones. If marketing can encourage us to buy a Ferrari, can it also persuade us to drive it safely – or resist the temptation to steal one?

Relationships and interactions

Few businesses, or people, can do everything by themselves (see Marketing Contexts); therefore a key element in marketing – indeed *the key element –* is building relationships. Increasingly companies realize that customers are their most important asset and view customer relationships as opportunities that need to be managed. The essential aim of relationship marketing strategies is of course value creation (see Marketing Contexts: Marketing values) *for both parties* through the formation and maintenance of relationships with external marketplace entities. The most important of these is usually with customers, but those with other stakeholders and partners that can influence and help companies' marketing operations are also important.

The relationship marketing approach has grown in popularity and attention significantly in the last decade, particularly since the seminal articles in the USA by Webster (1992) and Morgan and Hunt (1994). Its roots go back to European academics in the 1970s, studying the conditions and behaviour in industrial and services marketing, notably in Sweden and Finland, where they found long-term relationships between buyers and sellers to be particularly important to each party. They concluded that these 'interactions' were also critical in explaining marketing behaviour and the development of markets. This was labelled by the industrial marketing group, IMP, as the *interaction* approach. This led some of them to look at the wider phenomenon of *sets* of interconnected relationships known as the '*markets as networks*' approach (see Marketing Contexts: Views of markets).

For businesses, the possibility of and need for the new relational approach to marketing has arisen for a number of reasons: more intense, often global, competition; fragmentation of mass markets through IT and communication technologies; ability to collect and analyse more data about individual customers; a generally high level of product quality that is forcing companies to seek competitive advantage in other ways; more demanding customers; and rapidly changing customer buying patterns (Moller, 2010).

Consequently, companies have sought new ways of establishing long-term profitable relationships with customers and, ultimately, ways of maintaining these relationships in order to *retain customers* that they attract. Achieving better customer retention requires a good understanding of the reasons for their switching from one company or brand to another in the first place. In her exhaustive survey, Rowley (2005), identifies many 'triggers' to customers' switching, such as changes in circumstances that redefine the offering, changes in personal circumstance (such as a move in location), better deals elsewhere, service delivery or product failure, inadequate service or product recovery arrangements, or when a new product from a competitor offers better value.

Customer retention has been recognized as one of the most important aspects of marketing; indeed Dawkins and Reicheld (1990) argue that the ultimate goal of customer retention is to achieve 'zero defections' of profitable customers. It may be an apocryphal statistic, but it is nevertheless frequently quoted that it can be four times more expensive to win a new customer than to retain an existing one. Even if attracting new ones is not as expensive as this, once they have 'won' them the company will still incur the additional costs of bringing the new customers to the same level of profitability as existing or previous ones. Partly because of these efforts to improve customer retention and reduce defections, there has been a notable shift in marketing from transactions (i.e. sales) to relationships (i.e. retention) as companies move from short-term *transaction-orientated* goals to long-term *relationship-building* goals. The key differences between these approaches are shown in Table 2.1.

> *The interaction approach is based on the idea that business markets aren't made up of a large number of individually insignificant customers. Nor do they consist simply of action by suppliers – who assemble a marketing mix and launch it towards a group of passive buyers, whose only reaction is to choose whether or not to buy. Instead the process is one of interaction between active buyers and sellers that are individually significant to each other.*
> *Ford, 2004*

Table 2.1 Key differences between transactional marketing and relationship marketing

Transactional marketing	Relationship marketing
Focus on single sales	Focus on customer retention
Orientation to product features	Orientation to customer value
Short timescale	Long timescale
Little emphasis on customer service	High emphasis on customer service
Moderate customer contact	High customer contact
Quality is primarily a concern of production	Quality is the concern of all
Limited customer commitment	High customer commitment

Source: adapted from Payne (2000)

Grönroos (1994) developed the marketing strategy 'continuum', shown in Figure 2.1, where various types of goods and services can be placed depending upon their characteristics.

Grönroos (1994) suggests a transaction-type strategy for fast-moving consumer goods (FMCGs) and a relationship strategy for service firms. However, due to supplementary services to products, and vice versa, items may move along this continuum depending on what they comprise. For example, airlines may take

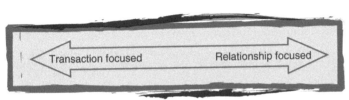

Figure 2.1 Marketing strategy continuum. *Source*: Grönroos (1994)

you from A to B but will offer you various in-flight products which augment the core service; on the other hand, supermarkets provide an outlet for consumer goods but provide various ancillary services, such as collect by car or being helped at the checkout. Due to the proliferation of relationship marketing strategies, it is evident that contemporary firms are trying to position themselves at the right-hand, relationship-focused end of the continuum.

Definition and characteristics of marketing relationships

One of the most popular definitions of what is known as relationship marketing is provided by Grönroos (1994). Note the role in Grönroos's definition of the concept of promises. He also states that 'giving promises may *attract* new customers and initially *build* relationships. However, if promises are not kept, the evolving relationship cannot be *maintained* and *enhanced*.' Therefore, this definition implies other characteristics that are essential in the development of relationships, a key one being the concept of *trust*, which underlies most of the theories of marketing relationships development, including the most widely referenced paper on the subject by Morgan and Hunt (1994).

Grönroos (1994) describes trust in terms of beliefs and intentions. First, he argues that there has to be a belief in the other partner's trustworthiness that results from the expertise, reliability or intentionality of that partner. Second, he views trust as actual behaviour or a behavioural intention that reflects the degree of reliance on the other partner, thus involving vulnerability on the part of the trustor.

So far in this chapter we have described what is meant by marketing relationships and the characteristics of relationship marketing. The role of relationships in creating value and future developments in relationship marketing will be discussed in the next subsections.

Relationship marketing and customer value

The ability to generate and deliver value *above and beyond* the product or service is critical for today's businesses. However, it is much less clear how managers

> *There has been a shift from a transactions to a relationship focus . . . From an academic or theoretical perspective, the relatively narrow conceptualization of marketing as a profit-maximization problem, focused on market transactions, seems increasingly out of touch with an emphasis on long-term customer relationships and the formation and management of strategic alliances . . . The focus shifts from products and firms as units of analysis to people, organizations, and the social processes that bind actors together in ongoing relationships.*
> Webster, 1992

can identify what this value is *in the eyes of their customers*, and how they can develop and mobilize the necessary competencies for generating this value (see Marketing Contexts: Marketing values). It is in this task that there is significant potential of the relationship marketing approach for identifying and delivering customer value.

In the past the formula for identifying customer value seems to have been to listen to your customers and learn from previous mistakes. However, the rapidly changing marketing context (see Marketing Contexts) means that managers are frequently confronting totally new situations, which reduces the value of lessons from the past. Customers can only communicate existing preferences and needs, which provide very few clues or visions for the future. Technology is changing the patterns and possibilities of production and consumption (see Creating Solutions), thus creating new learning cycles for suppliers and their customers. Inter-industry competition with new players reaching across established industry sectors (e.g. supermarkets as banks; AA as insurance; mobile phone as camera) challenges established competitive marketing approaches. In these constantly changing conditions, experience counts for less and managers must always be learning; they must be able, as it were, to remember to forget! The internet and e-commerce have created a new market space for buying and selling that requires different organizational and marketing competencies (see Moving Space). Information technologies have increased customer knowledge and therefore their level of expectations from their suppliers (see Creating Solutions).

These dramatic changes require marketers to reassess their understanding and calculation of what constitutes 'value' to their customers and how this value can be produced and delivered (see Marketing Contexts: Marketing values) – specifically detailed attention to customer, shareholder and employee value; appreciation of the knowledge potential underlying such relationships; and mutual understanding and careful positioning of relationships to provide possibilities for firms to reinvent the future *with* their customers, employees and shareholders. This is the formula for firms to achieve sustainable competitive advantage for the future that the relationship marketing approach advocates because, while products/services can be copied easily by competitors, long-term relationships are difficult to imitate.

Future developments in relationship marketing

One study by Veloutsou *et al.* (2002) reported predictions for the development of relationship marketing practices as a step towards the development of a system that could suggest to academics and practitioners appropriate

> *The aim of relationship marketing is to establish, maintain and enhance relationships with customers and other partners, at a profit, so that the objectives of the parties involved are met. This is achieved by a mutual exchange and fulfillment of promises.*
> *Grönroos, 1994*

strategies to future realities. The forecasts were based on the application of the scenario planning technique by a group of leading experts in the field (academics) who attempted to forecast the developments of relationship marketing under various scenarios. In total, sixteen factors were identified as very influential in shaping the trends of relationship marketing. The first seven factors are relevant to changes in the nature of the firm's relationships with the various internal and external markets and the requirements of these markets. The remaining nine report changes in the operation and delivery processes of the relationship management chain. Table 2.2 lists these factors, their description and the future possibilities.

Table 2.2 Potentially influential factors in the advancement of relationship marketing

Factor	Description	Possibilities
Brand trust	The degree to which back-up for the branding strategy is derived more from the human element than from attributes of the product/service itself	• Deriving more from the interaction with the contact personnel (human element) • About equal from human element and brand attributes • More from brand attributes
Value to consumer	Precise significance to consumer of exceeding expectations	• Become more important • Be of similar importance • Become less important
Prosumption	Involvement of consumers in design/production of product/service	• Increase • Stay the same • Decrease

(Continued)

Trust and commitment

Commitment and trust are 'key' to relationship marketing, because they encourage marketers to (1) work at preserving relationship investments by cooperating with exchange partners, (2) resist attractive short-term alternatives in favour of the expected long-term benefits of staying with the existing partners, and (3) view potentially high risk actions as being prudent because of the belief that their partners will not act opportunistically. When commitment and trust – not just one or the other – are present they produce outcomes that promote efficiency, productivity and effectiveness.
Morgan & Hunt, 1994

Table 2.2 (*Continued*)

Factor	Description	Possibilities
Nature of relationships	Critical definition of the type of customer–company relationship which will determine strategy	• Increase • Stay the same • Decrease
Parity markets/products	Lack of perceived differentiation as seen by consumers	• Become more commonplace • Occur as often as at present • Become less commonplace
Company networks	Association of brands with networks of companies rather than single companies	• Increase • Stay the same • Decrease
Sales as natural outgrowth of relationship management	Evolution of relationship management to the extent that the selling function becomes a natural result of the relationship	• Become more likely • Be as likely as at present • Become less likely
Diagonal integration	IT-driven process by which firms move into new fields, achieving new synergies and economies of scope	• Increase • Stay the same • Decrease
Global individualism	Combined effects of mass customization with global 1:1 marketing	• Accelerate • Move at a constant pace • Decelerate
Detrimental impact of artificial relationship management	Poor implementation of relationship management programmes, which has a detrimental effect on markets	• Increase • Stay the same • Decrease
Customization	Degree of individualized tailoring of a product/service offering	• Increase • Stay the same • Decrease
Database marketing	Aggregating customer information for subsequent analysis	• Increase • Stay the same • Decrease
Aggregation of customer relationship	Management of customer interactions to provide incremental value	• Increase • Stay the same • Decrease

(*Continued*)

Factor	Description	Possibilities
New media	The opportunities offered by new technology to increase personal communication with customers	• Increase • Stay the same • Decrease
Management processes	Combining previously independent management functions to produce a synergistic effect	• Become more common • Happen as often as it does now • Become less common
Company–customer interface	Process related to managing all points of contact between company and customer	• Increase • Stay the same • Decrease

Source: Veloutsou *et al.* (2002)

How to build relationships – the implementation of relationship marketing

Until recently, discussion on relationship marketing in several business contexts, including that of business-to-customer, has focused on the concept of *the relationship* itself – its attributes and stages (Bagozzi, 1995). However, it has paid insufficient attention to the aspect of relationship management as a *core organizational process* that extends throughout the organization and enhances the implementation of relationship marketing strategies (Sheth & Parvatiyar, 2000). The essence of such an *organizational process* is value creation through the formation and maintenance of relationships with external marketplace entities, particularly consumers, and is captured in the notion of customer relationship management (Srivastava *et al.*, 1999). Easy to say, but hard to put into practice.

An operational framework to assist firms' implementation of their relationship marketing has been constructed by Payne (1995), which takes the form of a detailed planning template called 'the relationship management chain' (see Figure 2.2) to operationalize the six-market model (see Marketing Contexts). The focus of this template is customer value. It delineates the various managerial processes that need to be undertaken by the firm to define the value proposition, identify appropriate customer value segments, design value delivery systems and evaluate its value performance. In the model, all these processes are based on the fundamental construct of customer value as the cornerstone concept in relationship marketing.

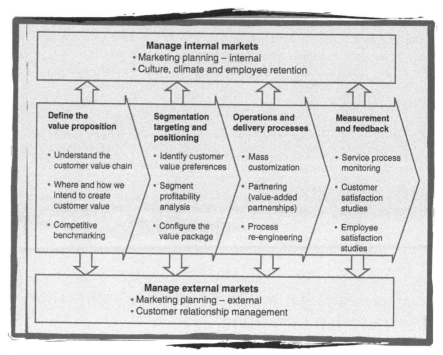

Figure 2.2 The relationship management chain. *Source*: Payne (1995)

With the recent development of the customer relationship management field, these techniques assist the implementation process of the relationship marketing principles. As such, they help to directly address Fournier *et al.*'s (1998) criticism that 'relationship marketing is powerful in theory but troubled in practice'. However, the success of most of these techniques depends upon the collaboration of the final customer. Therefore, to truly address the above criticism we need to understand how change in the marketplace could affect the willingness of customers to participate and willingly provide information.

Contemporary marketing practice (CMP)

Brodie *et al.* (1997) examined the extent to which contemporary organizations are carrying out relational marketing *in practice*. They investigated a number of companies across a range of industries, countries and types of markets, and concluded that many companies, while moving towards a relational focus, still practice transactional marketing, and many others practice both relational and transactional methods. They found the extent to which they use either one method or a mixture of methods depends largely on the nature of the business and the products and services on offer.

CMP research programme

- Started at the University of Auckland, New Zealand, in 1996 and extended to Canada, Finland, Sweden, Ireland, Argentina, Thailand, UK, Germany, USA, South East Asia, Africa and Eastern Europe.
- Objective: 'to profile marketing practice in a contemporary environment, and to examine the relevance of relational marketing in different organizational, economic and cultural contexts' (Brodie et al., 1997).

The contemporary marketing practice (CMP) framework combines and compares the traditional transactional marketing literature with a synthesis of the relational literature both in North America (e.g. Berry, 1983; Morgan & Hunt, 1994; Sheth & Parvatiyar, 1995; Webster, 1992) and in Europe (e.g. Grönroos, 1994; Gummesson, 1999; Håkansson & Snehota, 1995). (For further details see Brodie et al., 2008.)

The early CMP studies identified the need for a richer, multidimensional approach to understanding companies' implementation and practice that incorporates both transactional and relational aspects of marketing. The next step was the development of a classification scheme that accurately reflects the different marketing practices, which uses four rather than two different aspects of marketing practice to distinguish between traditional marketing management and relationship marketing.

Based on the 'clusters' of observations of types of marketing methods found in their wide-ranging sample of firms around the world, the CMP group's classification scheme consists of four aspects of practice:

1 Transaction marketing (TM) – managing the 4Ps to attract and satisfy customers.
2 Database marketing (DM) – using technology-based tools to target and retain customers.

3 Interaction marketing (IM) – developing interpersonal relationships between individual buyers and sellers.
4 Network marketing (NM) – positioning the firm in a connected set of inter-firm relationships.

By using research with multiple perspectives, the relative importance of different marketing practices could be examined. The implications of this approach were illustrated in an article published in the *Journal of Marketing* (Coviello *et al.*, 2002). The study examined 308 firms in the USA and four other Western countries to understand how different types of firms relate to their markets. What was important about the results was that there were three groups of firms: those that had marketing practices which were predominantly *transactional*; those that had marketing practices which were predominantly *relational*; and those that had marketing practices that were 'both transactional and relational', which they called '*pluralistic*'.

Each group comprised approximately one-third of the sample and included all types of firms (consumer goods, consumer services, business-to-business goods and business-to-business services). The comparative analysis (see Table 2.3) does not show a dominance of a relational approach with any of the groups of firms. While there is some support for consumer service firms being more relational (service-centred logic), what is of interest is that there are many exceptions and, furthermore, that all types of firms were reported in the pluralistic cluster (goods- and service-centred logic). Of the firms in the sample, this included 50 per cent of the B2C goods firms, 35 per cent of the B2B goods firms, 30 per cent of the B2C service firms and 33 per cent of the B2B service firms.

According to Brodie *et al.* (1997), their analysis fails to clearly identify specific types of firms which are dominated by more than one type of marketing practice, and simply highlights that all four types of marketing are in evidence and

Table 2.3 Approach to marketing by firm type

Cluster	Consumer goods (%)	B2B goods (%)	Consumer service (%)	B2B service (%)
Transactional *n* = 103	38.9	34.9	40.6	26.7
Relational *n* = 98	11.1	30.2	29.0	40.8
Pluralistic *n* = 107	**50.0**	**34.9**	**30.4**	**32.5**
Total	100.0	100.0	100.0	100.0

Source: Coviello *et al.* (2002)

practiced by most firms to varying degrees. What is more challenging is that the firms that reported the pluralistic marketing practices had superior performance characteristics.

The CMP research project by Coviello *et al.* (2002) examined changes in marketing practice in the USA, Canada, Finland, Sweden and New Zealand. Specifically, they sought to identify the extent to which the relational approach to marketing is being practiced and whether it is replacing the transaction approach. While results confirmed that firms were placing a greater emphasis on relationship marketing, they *did not indicate there was a 'paradigm shift' from transaction marketing to relationship marketing*. Rather, their research showed that, for all types of firms (i.e. goods versus services and consumer versus business-to-business), three profiles of marketing practices were present: a transactional, a relational and a pluralistic cluster. Studies in transition economies (e.g. Russia and Argentina) suggest that Coviello *et al.*'s (2002) results are not limited to developed countries but reflect a worldwide trend (Pels *et al.*, 2004).

Building loyalty and engagement

Beyond understanding and serving customers, marketers attempt to develop their relationships with them in order to build loyalty on the part of customers towards the company, brand, retailer or supplier. They try to achieve this by various means including through improving the quality of customers' interactions and engagement with them.

Loyalty is not a one-dimensional concept, however. Not only are there different types and levels, but there is no agreement about what is meant by customer loyalty. The main issue in marketing centres on whether loyalty is *an attitude* (a state of mind) or *a behaviour* (e.g. demonstrated through repeat purchases). And of course not all customers are the same, so they are found to exhibit varying degrees of loyalty. O'Malley (1998) identifies four different levels:

1 'No loyalty.' This situation is apparent when customers are not loyal to any brand or location at all and visit stores on a random basis, dependent on time and availability.

2 'Spurious loyalty. Viewed as a temporary loyalty. Spurious customers are often categorized as promiscuous, likely to patronize a particular outlet or brand on the basis of its promotional offers or convenience or location, and are easily influenced by competing offers from attractive alternatives. As a result, it is

considered relatively easy to encourage switching behaviour where spurious loyalty is evident.

3 'Latent loyalty.' Occurs when a customer has a high relative attitude towards the company or brand but this is not evident in terms of their purchase behaviour. Whatever the explanations for latent loyalty (e.g. inconvenient locations, peer influence or stores out of stock), such behaviour does not give the consumer an opportunity to display preferential purchase actions.

4 'Sustainable loyalty.' The customer displays high repeat-purchase behaviour, which is associated with a strong preference for a particular store and its facilities and services. It is said that this state is attained 'when the company has developed and communicated a proposition that clearly has long-term benefits for the consumer' (O'Brien & Jones, 1995) and where the consumer has made a conscious decision to purchase from that store on a long-term basis.

O'Malley (1998) argues that the role of so-called 'loyalty schemes' which many firms offer customers is restricted to situations where no loyalty or spurious loyalty is evident, and she doubted their usefulness beyond these stages, i.e. latent or sustainable loyalty. An alternative approach to categories of loyalty is the seminal 'loyalty ladder' proposed by Christopher et al. (1991) (see Figure 2.3),

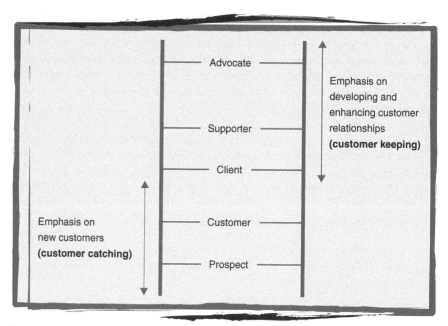

Figure 2.3 The relationship ladder of customer loyalty. *Source*: Christopher et al. (1991)

which explicitly associates levels of loyalty with different types of relationships with customers.

Christopher *et al.* (1991) proposed that customers move through a series of stages; they begin as 'prospects' that then become customers, then regularly purchasing clients, then supporters of the company, and finally active and vocal advocates for the company. This 'loyalty ladder' introduces a notion of increasing customer commitment to the firm and its offers as a customer advances up the loyalty ladder, and that customer service plays a pivotal role in achieving this progression up the loyalty ladder (Christopher *et al.*, 1991).

While researchers and practitioners recognize that there are different types and levels of customer loyalty, there is no agreement about what is meant by the term. The main dispute centres on whether loyalty is an attitudinal or a behavioural phenomenon. The behavioural perspective on loyalty usually uses a pattern of repeat purchase occasions as a measure of loyalty, particularly the so-called 'Enis–Paul' index. Dick and Basu (1994) considered that the behavioural approach to customer loyalty is problematic in that these measures make no attempt to understand the factors underlying repeat purchase. Because some degree of psychological commitment on the part of the consumer is also a necessary ingredient of true loyalty, Reicheld (1994) recommended that retention rate and share of total purchases should be used. To most, the notion of loyalty conjures up ideas of commitment, affection or fidelity (McGoldrick & Andre, 1997).

The area of loyalty that has been subjected to most research and early theories is mainly concerned with explaining customer loyalty to individual product brands and retail stores. These types of models of store loyalty are of particular interest to retailers, who are keen to ascertain whether different social groups command higher loyalty and whether this is related to particular social circumstances, demographic factors, brand loyalty or the number of stores used. Several studies have found that store loyalty is essentially negative in terms of customer attitudes because behind the appearance of behavioural loyalty (i.e. repeat purchases) may in fact be certain customers' limited resources, lack of money, time and transport, or choice. In other words, such customers are forced to use one store through lack of alternatives, endorsing the 'forced choice' view of store loyalty (East *et al.*, 1995).

Consumer engagement is a more recent approach to relationship building in marketing which has been developed from the well-established notion of employee engagement (Saks, 2006). 'Engagement' is conceptually distinct from involvement or mere participation, according to Brodie *et al.* (2011), because it doesn't explicitly embody interactivity and experience. Also, similar to loyalty, engagement is seen as a multidimensional concept (with cognitive, emotional and behavioural dimensions) where different conditions lead to differing levels of engagement (Van Doorn *et al.*, 2010).

There has been some critique of modern marketing techniques under the label of relationship marketing that may apparently promote loyalty and engagement on the part of the customers only with the aim of controlling customers' behaviour and encouraging them to buy more of their offerings or pay more for them through locking them into such schemes. Far from engaging positively with consumers and rewarding them for their loyalty, marketers' techniques of advertising, packaging, product placement, loyalty schemes and sponsorship programmes are designed at best to influence, at worst to manipulate and control, customers' purchasing behaviour. This may be more of a problem for certain types of product categories where consumer information is poor. For example, many technology-based consumer products for communication, computing and entertainment that have proliferated in recent years require so much specialized knowledge that consumers have neither the time nor the inclination to acquire all the necessary skills to make informed decisions about their technical requirements.

In the UK there have been many complaints about home energy companies' lack of transparency in their pricing and provision which compounds consumers' inability to make informed choices and inhibits them from switching providers. Similarly, financial products such as mortgages, life insurance and savings schemes are almost impossible to discriminate between (Knights *et al.*, 1994). As Zwick and Cayla (2011) argue, marketing rhetoric may espouse the merits of engagement and loyalty, but many consumers have been locked into loyalty schemes, contractual restrictions on services/insurance and other marketing efforts to promote consumer products which are well researched, extensive, expensive and solely aimed at maximizing the returns on their loyalty for the producers, irrespective of the best value for consumers (see Marketing Contexts: Marketing values).

FURTHER READING

Overview of development of the relationships-as-networks approach

Håkansson, H., Ford, D., Gadde, L.-E., Snehota, I. & Waluszewski, A. (2009) *Business in Networks*. John Wiley & Sons: Glasgow.

Moller, K *(2010)* 'Relationships and Networks' *in* Baker M. and Saren M. (Eds) *Marketing Theory: a student text* (3rd edn) Sage Publications; London, Chapter 14.

Relational approach to marketing

Christopher, M., Payne, A. & Ballantyne, D. (1991) *Relationship Marketing: Bringing Quality, Customer Service and Marketing Together*. Butterworth-Heinemann: Oxford.

Ellegaard, C., Medlin, C. J. and Geersbro, J. (2014) "Value Appropriation in Business Exchange: Literature Review and Future Research Opportunities", *Journal of Business & Industrial Marketing*, **29** (3), 185–198.

Gummesson, E. (1999) *Total Relationship Marketing*. Butterworth-Heinemann: Oxford.

Concept of customer loyalty

Dick, A. S. & Basu, K. (1994) Customer loyalty: towards an integrated framework. *Journal of the Academy of Marketing Science*, **22** (2), 99–113.

O'Malley, L. (1998) Can loyalty schemes really build loyalty? *Marketing Intelligence and Planning*, **16** (1), 47–55.

Reicheld, F. F. (1994) *The Loyalty Effect*. Harvard Business School Press: Cambridge, MA.

Customer engagement and retention

Brodie, R. J., Hollebeek, L. D., Juric, B. & Ilic, A. (2011) Customer engagement: conceptual domain, fundamental propositions and implications for research. *Journal of Service Research*, **14** (3), 252–271.

Resnick, E. (2001) Defining engagement. *Journal of International Affairs*, **54** (2), 551–566.

Rowley J. (2005) The four Cs of customer loyalty. *Marketing Intelligence and Planning*, **23** (6), 574–581.

Saks, A. M. (2006) Antecedents and consequences of employee engagement. *Journal of Managerial Psychology*, **21** (7), 600–619.

Van Doorn, J., Lemon, K. E., Mittal, V., Naß, S., Pick, D., Pirner, P. & Verhoef, P. C. (2010) Customer engagement behavior: theoretical foundations and research directions. *Journal of Service Research*, **13** (3), 253–266.

Building social relationships

Gerard Hastings

Marketing relationships: social or antisocial?

Marketing is as old as human society. Its key principles of cooperation and mutually beneficial exchange were deployed by our earliest ancestors to overcome the disadvantages of being a relatively weak species, coping with a challenging environment among many stronger and better adapted animals. Our key superiority – our large brains – enabled us to work out that our chances of survival would be greatly enhanced if we pooled our resources and learnt to operate collectively; if we could find win-wins. It takes team work to hunt and kill an elk or to colonize and cultivate a piece of ground, and team work requires rules, mutual respect and sustainable relationships. Marketing has grown out of these fundamental needs. It is not something that emerged from the US business schools in the middle of the last century but a timeless protocol for cooperation, mutual benefit and advancement. In complex modern societies where human needs have fragmented and populations are extensive, marketing can enable business to keep in touch with their customers and customers to express their wants and needs. The core principle of mutually beneficial exchange has survived through to the present day.

This reassuring story, however, has taken an alarming turn. Mutually beneficial relationships depend on a degree of balance, especially in terms of power. In the last few decades (coincidentally or otherwise since marketing was codified and promulgated in business schools) the corporate sector has grown with disturbing rapidity. Corporations have become some of the largest and most powerful organizations on earth, dwarfing many countries. Lou Pingeot (2014), using data from the World Bank and *Fortune* magazine, shows that '110 of the 175 largest global economic entities in 2011 were corporations, with the corporate sector representing a clear majority (over 60%) over countries'. The revenues of Royal Dutch Shell, ExxonMobil and Wal-Mart each exceed the combined GDP of the 110 poorest countries – that is more than half of all nations. Furthermore, mere size understates the problem. Network analysis makes it clear that interconnections between transnational corporations further concentrate power to the extent that fewer than 150 companies control 40 per cent of this corporate wealth, and 737 control 80 per cent of it.

In these circumstances the idea of mutually beneficial exchange or supportive relationships becomes difficult to sustain. As Figure 2.4 illustrates, the adolescent

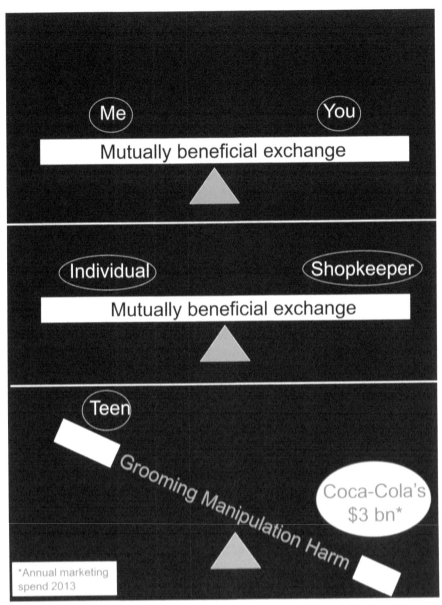

Figure 2.4 How corporate power distorts marketing relationships

cannot make empowered decisions about her consumption of sugar when Coca-Cola can muster $30 billion worth of persuasion; when even the Olympic Games can be hired into the marketing team. And beyond the overt ad-spend, a company of Coca-Cola's wealth can also buy stakeholder fealty – it can influence the social context of our decision-making. As Arundhati Roy reminds us (quoted in Gupta, 2011), 'Corporations that are turning over these huge profits can own everything: the media, the universities, the mines, the weapons industry, insurance hospitals, drug companies, non-governmental. They can buy judges, journalists, politicians, publishing houses, television stations, bookshops and even activists.'

As the Coca-Cola example illustrates, the malevolent effects of corporate marketing are particularly apparent in the harm being done to public health. Experts now routinely refer to 'industrial epidemics' – diseases that are a by-product of unhealthy consumption. Non-communicable diseases caused by tobacco, alcohol, processed foods and soft drinks are now killing far more people than communicable diseases like Aids or TB. Smoking alone will soon be seeing off 10 million people every year. Marketing in this toxic, lopsided form is persuading us to kill ourselves.

Furthermore, this harm to the individual is matched by much broader societal harm. What the excess consumption of sugar and fat is doing to our health, the excess consumption of stuff in general is doing to our planet. As climate scientist Stephen Emmott (2013) points out, 'We need to consume less. A lot less. Less food, less energy, less stuff. Fewer cars, electric cars, cotton T-shirts, laptops, mobile phone upgrades. Far fewer.' But no corporation can sign up to the idea of shrinking consumption; their business models assume perpetual growth and corporate marketing is designed to deliver it. This explains why, as Emmott continues, 'every decade global consumption continues to increase relentlessly', leading him to conclude starkly that 'we are f**ked'. His pessimism (and his language) may be shocking but it's difficult to deny his point.

So what can be done?

We can start by recognizing the paradox that lies at the heart of this story. The immense power of Shell, Wal-Mart and Coca-Cola is founded and built on our voluntary collaboration. No one forces us to drink brown sugar water or buy gas-guzzling SUVs. Corporate marketers may have daunting budgets and unnerving political influence but there is a real limit to their ability to compel us to go shopping. For the most part we choose to do so. By the same token, we can choose not to. We just need to start thinking more critically about the motivations, methods and consequences of our corporate serfdom. Therein lies hope.

And there is a second source of hope. Marketing, as we have discussed, long predates the corporation and climate change. It is an amoral technology for influencing human behaviour and, in its progressive form, enhancing human cooperation. If marketing can encourage us to buy a gas guzzling automobile, it can also persuade us to drive one safely – or resist the temptation to steal one. This benign purpose can be rediscovered and reinvigorated by applying marketing ideas, not to our consumption habits, but to other behaviours that it might be in both our individual and our collective interests to change. Our own health is one example; similarly blights like drink driving, racism and crime can all be attributed to our behaviour, as indeed can climate change.

These two ideas – the critical analysis of the corporate power and the active encouragement of prosocial behaviour – come together in the discipline of social marketing. As Lazer and Kelley's (1973) original definition explains, social marketing is concerned with the application of marketing knowledge, concepts and techniques to enhance social as well as economic ends. It is also concerned with the analysis of the social consequences of marketing policies, decisions and activities. Or more succinctly: social marketing critically examines commercial marketing so as to learn from its successes and curb its excesses.

The following two cases begin to put these principles into practice.

Building relationships to empower teenagers

NE Choices was a major drugs prevention programme which targeted 13–16 year olds in the north-east of England between 1996 and 1999. It was built around a high school drama initiative with additional community, school governor and parent components. As the name of the initiative implied, it aimed to enhance the critical capacity of young people in north-east England around illicit drugs and thereby improve their decision-making.

The programme was heavily informed by social marketing and so had a strong consumer and stakeholder orientation. This was driven by a comprehensive programme of market research to guide the development of NE Choices, ensure it was properly delivered, and evaluate its impact in terms of both consumer satisfaction and behaviour change. It also showed that relational thinking can be just as – if not more – relevant in drugs prevention as it is when selling beans and cars.

The programme was remarkably popular with the market. Both the core customers (the young people) and the other stakeholders strongly endorsed it. The impact evaluation showed, for example, that the vast majority of children felt the programme was enjoyable (89 per cent), thought provoking (88 per cent) and credible (84 per cent), and that the drama was realistic (79 per cent) and empowering (e.g. 88 per cent agreed that 'it encouraged us to speak our own minds').

Good customer relationships were being developed:

- Meaning and messages were jointly negotiated rather than imposed.
- Customized spin-off products were carefully developed and successfully delivered to important customer subgroups.
- Comprehensive research ensured that the programme did things *with* young people, rather than *to* them. This resulted in the production of a key relationship marketing tool: a comprehensive database for what is an elusive and vulnerable group.
- The young people trusted the programme and its brand, as the impact evaluation data shows.
- They also showed considerable commitment to NE Choices. For example, the last stage of research had to be conducted by mail as a proportion of the young people had, by then, left school. The vast majority were prepared to provide contact details and 70 per cent completed the sensitive and complex (40-minute) questionnaire.

Furthermore, three of the strengths which emerged from the impact evaluation are known to be markers for successful knowledge, attitudes and behaviour change: reaching a range of stakeholders and settings as well as the core customers; the successful use of drama in education to engage the audience; and being non-didactic. NE Choices was not only building strong relationships with what is typically a cynical and hard-to-reach group, it was – and this will come as no surprise to the marketer – beginning to deliver on the bottom line of behaviour change. More importantly, in the long term the young people in NE Choices had been encouraged to think for themselves and make their own decisions about drugs. Given the raft of problems we face as a species, this empowerment is arguably more valuable than any individual behaviour change.

Undermining abusive marketing relationships

In contrast to those created in NE Choices, marketing relationships can be extremely abusive, as the tobacco industry all too ably demonstrates. In the UK, new smokers are almost always children – 80 per cent take up the habit before their eighteenth birthday. One in two of those of us who don't manage to break the habit will die as a result, and the addictiveness of nicotine (it's a match for cocaine and heroin in this department) is more than likely to defeat attempts to quit.

Study after study (Lovato *et al.*, 2004 provides a good review) has shown that tobacco industry marketing acts as a recruiting sergeant, capturing and retaining new smokers. This is no accident. As a now infamous planning memo by the tobacco manufacturer R. J. Reynolds stated, 'if our company is to survive and prosper over the long term, we must get our share of the youth market' (Pierce *et al.*, 1999).

However, social marketing, and the sophisticated understanding of relationship building it provides, has helped redress the balance and removed most tobacco marketing from the UK. Specifically, three steps were involved. We had to: (i) build the evidence base of a link between tobacco promotion and youth smoking; (ii) develop good marketing relationships with politicians and other key stakeholders; and (iii) analyse the competition and destabilize their marketing relationships.

The evidence base

The tobacco industry has traditionally argued that advertising has no effect on consumption. Tobacco is a mature market, sales for it are stagnant, if not in decline, and therefore advertising cannot be increasing demand. The only effect it has is on brand switching among adult smokers.

The social marketer can approach this argument with a knowledge of segmentation and see that suggesting that there is just one homogeneous market for tobacco is naive. There are actually many markets: young smokers, roll-your-own smokers, cigar smokers and so on. Some of these may be shrinking but others are growing. The social marketer might also deduce that advertising is likely to have varying effects on different segments. For example, established, older smokers are much more likely to be influenced by their need for nicotine than seductive messages. We know that young smokers, on the other hand, are driven by psychosocial needs – to look cool, rebellious and independent, for example – and therefore might be expected to be more susceptible to branding and other image-based appeals. The social marketer would also recognize that the issue here is integrated marketing communications (IMCs), or even marketing as a whole, not just advertising. Finally, a marketer understands that IMCs are only going to be one influence (and a relatively modest one at that) on teen smoking.

All these insights help build better research to establish the evidence base: you need to focus on teenagers, use a wide array of marketing practices and build sophisticated models of effect to be tested on samples that are large enough to detect small differences.

Building relationships

Politicians need hard evidence to protect themselves from tobacco industry lobbying. This is partly a matter of doing research but also of disseminating it. The first requirement is to publish in respected scientific journals, such as the *British Medical Journal* and the *Journal of Marketing*. Data and research that appears in such outlets is virtually unimpeachable. Secondly, there is a need to use more popular outlets, especially the quality media. This convinces the politician that the issue has public support.

Destabilizing the competition's relationships

Marketers are keen on competitive analysis. In this case, the core concern is the tobacco companies' relationship with smokers and especially young, starter smokers. Many of the anti-smoking campaigns that have run over the last 50 years can be seen as indirect attempts to undermine these, but one recent US campaign tackles the job head on. The Truth campaign has deliberately set out to attack the tobacco industry, highlighting their unscrupulous business practices and deliberate attempts to attract youngsters to the habit. (See www.thetruth. com for more information.)

Young people in the USA demonstrating the impact of tobacco marketing

The need for systemic change

NE Choices and the UK's success in containing tobacco marketing do bring hope. However, in this era of industrial epidemics and a planet straining under the burden of gross over-consumption, we need to move beyond ad hoc initiatives: systemic change is needed. Such change can be built on three pillars.

First, corporate marketing needs to be contained by independent, comprehensive and robust regulation. The purpose should be to radically reduce everyone's exposure to commercial marketing, and corporate operators should not be involved in developing or deploying these new rules, merely in obeying them. The tobacco marketing success can and should be extended into other markets.

Second, commercial marketing needs to be countered with alternative perspectives and robust deconstruction. We need to create a world in which consumption is not presented as the solution to all our problems. As we have seen, the Truth campaign in the US did exactly this for tobacco companies.

Third, and most importantly, critical capacity needs to be built in the population. Small steps in this direction have been taken with media literacy but the idea has to be pushed much further, addressing not just advertising but the whole neoliberal business system. The marketing mix, stakeholder marketing and the fiduciary imperative which requires corporations to prioritize profit each need to be unpacked and critiqued. Not so much media literacy as marketing literacy.

Figure 2.5 The three Cs – containment, counteraction and critical capacity

These three Cs of containment, counteraction and critical capacity are mutually dependent: regulation without public support is severely weakened, while a politician's inclination to regulate is greatly increased by popular demand – and both are aided and abetted by effective counter marketing (see Figure 2.5). The move to smoke-free public places in Scotland during 2006 perfectly illustrates this strategic potential: the near-perfect alignment of public and parliament defeated a notoriously powerful multinational industry and delivered what many would consider to be the greatest single achievement of the Scottish Government of this period.

FURTHER READING

Bakan, J. (2004) *The Corporation: The Pathological Pursuit of Profit and Power.* Penguin (Canada): Toronto.

Emmott, S. (2013). *10 Billion.* Penguin: London.

Farrelly, M. C., Healton, C.G., Davis, K.C., Messeri, P., Hersey, J. C. & Haviland, M. L. (2002) Getting to the truth: evaluating national tobacco countermarketing campaigns. *American Journal of Public Health,* **92** (6), 901–907.

Gupta, A. (2011) Arunhati Roy: The people who created the crisis will not be the ones who come up with a solution. In *The Guardian,* 30 November 2011. www.guardian.co.uk/world/2011/nov/30/arundhati-roy-interview

Hastings, G. (2003) Relational paradigms in social marketing. *Journal of Macromarketing,* **23** (1), 6.

Hastings, G. & Domegan, C. (2013). *Social Marketing from Tunes to Symphonies,* 2nd edition. Routledge: London.

Hastings, G. B. & Saren, M. (2003). The critical contribution of social marketing: theory and application. *Marketing Theory,* **3** (3), 305–322.

The role of communications

Julie Tinson

Introduction

Do you follow Kim Kardashian on Instagram? Do you aspire to her lifestyle, have an interest in her fashion choices or the new products she uses or develops? As Kim Kardashian has 34 million Instagram followers, it is likely that your views, behaviour and attitudes regarding this celebrity are replicated across an increasingly diverse populace. Marketers use celebrities and celebrities develop their own profiles – in an emotional and/or rational way – to communicate their message. The use of celebrities is one of the *indirect* ways in which organizations and their brands can begin to build a relationship with consumers (see Brand Selection). During the initial stages of 'courtship', organizations use celebrities they know their customers (potential and actual) aspire to be like and indirectly attract customers to the product, service, organization or brand.

> Marketing communications *provide the means by which products, brands and organizations are presented to their audience with the aim of initiating a dialogue, potentially leading to a relationship.*

The following sections describe the use, development and effectiveness of communications for relationship building and the varying degrees of communication used throughout the buyer–seller liaison. Despite doubts about the accuracy of the marriage metaphor for market relationships, this section uses the analogy of a romantic relationship to explore in a step-by-step fashion the ways in which consumers are attracted to a brand through to committing to a relationship, problems encountered, and possible dissolution at the end.

> The target audience *is people who, directly or indirectly, are chosen to receive communication messages.*

First encounter

In their attempts to 'seduce' consumers into a relationship, organizations use a variety of methods to communicate with their target audience. Approaches towards communications vary enormously between different cultures; thus, the means and style of communications depend partly on the country where the audience resides. As a generalization, it is commonly viewed that in the USA, for example, the communication messages tend to be more 'hard sell', whereas in France consumers expect to be seduced with more 'soft sell' messages. Similarly, in the UK consumers prefer more complex messages they can 'solve' which, it is argued, affords them the opportunity to feel intelligent and engages them with the message itself (Fowles, 1996). Of course, building any relationship in any country is never straightforward, and what is an attractive proposition to one person may be displeasing to another.

Q. How can organizations effectively initiate a relationship using a communications approach?
A. Initially, by using familiar language in their advertising an organization can demonstrate an understanding of the way in which their consumers interact with one another and, by association, suggest they too understand and are acquainted with the consumer. Similarly, the use of music (2016's John Lewis 'Tiny Dancer' advertisement is a good example of this) and specific colours will all indicate an immediacy or bond with the organization and consumer.

You say it best when you say nothing at all

If a consumer's eyes meet an advertisement across a crowded room and he/she *immediately* understands the message conveyed, this might be as a result of the use and recognition of the signs or symbols used in the piece of communication. This use of signs and symbols is known as *semiotics*. Semiotics is the study of the meanings and interpretations associated with signs and symbols. An example of how we use and interpret such signs in marketing communications would be if the male and female models in an advert were depicted standing close together; the assumption most observers would make is that they were 'intimate'. If a solitary model were standing in the rain, this might suggest loneliness. Of course, not all cultures translate messages in the same way and organizations differentiate their brand from that of the competitor by demonstrating they are aware of semiotics. Different signs and symbols have alternative meanings in different cultures. For example, if children raise their hands in the UK it is a sign of the child trying to attract attention but in other cultures it is a sign of rudeness.

> **Q.** How can ads suggest meaning without words?
> **A.** Through the use of space in the picture – for example, with greater spatial proximity implying intimacy between the people pictured closer together. Other means include: numbers – using the year a product was established (e.g. 'Guinness 1759' suggests a brand with longevity); time – business efficiency is often shown by a fast-moving man (such as Usain Bolt illustrating the fibre optic broadband speed offered by Virgin Media); clothing – Scottish people are usually depicted wearing kilts; and kinetics – sedentary lifestyles are often shown through the use of models lounging on sofas.

Not only adverts but also brands themselves usually incorporate symbolic pictures or 'logos' (see Brand Selection). For instance, McDonald's 'golden arches' symbol is a world-renowned logo. While driving on motorways in many countries, it is usual just to see the golden arches being advertised on service station billboards, with instant recognition among consumers as to what the brand represents (see Consuming Experience). Not all signs or symbols have positive associations, however.

> A brand is a name, term, sign, symbol, design or combination of these which is used to identify the goods or services of one seller or group of sellers in order to differentiate their offering from that of the competition.

Talking the same language

In 2014, the BBC reported that Britons spend more time using technology devices than they do sleeping and social media has increased the number of adverts to which individuals are exposed. As growing numbers of consumers become 'ad literate' – particularly young people – there is a need to make adverts increasingly abstract or creative to remain novel, innovative and challenging.

When organizations attempt to initiate a relationship with the consumer, the communications approach must be engaging, inspiring and involving to convince the consumer (or groups of consumers) that they are special and that the brand understands them.

Ad literacy *is the extent to which a consumer is familiar with and can 'read' various types of advertising, the signs used and the messages they contain.*

Creativity

An example of this creativity and innovation is exemplified in the following scenario (data compiled by whynot! thinkpeople, the creative shopper agency who developed the Anchor Baking Kits for Schools campaign). In 2015, as a consequence of TV programmes such as *Great British Bake Off*, there was a rise in the popularity of baking at home with a subsequent increase in the use of butter. The challenge for Anchor butter was to stand out on the shelf in major retailers next to cheaper alternatives like own-brand block butter. As an ingredient, the price of butter often wins over taste. In addition, competing brands like Stork are known for their heritage. How could Anchor increase their credentials and give families an emotional reason to trade up to Anchor?

An engaging, measurable and integrated brand promotion was designed to appeal to 'life jugglers'; 25–45-year-old family-focused women who, specifically when they cook, are in the mindset of nurturing, showing their loved ones they care through food and bringing families together through cooking and eating. Following research to generate insight around families with young children and baking, it was revealed that practical cookery would be part of the school curriculum for Key Stages 1–4 from September 2015. In discussion with primary schools it was discovered that they did not necessarily have all the necessary equipment they would need to teach children (5–11 year olds) how to bake and that schools were concerned about the cost implications.

Adopting an innovative and creative approach, Anchor launched Baking Kits for Schools in March 2015 to provide schools with the tools they needed to support the learning of the children and to associate Anchor as the 'butter of choice' for baking. As the children would also come home and share what they had learnt at school, usage would be extended into the home environment, driving penetration of Anchor. Over 22,000 primary schools were contacted via email, mailout packs and follow-up phone calls. This approach allowed as many schools as possible to be recruited supported by bold PR around the campaign. Five thousand responses were expected from teachers, with fifteen baking kits going out to everyone that signed up. Baking kits included all the essentials: a spoon, a bowl and an apron.

At the centre of the campaign was an on-pack promotion that ran across 4.5 million packs in major retailers. 10p or 5p from every promotional pack of Anchor butter sold was automatically donated to provide free Anchor baking kits to participating schools. Shoppers who were keen to engage further could nominate their local school and also enter prize draws to win additional equipment for them. These layers of participation were important to create appeal across the target demographic, who are known for being time poor but also enjoy embracing schemes that benefit their family. A microsite was also developed to support the campaign which helped Anchor engage with the registered schools and customers interested in the promotion. As primary schools were the prime target, the overall look and feel was fun, colourful and engaging, e.g. there were recipes to try out at home and stories written by children about their baking experiences. Posters were put up in schools and flyers sent to parents to draw and maintain attention as well as reinforce the message.

The campaign prompted an impressive 6,033 primary schools to sign up from all over the UK, a figure that exceeded the original objective. A total of 92,500 kits went out to schools and 4,267 people entered to win a kitchen makeover. The click-to-open rate of the email communication was 26 percent versus the industry average of 5 per cent. On Facebook alone over 1.9 million views were achieved across four promoted baking posts. A total of 28 PR pieces were seeded in the press which reached 11.2 million people. Neilson and Kantar data shows value +17%, volume +48% and penetration +39% year-on-year for Anchor Block, further demonstrating the success of the promotion.

In addition to these results, multiple photos and letters were received from primary schools saying how much they appreciated their baking kits. Incremental kits were also sent to Beaver and Scout groups that had been in touch, as well as schools that had missed the registration period, to show the commitment to the cause from Anchor in ensuring no one missed out.

Advertising *is the use of paid mass media to deliver marketing communication messages to target audiences.*

Initiation

What is important about this scenario for building relationships through communication?

- The consumer must be attracted to the communication (impact/innovation/creativity).
- The consumer must want to be involved with the product/service/brand.
- The language/signs must be understood by the consumer. It should say, 'I know and understand you.'
- The consumer has to trust the organization to engage in the initial relationship.
- The message must be credible.

Figure 2.6 demonstrates the types of agencies that exist for developing different types of communication approaches. *Above-the-line* is a term used to describe advertising promotions that employ commission-paying mass media (TV, press, cinema) and *below-the-line* is where use is made of non-commission-paying media. The use of the below-the-line term is fairly limited in the current climate, however, as it covers such a broad range of promotional activity. *Through-the-line* agencies deal with both above- and below-the-line activity. Examples of the major players are highlighted in Table 2.4.

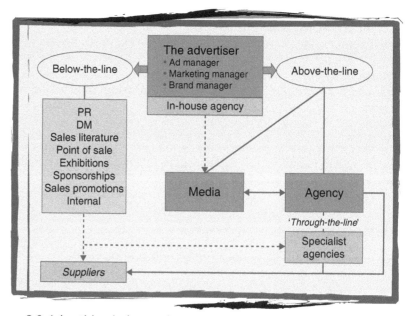

Figure 2.6 Advertising industry players

Table 2.4 Examples of major industry players

Specialist agencies	• Direct marketing
	   – WWAV Rapp Collins
	   – Brann
	   – Grey Direct
	• Sales promotion
	   – Carlson Marketing Group
	   – Mosaic
	   – DraftWorldwide
	   – IMP Group
	   – Haygarth Group
	• PR
	   – Weber Shandwick
	   – Momentum
	   – Magic Hat
	   – Fishburn Hedges

In-house agencies	• IKEA • Calvin Klein • Bernard Matthews
Media selling houses	• Granada • Carlton • Sky
Media departments	• Universal McCann • OMD Media (Omnicom) • Walker Media
Advertising agencies	• Abbott Mead Vickers • JWT • Saatchi & Saatchi • Mother • McCann Erickson • TWBA
Through-the-line	• Craik Jones

Timing

When organizations want consumers to engage with their brand, product or service, timing is of the essence and, more often, alternative communication approaches are being used to deal with the issue of timing. Advertising with regard to mortgages, associated tie-ins, insurance and finance deals are particularly prevalent in relation to timing as these messages are only relevant if the target audience are in a position to use these services. Messages to dissuade consumers from engaging in harmful practices are also timely (i.e. the message ought to prevent harmful behaviour).

Q. What is key to successful communication with new customers?
A. Timing is key if a consumer is to engage with any relationship. This may be because the product is cyclical (fashionable for short periods of time) or because the consumer previously did not have the age or experience or did not have the disposable income to be able to buy.

Ambient advertising *is when the medium used for communication becomes part of the message.*

Ambient advertising is becoming increasingly popular as a result of its immediacy and the ability it has to *overcome timing* issues. Ambient advertising often catches consumers 'off guard' and, as a result, has a greater probability of attracting the consumer's attention and of staying in the consumer's consciousness. When Nivea introduced their Nivea Sun Doll in 2015 in Rio de Janeiro it was to teach children the importance of using sunscreen. Nivea representatives went onto the beach and gave away the dolls to children as they were getting ready for a day of fun in the sun. These dolls actually burn (go red) when exposed to sunlight without protection. The timing was perfect because children could understand what would happen to them if they did not let their parents apply sunscreen and it supported the parents in their endeavour to protect their children. The *problem had been solved* for both the parents and children. And this of course is another key facet of communication – it resolves problems consumers may not even know they had (see Creating Solutions).

This type of communication method is often known as 'thinking outside the box'. It is particularly useful for media planning purposes, i.e. when to run an advertisement, which is the best advertising to break the product, which is the most appropriate magazine or social media/website. In order to answer such questions, the most frequently used criterion is that which will provide the most *reach* – the best coverage among the target audience. There are numerous trade sources which will provide a holistic view of the type of media that matches the type of consumer the organization is trying to reach (e.g. BRAD, TGI and Mintel).

> *Q.* Why is ambient advertising such an important communications tool?
> *A. Such is the immediacy of the ambient advertising approach that consumers can also be reminded about nuisances they were (un)aware existed. When deodorant cans replaced the hanging straps in the underground carriages, consumers were reminded how to prevent problems occurring.*

Different communication approaches will provide different levels of reach and often thinking outside the box produces maximum publicity. The Ice Bucket Challenge, designed to promote awareness of the disease ALS (amyotrophic lateral sclerosis) – which involved dumping a bucket of ice water on someone's head and nominating others to do the same – is an example of maximizing publicity for a cause. This activity went viral during July and August 2014 and those nominated for the Ice Bucket Challenge had 24 hours to comply or were obliged to make a financial donation to the charity. The additional reported funding received by the ALS Association as a consequence has been $100 million (source: ALS Association) and related charities have also benefitted from encouraging such consumer engagement.

Importantly, publicity can even be negative but still generate profit. In 2015 Protein World launched a £250,000 billboard campaign in the London Underground asking consumers to consider if they were 'beach body ready'. This relatively unknown company were reported to have made £1 million in just four days as a consequence of the backlash of negative publicity. Despite the message being considered to 'shame' those who did not have an 'ideal' body shape, with campaigners against the message defacing the posters and voicing their upset on Twitter, sales of the weight-loss collection exceeded their expectation. Interestingly, while receiving 378 complaints, the Advertising Standards Authority deemed the campaign not to be offensive or irresponsible. Although the advert was eventually withdrawn by Protein World as there were concerns that its health claims did not have EU authorization, the brand awareness had already increased expo-nentially. A new advertising campaign launched by Protein World in May 2016 adopted a similar approach to the initial billboard campaign.

- **Reach** *is the coverage or penetration of the potential audience and is a measure of how many members of the target audience will be reached by a medium or collection of media used in a campaign.*
- **Frequency** *is the number of times a member of the target audience is exposed to a media/message over a specified time period.*

Q. How often is it necessary to advertise to make sure the target audience receives the message?
A. Simplistically it is acknowledged that if a member of the target audience has seen an advertisement three times (the first time to raise awareness, the second to create interest and the third to induce desire) this would be enough to encourage intention to purchase.

Figure 2.7 illustrates the communication process, demonstrating the two-way nature of communications from sender to receiver and back again – that is, from the organization to the target audience back to the organization. The message is encoded (creatively, engagingly, using semiotics where appropriate) and a medium is chosen to convey the message (TV advertising, billboard, social media). If the target audience understands the message the organization has intended to send, communication has taken place. 'Noise' is any distraction that might prevent the target audience from receiving the message, e.g. too many other advertisements. The target audience will then 'feed back' to the organiz-ation in a number of ways: (a) through doing what the message asked of them (purchasing the product, giving blood, giving up smoking); (b) taking part in *post-campaign research*. If the feedback is appropriate, the organization will consider the campaign to have been successful.

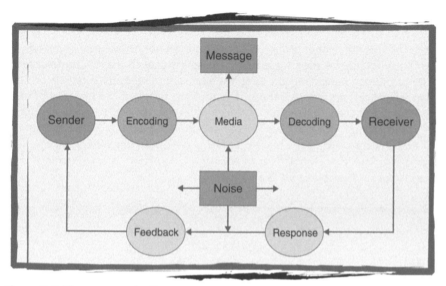

Figure 2.7 The communication process

Pre- *and* post-campaign research *occurs when advertising is researched prior to release or after the advertisements have run. Pre-campaign testing is used more frequently, although post-campaign research allows advertising to be tested in its natural environment.*

Communicating with new customers

Communication can also be used to facilitate an introduction between a brand and a new consumer. A consumer can seemingly fall into a relationship with an organization or brand but there is generally some form of communication to ensure the consumer believes the product or service has an attractive proposition. A PartyLite Candle evening or an Ann Summers 'home party' may be one such first or blind date where the host is generally a friend (or a friend of a friend) and the atmosphere jovial. As a consumer there is a feeling of safety (friends are also invited) and, as the host has invited the consumer to their home, it is likely a level of trust exists between the host and consumer. It is also likely that (an) *opinion leader(s)* will be present.

Opinion leaders *are predisposed to receiving information and reprocessing it to influence others.*

The personal and social consequences of any medium – that is, of any extension of ourselves – result from the new scale that is introduced into our affairs by each extension of ourselves.
McLuhan, 1964

This is an extremely clever form of communication as it uses existing relationships with 'lead customers' and, to a certain extent, appropriates them. This is a very *direct* communications approach. More often than not, there is an obligation to buy the product(s) as the host is also a friend. Further to this, the organization has a captive audience and the host has a considerable opportunity to tell the attendees about the background of the organization and the brand, what the brand attributes are (meaning, value, quality, symbols) and why the consumer wants the brand in their life. As with any first/blind date, the chemistry is essential and the longevity of the relationship is generally dependent on the first impression. The importance then of ensuring a consistent message and/or consistent approach (*integration*) is very great.

> Integration *within a campaign should ensure consistency of message so as not to confuse the target audience and will provide added credibility as a result.*

Post-purchase communications

The initial post-purchase period in relationships is generally a time in which both parties are overlooking or at least more forgiving of faults and, as such, there is an excellent opportunity to overcome teething problems. Ideally this should be a honeymoon period for both parties as the customer enjoys the benefits of their new purchase. For the seller, it is the time for building a secure relationship foundation – based on trust. As both parties are typically more forgiving at this juncture, communication is usually used to combat negative post-purchase evaluation and is more indirect in overall approach. This is particularly true of high involvement purchases (cars, holidays) where emotion and time spent deliberating choices are key factors in the decision-making and post-purchase evaluation.

> **Q.** What is the difference between the pre- and post-purchase periods in a consumer's relationship with a supplier?
> **A.** *The focus of the post-purchase relationship may simply rest on a few perceived user benefits.*

Another form of communications is also important at this stage. *Internal marketing communication* is critical for ensuring that employees are aware of the brand values, and even more importantly to ensure that they are able to *demonstrate* these brand values and attributes during their interactions with customers and others outside the firm, such as on social media, in phone calls, during deliveries, and when dealing with complaints or queries or service provision.

> Internal marketing *communication is the extent to which brand values communicated through external communications are supported by the values shown by those inside the organization, particularly those who interact with external groups.*

Additionally, the higher the level of involvement, the greater the level of reassurance is likely to be. Organizations are increasingly innovative in their approach to reassuring consumers of luxury and/or high involvement products. Land Rover, for example, offer their customers a 'vehicle health check' which personalizes the car and recognizes the importance placed on the product by the consumer. This health check is captured on film and is sent as a file to the customer to set their mind at rest that (i) the service has been carried out and (ii) the vehicle is 'healthy' and less likely to break down.

> *Q.* How can advertising support consumers after the product or service has been purchased?
> *A. In bouts of negative* post-purchase evaluation, *the customer would be able to support their own beliefs with the positive visual association provided by the advertising. Similarly, the advert may also encourage a potential target audience to change their attitudes and values towards the brand.*

> • Post-purchase evaluation *occurs once a product has been purchased and is the time when cognitive dissonance is likely to occur.*
> • Cognitive dissonance *is when a consumer is dissatisfied with the product because it doesn't perform appropriately or when they wish they had purchased a superior product.*

Encouraging loyalty

As with all relationships, proportionately the greatest amount of time, money and effort has usually been spent on the initial 'honeymoon', i.e. post-purchase, period. But nowadays firms are increasingly realizing that maintaining a relationship and keeping it fresh is as important as developing it in the first place. The introduction of customer 'loyalty' cards has allowed organizations to collate and continuously update information from customers about their personal details and circumstances, income and spending, their household composition and buying behaviour (see Relationships and interactions, Building loyalty and engagement). As a result, they are able to monitor what individuals consume, how often they consume and the extent to which they are interested in *sales promotions* and special offers. They are then able to tailor promotions especially for groups of consumers (segments) in order to maximize sales and generate more repeat purchases.

> **Q.** Does loyalty suggest that the consumers will only buy one brand or use one retail outlet?
> **A.** *Loyalty rather assumes that consumers will not shop elsewhere – but consumers are loyal for a variety of reasons (convenience, lack of choice, type of existing product prevents buying parts elsewhere, etc.). Marketers should beware of consumers' spurious loyalty (see Relationships and interactions).*

> Sales promotion *is a widely used term covering many promotional activities but excludes advertising. It is generally associated with free offers, price deals and premium offers.*

There are outlets, such as The Bear Factory, that take building relationships very seriously indeed. They are unique in their interactive approach to constructing the product and the 'relationship' is encouraged immediately. The shop sells soft toys but, as a consumer, you are expected to choose the type of soft toy (monkey/dog/bear), the stuffing and the 'heart'. You are encouraged to make a wish as you put the heart into the soft toy before the toy is stitched. You must choose a name for the toy and you are issued with a birth certificate once you complete the details of the individual who is to receive the toy (including their date of birth).

This information is then processed and the recipient of the gift will get regular 'personal' direct marketing, including reminders about the soft toy's birthday (they have an extensive product range on clothing for the toys) and birthday cards for the recipient of the soft toy. Maintaining and developing the relationship is made easy through the use of interactive purchasing and clever database marketing. The Bear Factory have also expanded their offering online.

> Direct marketing *refers to all communication approaches that generate a series of communication messages and responses with actual or potential consumers.*

Information and databases

While a customer database holds considerably more information than an address book, the principle is the same. An address book contains names, addresses and telephone numbers of all the people known to the owner with, perhaps, some additional information on their likes/dislikes. A customer database holds information on members of a target audience including age and lifestyle. Databases can be created (using a sales promotion, for example, and by collecting names and addresses of competition entrants or using existing/previous customers) or can be rented or bought (from the Royal Mail or a variety of other suppliers). Advances in information technology (see Creating Solutions: the role of IT) enable computerized databases to contain many levels and therefore an organization can easily retrieve their best customers, see who is responsive to which type of communication approach and how often, and when these customers buy the product or service (Evans, 1998). Supermarket loyalty cards are an example of database collation and management, with supermarkets tailoring relevant sales promotion for specific groups within the target audience.

> Database management *is the cooperative management and upkeep of precise customer and potential customer information (in addition to competitor information, market information and internal company information).*

Q. What is the benefit of database management?
A. There is some monitoring and a proactive approach towards the relationship by the organization. If a financial services provider has given a loan to a consumer, for example, they can manage the relationship by monitoring repayments and by checking before completion of the loan period if the customer wants another loan or another banking product (e.g. credit card). In this way the consumer knows the organization is still interested in them and the dialogue is a way of maintaining and developing the relationship.

Q. What are the problems associated with database management?
A. There are problems of privacy, where the consumer feels the organization is being intrusive in its communications approach. It may be a factor in customers straying from the relationship.

Q. How committed are consumers?
A. Temptations to switch brands or suppliers are everywhere and as a consumer it is relatively easy to be promiscuous.

Discouraging/encouraging switching behaviour

Financial service providers who offer no or low APR on credit cards to attract new consumers often find that when they increase their rates many of their 'new' consumers move their credit card debt to other financial service providers offering the lowest rate. These customers are sometimes pejoratively referred to as 'rate tarts' and in this scenario there is little the organizations can do to prevent this happening time and again. A tie-in may be an option but it might dissuade genuine new customers from applying for a credit card and competition in the financial services sector is fierce.

Indeed, there are organizations that encourage switching. Utility providers, for example, constantly urge customers to switch their gas or electricity suppliers, offering comparison websites to allow the best deals to be researched. While customers tend to be apathetic about switching their utility providers, some firms clearly benefit from encouraging more consumer switching. For competitors who are followers rather than leaders, it is advantageous when consumers can be easily dissuaded from continuing a relationship with an existing service provider. With competitors using communications emphasizing charm versus familiarity, charisma versus boredom, the consumer may be tempted to risk their existing relationship.

A long-term relationship will involve many changes, with the consumer modifying, adapting and becoming more experienced as time goes on. Communication approaches, alternative messages and media vehicles used must reflect the permutation in external factors (economic changes, cultural shifts), micro factors (competition, suppliers and distributors) and – importantly – changes in the consumer's experiences. As the consumption of soft drinks has altered significantly in recent years, with consumers realizing the benefits of drinking mineral water as opposed to high-sugar and low-fruit substitutes, it has been important for organizations to address these changes. For

example, in 2016 Coca-Cola spent £10 million on their 'classic Coke' relaunch, and Coke Zero has been rebranded as Coca-Cola Zero Sugar in a deliberate attempt to emphasize the difference between sugar and no sugar drinks.

Q. Why do marketing relationships end?
A. Consumers and service providers may cite irreconcilable differences and separate for a number of reasons. Companies may become complacent about their consumers, expecting them to remain loyal even when they have failed to develop, adapt and modify their product or service. Trial purchases with other brands may have alerted the consumer to better quality, superior service, additional brand attributes or product features the current provider does not offer.

Marks & Spencer, regarded as synonymous with British culture, have been going through yet another period of change to revive their clothing and homeware business. They have recognized that their target audience are interested in the style, fit and quality of clothing and that they also need to modify and adapt their service provision. While a move towards fashionable contemporary clothing may entice shoppers, some of the target audience is unlikely to return to Marks & Spencer as a result of the subsequent discontent felt during the years of indifference towards the developing needs of the consumer. However, some will have an emotional bond with the brand and will be forgiving.

> Brand identity *is the position the organization wants to believe they hold in the minds of the consumer. This identity is encapsulated in the logo, signage, uniform and letterheads of an organization, and reflects enduring qualities to be aspired to.*

Many of the problems faced by Marks & Spencer and many other organizations are largely attributable to the difference between *brand identity* and *brand image*. While the organization might believe consumers are loyal, the consumers may be looking elsewhere for service as the brand identity may not be credible, reliable or comprehensive.

> Brand image *is the actual perception of the organization held by the consumer. The perception rather reflects superficial qualities and existing associations. Problems occur when the gap widens between identity and image.*

Maintaining a dialogue between the organization and the customer is crucial if switching is to be discouraged and avoided. In any case, of course, some consumers will prefer the familiarity of their existing organization, i.e. 'better the devil you know'. For suppliers, it is important to leave the door open and make it as easy as possible for consumers to return to the brand, service or product if they so wish. BT, for example, have previously used their advertising to demonstrate how easy it is to reconnect, and mobile phone service providers offer consumers the opportunity to restart their contract with their existing mobile phone number for up to six months free of charge. As it is considerably cheaper to retain an existing consumer than to find a new one, these tactics are in the interests of the organization.

In some cases the dissolution of the marketing relationship may be unavoidable. The consumer may have different needs and tastes and the organization or brand may simply be catering for a different audience. In cases where consumers have received poor service, they may leave the organization without (a) telling the organization they are leaving or (b) telling the organization why they are leaving. The best the marketer can do in terms of utilizing communications with the 'ex-customer' is to provide them with an opportunity for feedback and reflection on their reasons for leaving. Investment in evaluation is key to understanding what went wrong and how to alter marketing and operations so that other customers can be prevented from switching. The most serious implication for the firm is not just the loss of one customer but that their own lack of understanding and insufficient knowledge of the reasons for their behaviour will fail to improve the service provision for *existing consumers*. The question then becomes: how long will they stay?

As previously explained, communication approaches must be timely in order to be effective. In the UK, for example, some universities are finding it increasingly difficult to differentiate themselves even through branding, and it is extremely important for this 'sector' (represented by Universities UK) to retain their existing customers (students). In order to maximize retention rates, exit interviews (as part of student retention schemes) are being conducted with consumers to find out why they are leaving university. This information (regarding service, contact, finance, personal matters and quality) is fed back into the organization where improvements are often made for both existing students and potential recruits. This may be through the introduction of more student services or through the modules being delivered to the students who remain registered.

However, organizations are also becoming more picky about their long-term partners.

Q. How do organizations deal with consumers they do not want to have a relationship with?
A. A process known as 'de-selection' is regularly occurring in many consumer and business-to-business markets, and organizations are very selective about the consumers to whom they offer their business. Communication approaches reflect this 'de-selection', where customers who will be less profitable are encouraged not to continue the relationship.

> De-selection *is where service providers consider which relationships are more profitable for them (or are too costly for them to continue with) and stop providing a product or service, or make the product or service too costly in order to discourage the relationship.*

Direct marketing is usually employed in the financial services sector to suggest new accounts and existing accounts become 'closed issue' – that is, the bank does not take on new customers for that account and lowers the interest rate to maximize profit. De-selection needs to be a formal and considered process, and not merely one where customers close accounts and are not 'rescued' at the point of closure.

Greater expectations?

Having been through a relationship, are consumers more experienced?

> *Q.* Are consumers more determined to make new relationships work or are they more fickle and promiscuous as a result of their experience?
> *A. The answer is as individual as consumers are and, with the diversification of target audiences across consumer markets, it is becoming increasingly difficult to segment the market. However, organizations continue to strive to reach their customers through communication messages and varying communication approaches – some examples of which have been outlined earlier in this section.*

Reinvention

In conclusion, it may be necessary to reinvent a brand in order to make it appealing to existing or potential consumers. As a greater distance between the producer and consumer is often the reason a relationship fails, minimizing the gap between brand identity and brand image is essential to maintaining a successful brand. Using communications to build relationships and to develop and maintain a dialogue with the consumer is key if the brand is to remain current and credible.

Johnson & Johnson relaunched its baby care business in 2016 as they realized that new mothers are now switching to all-natural products – typically made by smaller companies for a higher price. Despite Johnson & Johnson being the 'go to' products for parents since 1893, our younger generation of consumers prefer simpler, more 'wholesome' ingredients. And these shifting tastes of younger consumers (often dubbed 'millennials') have affected a number of other well-known organizations. McDonald's, Gap, Avon and Heinz have all been subjected to new competition, primarily from high-quality, naturally sourced items. Reviewing the expectations of the target audience on a regular basis and tracking their purchase preferences can lead even the most established organizations and brands down the path of reinvention.

Therefore, the significance of using communication approaches to build relationships is about narrowing the gap between the producer and the consumer. Figure 2.8 highlights the issues associated with brand identity and brand image, with the examples discussed in this section demonstrating the difficulty producers have in 'getting close' to the consumer.

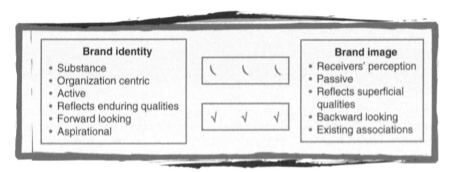

Figure 2.8 Differences between brand identity and brand image

This section has considered the effectiveness of communications and building relationships through communications using a direct approach (for example, a PartyLite Candle evening or The Bear Factory) or an indirect approach (for example, the use of celebrities). Ad literacy – the extent to which the target audience is familiar with the communication messages used by organizations – was addressed through discussion of language used to familiarize the customer with the brand. The use of branding (semiotics, attributes and values associated with brands) is also a key feature of building relationships, and the appropriate use of communications in order to maximize impact was also explored through the whynot!/Anchor example. Immediacy of the communications message was considered through the description of ambient advertising. The necessity for communications to be more creative, abstract and engaging was the focus of many of the examples provided, with organizations that thought 'outside the box'

used to demonstrate developments in the communications arena. Of course, effective communication messages are only really successful when married with appropriate media planning schedules – reach and importance of suitable media selection was also briefly explored. As the relationship between an organization and a customer develops it is essential to maintain a dialogue and this was particularly evident through the examples of database management.

Finally, enjoying relationships with brands as a consumer will probably be the result of considerable research on behalf of the organization. As with any relationship, knowledge is power and effective communications can only be successful as part of a two-way communications process. Organizations need consumers to assist in developing, adapting and co-creating a powerful experience.

Happy relationship building.

FURTHER READING

Beard, F. K. (2013) How practices have changed in two decades. *Journal of Advertising Research*, **53** (3).

Hutter, K. (2015) Unusual location and unexpected execution in advertising: a content analysis and test of effectiveness in ambient advertisements. *Journal of Marketing Communications,* **21** (1).

Johns, R. & English, R. (2016) Transition of self: repositioning the celebrity brand through social media – the case of Elizabeth Gilbert. *Journal of Business Research*, **69** (1).

Kim, K. K., Williams, J. & Wilcox, G. (2016) 'Kid tested, mother approved': the relationship between advertising expenditures and 'most-loved' brands. *International Journal of Advertising*, **35** (1).

Kozinets, R. V. (2014) Social brand engagement: a new idea. *GfK-Marketing Intelligence Review*, **6** (2).

Mora, J. D. (2016) Social context and advertising effectiveness: a dynamic study. *International Journal of Advertising*, **35** (2).

Ogilvie, M. & Mizerski, K. (2011) Using semiotics in consumer research to understand everyday phenomena. *International Journal of Market Research*, **53** (5).

Wagler, A. (2013) Embracing change: exploring how creative professionals use interactive media in advertising campaigns. *Journal of Interactive Advertising*, **13** (2).

Yang, S., Lin, S., Carlson, J. & Ross, W. (2016) Brand engagement on social media: will firms' social media efforts influence search engine advertising effectiveness? *Journal of Marketing Management*, **35** (5–6).

Ten of the best websites, blogs and social media

www.nytimes.com (media and advertising section)

www.fortune.com

www.advertisingage.com

www.thedrum.com

www.campaignlive.co.uk

www.sethgodin.typepad.com

twitter.com/markritson

www.oystercatchers.com

www.marketingprofs.com

www.storyneedle.com

Ten of the best agencies

Anomaly

Mother

IDEO

R/GA

We Are Social

Droga5

SapientNitro

Mediacom

Fred & Farid

72andSunny

A network perspective to business relationships

Jaqueline Pels

I n this section we look at the role of networks in building market relations and the various business institutions that participate and support them.

What does the term 'network' mean?

A marketing network is essentially a set of interlinked business relationships. Networks are a subset of an ecosystem. Ecosystems include a wider set of relationships between business and non-business (e.g. government, non-governmental organizations) institutions. Let's work through *an example* of what happens in the marketing network when you make an internet purchase.

Suppose you log on to Dell.com or any other website to buy a product. If it is not a standardized offer (i.e. the same item for each customer, such as a book) then you will have to help build *your own* product solution, say for a PC, where you can select different combinations of screen, stack, printer, sound card, extra memory, etc. This means that, through a menu-selection process online, you have to provide the company with specifications of what you want so that the product can be assembled. Sometimes, when you have finished specifying your requirements and check the price, you realize that it is too expensive – so then you go a couple of links back and alter some of the selections in your original specification in order to get the best product–price combination that you can afford. This online product–price specification process creates a dialogue between you, the customer, and Dell, the supplier (see Figure 2.9). And *dialogue* is one of the *key characteristics* of a marketing relationship (see The role of communications).

Continuing this example, if eventually you reach a satisfactory product solution and decide to buy the PC, you fill in payment details, then press 'buy' and wait for the product to be sent to you. This is the end of *your* troubles or concerns as the customer. But they now become more pressing for the supplier. From

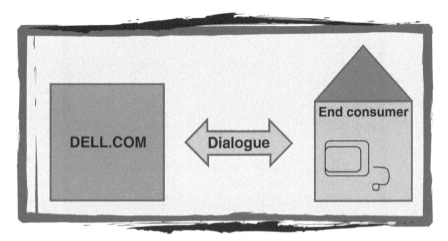

Figure 2.9 Dialogue between supplier and consumer

that moment of purchase, Dell or the organization from which you bought the product needs to start organizing a series of operational actions in order to ensure delivery of the product to you promptly. Your single purchase act will trigger a whole set of decisions and activities by the seller. It could be that some of the components for the computer are not manufactured in the company and that these must be shipped in from suppliers (e.g. Intel microprocessors). In this case there must be a fast and efficient *information system* installed between the two firms (see Creating Solutions: Information technology and innovation) and *trust and commitment* between the parties must be high (see Relationships and interactions). Furthermore, once the PC is assembled it needs to be delivered to you, thus contracts and agreements with external suppliers of transportation must be made. If we were to go into details, this description would become more and more entangled and specific. This set of interconnected and interdependent business relationships is what we call a *network* (see Figure 2.10).

This example of an internet-based PC purchase describes a small and specific network directly involving only the supplier–manufacturer–consumer linkages. Traditionally the supplier-to-manufacturer part of the link would have been discussed under the title of 'supply' or 'procurement' while the manufacturer–consumer link would have been labelled as 'marketing' or 'retailing'. The value of the *network* perspective is that it looks at the *whole set* of relationships involved *simultaneously*, from the source of raw materials right through to delivery of the final product to the customer (see Moving Space: Moving materials through market space).

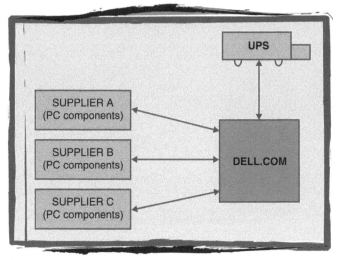

Figure 2.10 Example of a network

Furthermore, if we were to look at Figure 2.10 from a wider perspective and we were able to *zoom out* further from the supplier–manufacturer–consumer link, we would see many other relations (that is, dialogues) occurring with other actors. *We would be seeing the broader network* as in Figure 2.11. In the Dell.com example, it implies that looking at the broader network will more accurately identify all the relationships and *institutions* involved in the supply and delivery of the product to the customer – first stimulated by the act of purchase (see Consuming Experience) – including understanding which are all the institutions involved in the process

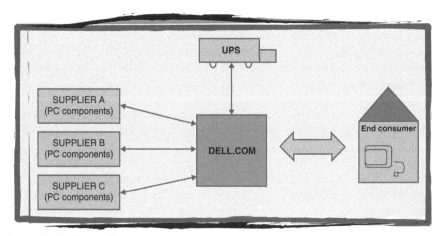

Figure 2.11 View of the broader network

of: designing the most user-friendly website, defining the set of suppliers of PC components, establishing the security that will allow buyers to purchase over the internet, guaranteeing the delivery process, etc.

Types of business institutions in marketing exchanges

Business institutions are organizations that transform inputs into outputs. There are three types of business institutions: households, private firms (retailers, competitors, suppliers, etc.) and public firms. Between these institutions, two different types of exchange can take place: (1) market exchanges and (2) relational exchanges.

1 In a *market exchange* the parties are independent and *choose* to interact with the counterpart because they perceive a benefit in engaging in this form of exchange. Once again, if we look at our Dell.com example, it is quite likely that before deciding to purchase a Dell PC the buyer has looked at and searched other websites, and furthermore it is possible that our potential buyer has even gone to visit some offline stores. This type of exchange has strong assumptions. It believes that both the buyer and the seller are seeking to maximize their utility and that both parties/institutions have other options (i.e. other buyers or other sellers). Furthermore, each exchange is seen as independent from previous and future market exchanges.
2 *Relational exchanges* go beyond the pricing incentives. They seek to build social bonds on top of any financial bond that may exist. What holds the relationship together is the knowledge that the actors have about each other. There is a beginning of a dialogue and both parties benefit from giving and receiving information. This is the case when we provide Amazon.com with information about a topic we are interested in (e.g. the Harry Potter saga) and Amazon.com then sends us updates on the latest books, games, etc. related to our interests. It is important to notice that this information exchange might not lead to a sale. These are relationships that are solidified through structural bonds – in other words, creating special adaptations for a specific relationship that cannot be transferred to other relationships. This is the case for a consultancy firm that builds a special task force to serve a customer. The skills required to solve the problems of customer 'A' will differ from those required to solve the problems of customer 'B'; thus, the task forces will be integrated by different team members.

Choosing a relationship

Let us return to the Dell.com PC purchase example. Dell.com's core business is not producing computers, it is offering consumers the possibility of building their own PC with the certainty that they can access the latest technology. Thus, their competitive advantage will be high flexibility at low costs. Dell.com could choose between three options: producing all the PC components themselves, buying them in the market, or developing a relationship with certain suppliers. Let's analyse these three alternatives.

1 If they choose option 1 (producing PC components themselves), they will have full control of the process and will not need to adapt to another institution (the supplier). However, costs will probably be very high as the industry is a very dynamic one and to be in the forefront of it requires indigenous investments. As we can see, the do-it-yourself option doesn't seem to be the best alternative.

2 If Dell.com choose option 2 (the market exchange), they could obtain low costs by having a different supplier bid for each component. But let us remember that Dell.com do not sell standardized PCs, they sell tailor-made PCs, and if they are going to purchase components on a bidding system, most likely the supplier will require them to buy batches of PC components in exchange for the low prices. Unfortunately, Dell.com do not know ahead of time the specifications of the PCs they are going to sell on a particular day. Thus, to have control and be flexible they will have to have high stock and thus the cost advantage obtained in the bidding process might be lost.

3 If Dell.com choose option 3 (the relational exchange), in order to obtain the required levels of cost, adaptation and control the company will need a partner that sees itself as part of a larger network. This partner will understand that its own success depends on Dell.com's success and that both partners need to adapt to the end consumer's requirements. In other words, adaptation will be natural as the supplier and Dell.com will probably develop a 'just in time' (JIT) programme. Control will not be the result of strict and rigorous contracts but of the commitment both institutions have. Finally, costs will not be dependent on volume. To find such a partner is not easy. As suggested before, the fundamental requirement for a successful relational exchange is mutuality.

Relations, exchange and networks

Because relationships are connected, change in one of the relationships is likely to affect other relationships. Suppose Coca-Cola suggest to Sainsbury's that they have a special in-store display. Before agreeing, Sainsbury's should take into consideration how the other soft-drink suppliers will react because if the Coca-Cola initiative is successful (and let us remember that Coca-Cola is engaging in it in order to be successful) this will affect negatively the other soft-drink firms and Sainsbury's needs to think about the big picture. On the other hand, Coca-Cola must also consider how the other retailers will react. This is called *network thinking*.

In the Coca-Cola–Sainsbury's case, the *activity* that is being connected is a promotion. We have already discussed that both Coca-Cola and Sainsbury's need to consider the impact of this activity on other business institutions they are interacting with. However, they also need to coordinate this activity with other activities that they are involved with and that are taking place at the same time. Probably Coca-Cola will be supporting this in-store display with some advertising; thus, the timing of both activities must match. On the other hand, it is quite likely that Sainsbury's will also have some other in-store activities occurring, such as a product sampling. Sainsbury's needs to make sure that these two

in-store activities are harmonious (e.g. free cheese sampling and the Coca-Cola special offer) and that there are not too many in-store activities simultaneously that would distract purchasers. Such activities involve the technical, administrative and commercial actions of a company which can be connected in different ways to those of another business institution.

It is important to notice that not only activities are being connected. Actually, Coca-Cola needs Sainsbury's *resource* (the store) to reach the end consumer with its promotional activity and Sainsbury's needs Coca-Cola's resource (the actual discount the promotions involves) to provide its customer with a financial benefit that will attract buyers to its stores.

So networks connect sets of business institutions' activities and resources with the ultimate aim of providing a benefit (value) to end consumers. But one key question then is where and when do networks end? This is no easy question. It depends on where and what we are looking at.

- If we were thinking in very restricted terms (i.e. selling and buying goods) then our network would be limited to the set of buyer–seller relationships the focal firm has – see Figure 2.9 in our Dell.com case – just the Dell.com–end consumers network or the suppliers–Dell.com network.
- If we were thinking in more ample terms (that is, all types of exchanges) then we would have to consider a more ample and extended network which included the customer's customer, suppliers, suppliers' suppliers and even non-business institutions such as governments (see Figures 2.10 and 2.11 in our Dell.com case) – the set of suppliers–Dell.com–UPS–end consumers–other institutions.

In other words, the limits of a network of institutions that create value are variable, depending on the view and level of focus on the marketing operation. If it is a global view then obviously the network of business/non-business institutions is very large, but usually we are looking at the network involved in the supply of a specific product or associated with a specific company, or at most in one industry or business sector.

At the level of the single firm, the marketers need to understand which are their customers (both intermediaries and segments of end consumers), their suppliers (both direct and indirect suppliers) and the other non-business institutions that may be related to a given value-creating process (government, press and media, user groups, environmentalists).

In this section we have tried to explain how building relations can be understood in terms of the institutions involved and the network approach to analysing the links between market relationships. This means identifying the set of institutions that participate in the marketing process through their activities and resources. However, we have also acknowledged that business institutions might choose not to be engaged in relational exchanges and favour a more market or trans-actional approach (see Relationships and interactions).

Key definitions

1 A *network* is a set of interconnected and interdependent business relation-ships.
2 *Institutions* are business organizations that transform inputs into outputs, as well as non-business organizations.
3 A *market exchange* is the simultaneous transaction of valued goods, servi-ces and ideas between two parties (business institutions) that are capable of accepting or rejecting the values offered.
4 A *relational exchange* can be based on: (i) a financial benefit, (ii) a social bond or (iii) a structural bond.
5 The fundamental requirement for a successful relational exchange is *mutual-ity*.
6 *Networking* implies taking into consideration how changes in one relationship may affect other connected relationships.
7 *Networks create value* by connecting institutions, their activities and their resources.
8 The *limits of a network* of institutions are subjective.

FURTHER READING

Christopher, M., Payne, A. & Ballantyne, D. (2013) *Relationship Marketing: Bringing Quality, Customer Service and Marketing Together*. Butterworth-Heinemann: Oxford.

Ford, D., Gadde, L. E., Håkansson, H. & Snehota, I. (2011) *Managing Business Relationships*. Wiley: Chichester.

Hollensen, S. (2015) *Marketing Management: A Relationship Approach*. Pearson Education: Harrow.

Mele, C., Pels, J. & Storbacka, K. (2015) A holistic market conceptualization. *Journal of the Academy of Marketing Science*, **43** (1), 100–114.

Möller, K. & Wilson, D. (eds.) (1995) *Business Marketing: An Interaction and Network Perspective*. Kluwer Academic: Norwell, MA.

Pels, J. (1999) Exchange relationships in consumer markets? *European Journal of Marketing*, **33** (1/2), 19–37.

Sheth, J. N. & Parvatiyar, A. (2000) *Handbook of Relationship Marketing*. Sage: London.

References

Bagozzi, R.P. (1995) Reflections on relationship marketing in consumer markets. *Journal of the Academy of Marketing Science*, **23** (4), 272–277.

Berry, L.L. (1983) Relationship marketing. In: *Emerging Perspectives of Services Marketing* (L.L. Berry, G.L. Shostack & G.D. Upah, eds.). American Marketing Association: Chicago.

Brodie, R.J., Coviello, N.E. & Winklhofer, H. (2008) Contemporary marketing practices research program: a review of the first decade. *Journal of Business & Industrial Marketing*, **23** (2), 84–94.

Brodie, R.J., Coviello, N.E., Brookes, R.W. & Little, V. (1997) Towards a paradigm shift in marketing? An examination of current marketing practices. *Journal of Marketing Management*, **13** (5), 383–406.

Brodie, R.J., Hollebeek, L.D., Juric, B. & Ilic, A. (2011) Customer engagement: conceptual domain, fundamental propositions and implications for research. *Journal of Service Research*, **14** (3), 252–271.

Buttle, F. (1996) Relationship marketing. In: *Relationship Marketing: Theory and Practice* (F. Buttle, ed.). Paul Chapman: London.

Christopher, M., Payne, A. & Ballantyne, D. (1991) *Relationship Marketing: Bringing Quality, Customer Service and Marketing Together*. Butterworth-Heinemann: Oxford.

Coviello, N., Brodie, R., Danaher, R. & Johnston, W. (2002) How firms relate to their markets: an empirical examination of contemporary marketing practices. *Journal of Marketing*, **66** (3), 33–46.

Dawkins, P.M. & Reicheld, F.F. (1990) Customer retention as a competitive weapon. *Directors and Board*, 14 (Summer), 42–47.

Dick, A.S. & Basu, K. (1994) Customer loyalty: towards an integrated framework. *Journal of the Academy of Marketing Science*, **22** (2), 99–113.

East, R., Harris, P., Wilson, G. & Lomax, W. (1995) Loyalty to Supermarkets. *International Journal of Retail, Distribution and Consumer Research*, **5** (1), 99–110.

Emmott, S. (2013). *10 Billion*. Penguin: London.

Evans, M. (1998) From 1086 and 1984: direct marketing into the millennium. *Marketing Intelligence and Planning*, **16** (1), 57–67.

Evans, M., O'Malley, L. & Patterson, M. (2004) *Exploring Direct and Customer Relationship Marketing*. Thomson: London.

Ford, D. (2004) The IMP group and international marketing. *International Marketing Review*, **21** (2 February), 139–141.

Fournier, S., Dobscha, S. & Nick, D.G. (1998) Preventing the premature death of relationship marketing. *Harvard Business Review*, **76** (1), 42–51.

Fowles, J. (1996) *Advertising and Popular Culture*. Sage: London.

Grönroos, C. (1994) From marketing mix to relationship marketing: towards a paradigm shift in marketing. *Management Decision*, **32** (2), 4–20.

Gummesson, E. (1999) *Total Relationship Marketing*. Butterworth-Heinemann: Oxford.

Gupta, A. (2011) Arunhati Roy: The people who created the crisis will not be the ones who come up with a solution. In *The Guardian*, 30 November 2011. www.guardian.co.uk/world/2011/nov/30/arundhati-roy-interview

Håkansson, H. & Snehota, I. (eds.) (1995) *Developing Relationships in Business Networks*. Routledge: London.

Knights, D., Sturdy, A. & Morgan, G. (1994) "The consumer rules? An examination of the rhetoric and "reality" of marketing in financial services," *European Journal of Marketing*, **28** (3), 42–54.

Lazer, W. & Kelley, E. (eds.) (1973) *Social Marketing: Perspectives and Viewpoints*. Irwin: Homewood, IL.

Lovato, C., Linn, G., Stead, L.F. & Best, A. (2004) Impact of tobacco advertising and promotion on increasing adolescent smoking behaviours. *The Cochrane Library*, **2**.

McGoldrick, P. & Andre, E. (1997) Consumer misbehavior: promiscuity or loyalty in grocery shopping. *Journal of Retailing and Consumer Services*, **4** (2), 73–81.

McLuhan, M. (1964) *Understanding Media*. Routledge & Kegan Paul: New York.

Morgan, R.M. & Hunt, S.D. (1994) The commitment–trust theory of relationship marketing. *Journal of Marketing*, **58** (July), 20–38.

O'Brien, L. & Jones, C. (1995) Do rewards really create loyalty? *Harvard Business Review*, May/June, 75–82.

O'Malley, L. (1998) Can loyalty schemes really build loyalty? *Marketing Intelligence and Planning*, **16** (1), 47–55.

Payne, A. (1995) *Advances in Relationship Marketing*. Kogan Page: London.

Payne, A. (2000) Relationship marketing: managing multiple markets. In: *Cranfield School of Management, Marketing Management: A Relationship Marketing Perspective*. Macmillan: Oxford.

Pels, J., Brodie, R. & Johnston, W. (2004) Benchmarking business-to-business marketing practices in transitional and developed economies: Argentina compared to the USA and New Zealand. *Journal of Business and Industrial Marketing*, **19** (6), 386–396.

Pierce, J.P., Gilpin, E.A. & Choi, W.S. (1999) Sharing the blame: smoking experimentation and future smoking-attributable mortality due to Joe Camel and Marlboro advertising and promotions. *Tobacco Control*, **8**, 37–44.

Pingeot, L. (2014) *Corporate Influence in the Post-2015 Process*. www.misereor.org/fileadmin/user_upload/misereor_org/Publications/englisch/working-paper-corporate-influence-in-post-2015-process.pdf, accessed June 2017.

Reicheld, F.F. (1994) *The Loyalty Effect*. Harvard Business School Press: Cambridge, MA.

Rowley, J. (2005) The four Cs of customer loyalty. *Marketing Intelligence and Planning*, **23** (6), 574–581.

Saks, A.M. (2006), Antecedents and consequences of employee engagement. *Journal of Managerial Psychology*, **21** (7), 600–619.

Sheth, J. & Parvatiyar, A. (1995) Relationship marketing in consumer markets: antecedents and consequences. *Journal of the Academy of Marketing Science*, **23** (4), 255–271.

Sheth, J. N. & Parvatiyar, A. (2000) *Handbook of Relationship Marketing*. Sage: London.

Srivastava, R. K., Shrevani, T. K. & Fahey, L. (1999) Marketing, business processes and shareholder value: an organizationally embedded view of marketing activities and the discipline of marketing. *Journal of Marketing*, **63**, 168–179.

Van Doorn, J., Lemon, K. E., Mittal, V., Naß, S., Pick, D., Pirner, P. & Verhoef, P. C. (2010) Customer engagement behavior: theoretical foundations and research directions. *Journal of Service Research*, **13** (3), 253–266.

Veloutsou, C., Tzokas, N. & Saren, M. (2002) Relationship marketing: what if? *European Journal of Marketing*, **36** (4), 433–439.

Webster, F. E. (1992) The changing role of marketing in the corporation. *Journal of Marketing*, **56** (October), 1–17.

Zwick, D. & Cayla, J. (2011) *Inside Marketing: Practices, Ideologies, Devices*. Oxford University Press: Oxford.

EXPERIENCE

consuming Experience

We are all consumers. Unless we go and live on a desert island we cannot avoid consuming and thus playing a role in the marketing process. This chapter looks at the role of consumers in marketing, why and what they consume, and the various ways in which consumption is related to identity. Consumer culture plays a significant part in the creation and reproduction of people's tastes, dreams and aspirations. We discuss the influence of consumer subcultures and tribes on individuals' lifestyles, possessions and values. The concepts of consumer co-production and satisfaction are explained as well as the corollary of dissatisfied and disadvantaged consumers. The latest ideas about collaborative consumption, sharing and access are also introduced.

what is consumer?

Consumerism is often criticized for being materialistic, with an emphasis on the value and use of physical objects over non-material pursuits such as ideas, ideals and society. Yet, paradoxically, consumer culture is more and more a visual culture in which the consumer is bombarded with multimedia images, pictorial advertisements, 'sightseeing' vacations, brightly lit shopping arcades, entertainment 'spectacles', 'eye-catching' packaging. Much consumption is visual consumption (Schroeder, 2003); therefore, it is not just materials that are consumed but non-material images too.

Because the consumption process is more complex than it first appears, it is useful to look at the various explanations that have been proposed in order to be able to analyse from different perspectives in any given situation what it is that is being consumed.

Explanations of what is consumed
- *Materials and energy*
- *Labour*
- *Use or utility*
- *Experiences*
- *Culture*
- *Meaning and signs.*

Consuming materials and energy

It might appear obvious what the consumer consumes – physical materials that make up the products and services that they purchase and use. A car buyer consumes the car as they drive it around; we all consume the food we purchase as we eat it, or even as it sits in the fridge and rots! One definition of the product (Kotler, 1967) is '. . . anything that can be offered to a market for attention, acquisition, use or consumption that might satisfy a want or a need. It includes physical objects, services, persons, places, organizations and ideas' (see Creating Solutions). Therefore, it should be fairly clear from the wide range of the type of things that consumers consume – i.e. objects, services, people, places – and thus the physical objects that are 'used up' as they are consumed.

When you think about it, however, it becomes a little less clear what exactly it is that is being consumed in these marketing processes. One complication is that it is not only the car that is being consumed in the above example, so is petrol, so is the

road surface and the road *space*, so even is the air. Often, several things are consumed together, what are sometimes called 'complementary' products. The materials and energy in products are certainly consumed – although an ecological view would point out that they are in fact *transformed* into other forms of energy and matter, such as waste, gas, power, etc. (see Marketing Contexts: Marketing values).

It is not only these physical components that are consumed, however, because most products also have intangible features – such as after sales service, guarantees, instructions – which we know are important for customers (see Creating Solutions). In addition, many purchases now are not primarily physical products at all – for instance insurance, entertainment, education, health – therefore, the 'objects of consumption' cannot simply be the materials that comprise products.

Another aspect is that, from the customer's point of view, consumption is essentially an *experience*. How well they enjoyed the 'experience' of using it usually determines how satisfied the consumer is with the product. Also, in driving and even when eating, the consumer's time and some attention and effort are being 'consumed' as well. And what about the whole modern marketing phenomenon of branding (see Brand Selection): can people 'consume' a brand label simply by showing off the logo?

One way in which marketing has dealt with the multiple aspects of products that can be consumed is to think in terms of the 'total market offering'. According to the traditional marketing view, the product comprises a 'bundle of attributes' that can be analysed in terms of its constituent elements, including benefits, services and expectations, which together make up the 'total offering' to consumers (see Creating Solutions). Any or all these parts of the 'total' offering can be consumed.

Consuming labour

It may appear a strange way of looking at it nowadays, but in the eighteenth and nineteenth centuries most economists regarded the products and services that people purchased as a sort of 'jellied work', i.e. other people's labour that is solidified and stored as products. So when you purchased bread from the baker what you were buying was the *product* of all the labour activities that went into producing and delivering it, i.e. the farming and harvesting of the ingredients, the milling and milking, transporting and baking. The bread you buy is the outcome of this work and if you did not choose to buy it you would have to buy the materials and do the baking yourself. Buying the bread saves you work and this is what you pay for and consume.

This historical emphasis on the labour value of products fitted in with the times being influenced by the spirit of the Reformation, which valorized work as good in itself, as spiritually dignified, an act of homage. All this work produced 'goods' and therefore it figures that it was the work input that made them valuable.

You can still see how this labour view of consumption can be applied to today's products. For example, large parts of the labour function that were labelled as 'housework' and performed by 'housewives' or even by servants during the early twentieth century have now been incorporated in manufactured products and machinery. Home cooking has been substituted by ready-made and convenience food; home-cleaning work is mechanized by washing machines, dishwashers, vacuum cleaners, etc. Here some of the 'unpaid' house labour activities that Ivan Illich (1981) calls 'shadow work' have been in part transformed into objects of consumption within the market exchange nexus.

This example shows how consumers 'at home' use domestic appliances to per-form 'housework'. They are usually consuming them in order to help minimize the amount of work they have to perform, to make their housework easier and to save time. Thus today's products like the Hoover or Dyson vacuum cleaner

can also be regarded as 'packaged work'. The next stage of development is likely to trans-form work from these types of mechanized products to robotic products that will perform decision-making activities as well as physical functions. So, despite the apparently outdated nature of the original economists' view of con-suming labour, almost all products and services can still be viewed as labour 'saving' precisely because by buying them 'ready made' they save the consumer from the time and work involved in making them themselves.

Apart from these more obvious examples of labour-saving devices, however, there are many other consumption aspects of products or ser-vices that are not so well explained as work substitutes. For instance, all products consist of physical materials and, whether it is bread or a car, these material elements are required – as well as labour – to manufacture the product. For many products, the materials used to make them are much more expensive than the labour input. Whatever the proportional inputs, from the consumer's point of view it is not so much the labour involved in manufacturing a car that is consumed, it is much more directly the physical objects – metal, rubber, glass, oil, gas – that are 'used up' over time as they drive it.

So there is a fundamental problem with the 'consuming labour' idea nowadays. The 'total market offering' for any product – a car, bread, even for a Hoover – involves more aspects than simply labour saving; it includes the materials used to make it and features such as design, usability, storage, weight, access, effectiveness (see Creating Solutions). In other words, one of the elements that is central to consumption is its *use*. Indeed, one normally thinks of consuming a product *as* using it.

Consuming use or 'utility'

> *People don't buy drills, they buy holes.*
> *Kotler, 1967*

It seems obvious that consumers buy products in order to use them, and thus what is consumed is in fact the usefulness or 'utility' of the product. People pay for and judge a product's value in relation to how useful they find it or expect it to be. When a product has been consumed, it is 'finished' and is no longer useful. Once eaten, the bread has 'lost' its usefulness; when eventually becoming unroadworthy, the car is useless, except for scrap metal. The next time the consumer is hungry or needs to drive they have to purchase a new loaf of bread or another car in order to fulfil this use. It is therefore fundamentally the 'use' of products that they are consuming. The argument here is that it is this feature of 'utility' in products that the customer uses up in the act of consumption.

In marketing we view products as 'solutions' to customer problems or needs (see Creating Solutions). Products do not normally provide these solutions simply by the act of being purchased; it is only by *using* the car or the bread that the consumer's need for transport or food is satisfied.[1] To re-emphasize an earlier point, it is more accurately the experience of the use of the product that satisfies – this is the so-called 'interactionist' approach to consumer value (Holbrook, 1999) (see Marketing Contexts: Marketing values). Whatever the nature of the consumer's satisfaction, it is nevertheless the *use* of the product that is consumed during the process. This can best be explained by looking at the origins of the concept of 'utility', which are from economics.

---

[1] There is of course a partial solution to the hunger 'problem' which is satisfied by the act of purchase of the bread alone. That is, the *ownership and control* of the solution that buying the loaf transfers to the customer, who can now choose to eat at any time. But until it is eaten, *i.e. used*, the bread is not consumed; it remains in a condition of 'stored use'.

So central is the concept of utility to micro-economics for explaining consumer behaviour and choice between products that economic theory assumes that consumers seek to maximize their total utility from their combination of purchases. This requires a careful judgement as to the best combination of items to buy because the law of 'diminishing marginal utility' holds that the more a person consumes of a particular good, the less utility each additional item provides. For example, after a certain number of loaves of bread have been consumed, the satisfaction or utility derived from eating more bread decreases.

Thus, according to this view, products are judged by consumers according to their 'utility' but it is not a static measure – even for the same product. The degree of satisfaction you the consumer obtain from a product, e.g. a car, depends on how many cars you have and how much you use them. The usefulness of the car to you also then depends on how many you have and how much you drive. Therefore, utility is not static, it *changes* with use.

There are some major criticisms of the utility concept as a basis for understanding the nature of consumption:

1. It is entirely subjective, a personal view of the product's potential to provide functional consequences by the consumer, and not a property that the product inherently contains.
2. It is hard to distinguish from satisfaction, the fulfilment of a physiological or psychological need, which is something the consumer experiences (see Why consume? Motivation and stimulation).
3. The price or 'exchange value' of a product may have no relation to its utility. For example, bread is much cheaper than gold, but which is more useful?
4. Even when a product is bought primarily for its functional utility, the differentiating factor between alternatives can be a 'useless' attribute, like the brand name or the colour, which are also consumed.
5. It is hard to apply this concept to the whole area of financial services, where many products are purchased in order to retain or multiply their value, not for any functional use.
6. It is hard to apply this concept to aesthetic aspects of consumption, where people's aesthetic appreciation of a work of art or sculpture is by definition entirely *unrelated* to any practical use of the object.

Consuming experiences

In modern societies consumers demand more than just the functionality of physical products; they seek out and engage in consumption experiences which occur during events, recreation and leisure activities. According to Lanier and Rader (2015), experience has become a primary means by which we understand post-industrial consumer societies. Pine and Gilmore (1999), who are regarded as the founders of an experience economy theory for business, provide many examples of firms where their main product is the provision of experiences, for example restaurants, hotels, sports firms, professional football, music festivals, film and TV companies, tourist agents, artists, design houses and architectural practices. They coined the term 'the experience economy' to characterize these markets for experiences and the firms that provide experiences for customers, either alone or as an add-on to their main product.

Given this fundamental economic and cultural shift, there has been an increased focus on understanding consumption experiences, especially regarding the production and consumption of experiential market offerings (see Carù and Cova, 2007). Studies of experiential events of this type by consumer researchers include: white-water rafting described by Arnould and Price (1993); Celsi, Rose and Leigh's (1993) study of skydiving experiences; consumers' actions and interactions at a gay carnival (Kates, 2002); the re-enactment of the Mountain Men experience detailed by Belk and Costa (1998); ethnographic research into participants' experiences by Peñaloza (2000) at American rodeos; and Schouten and McAlexander's (1995) research into the communal experiences, rites and rituals of the new motor bikers.

One aspect of consumer behaviour that Pine and Gilmore do not take fully into account is that fundamentally an experience occurs in the mind of the customer. A firm or provider delivers an event of some sort that appeals to and potentially influences the customer, but the experience happens in his or her mind and body — a sensation, feeling or memory (Bitner, 1992; Hirschman & Holbrook, 1982). Furthermore, although it may be created by a single event like a football match or a stage play, the consumer experience is spread out over a period of time which includes pre-event and post-event experiences. Arnould, Price and Zinkhan (2002) divide these into four stages as follows:

1 The pre-consumption experience: searching, planning, imagining, anticipating.
2 The purchase experience: choice, packaging, payment, service encounter.
3 The core consumption experience: sensation, satiety, ease/ irritation, dis/satisfaction.
4 The remembered experience: nostalgia, souvenirs, narratives, pictures, reliving, memories.

A further complexity is that the experience varies from individual to individual or, indeed, for the same individual on different occasions and at different points in time.

Consuming culture

Viewing consumption as a cultural practice opens up a whole new perspective on what is being consumed. The term 'culture' used by sociologists covers people's common patterns of behaviour and values; it is learnt and shared with other people, and that culture influences how we behave and expect others to behave (Gronhaug, 1999: 111). When these cultural considerations are taken into account, consumer products become more than just materials, more than objects of use, and their demand derives more from their role in cultural practices than in the direct satisfaction of functional or material needs; 'they are goods to speak with, goods to think with' (Fiske, 1989). A pioneering work was Douglas and Isherwood's *World of Goods* (1978); they regard consumption and consumer choices as a source of meaning for people, as a social process that helps clarify and stabilize the constantly changing cultural (or social) categories.

Consumption is not solely an individual act – it encompasses and affects the whole society and culture. This is recognized by advertisers and market researchers who take into account a wide range of social and cultural factors in order to understand consumers' behaviour and product choices (see Creating Solutions). According to Douglas and Isherwood (1978), *all* consumer needs are culturally defined. They argue that even apparently basic physiological needs like hunger are *expressed* in a particular way that is determined by the culture. For instance, 'I am dying for a Big Mac' means 'I am very hungry' in today's Western culture; quite apart from language, this expression and desire would take a very different form in sub-Saharan Africa or in eighteenth century Russia.

Sociologists look at the role of consumption in making distinctions between social groups. Pierre Bourdieu, in his book *Distinction: A Social Critique of the Judgement of Taste* (1984), found that the way in which consumers classify goods differs according to social class and that their definition of 'taste' indicates closely their social class. For some products these distinctions were greater than others; these are called 'marker' goods. There were also gender differences in consumption – for example, working-class men chose steak for a special meal, whereas women chose fish.

Anthropologists have found that in all societies objects and material goods play a role in cementing social relations and people's consumption of products has a cultural function in self-expression, perceived security and attachment to society. This has been illustrated by Walendorf and Arnould (1988) in an anthropological study entitled 'My favourite things: a cross-cultural inquiry into object attachment, possessiveness and social linkage'. Products can be used by consumers to 'make a statement'; they are advertised and associated with particular 'role models' or celebrities (see Brand Selection); friends, family and peer groups influence how we view products.

Advertising appropriates cultural 'cues' in order to attach meaning to them, often drawing on well-known stories, characters and myths. Such 'mythic archetypes' have universal expression in countries' literatures and folk tales, and although these are periodically updated to suit local and contemporary conditions, they draw on a long historical lineage of common cultural meanings (Hirschman, 2000). Culture plays an even wider role in consumption according to the perspective of the consumer culture theory (CCT) developed by Arnould and Thompson (2005, 2015) which distils and integrates all of the culture-orientated strands of consumer research under one 'umbrella' theory. In this approach, consumer culture encompasses an interconnected system of commercially produced images, texts and objects that consumers use to make collective sense of their environments and to orientate their experiences (see The role of consumers, Consumer culture).

In a variety of ways, it is at least partly culture itself that people 'buy into' and consume. Not only are their choices and behaviour affected by culture, but also the meaning and values that they ascribe to the objects of consumption are reflections of both the historical and contemporary culture. This, however, begs one key question: how are these meanings and values 'transferred' from the culture to the products, and how do consumers interpret these? The obvious answer is through marketing and advertising in particular. In order to examine this question, the next subsection looks at meanings and signs as themselves the objects of consumption.

Consuming meanings and signs

We can see that products are not consumed simply for their functional use. Even a washing machine does more than wash – it carries other meanings for the con-

sumer, such as 'cleanliness' or 'comfort' or 'prestige'. Indeed, there is a strong argument that for some products the meanings are more important for consumers than their use. For example, the taste of Coca-Cola may be less important than what it stands for in the consumer's eyes, be that 'trust', 'reliability', 'the American dream', 'relaxation' or whatever. The meanings that consumers interpret or ascribe to products can therefore be regarded as part of what they consume. In consumer research, this has led to increased attention to various so-called 'interpretative' techniques of analysis in order to understand these meanings and the processes by which they occur in this consumer culture. These include hermeneutics (the study of meanings) and semiotics (the study of symbols and signs).

Originating in the linguistic structuralism of Saussure (1959), semiotics proposes that the underlying structures of cultural meaning within the social environment are constituted from systems of signs. For semioticians the sign is the essential unit of meaning within language and culture. The sign has two components, the *signified* and the *signifier*, which together link words, objects and ideas to meanings and values. Almost any object, custom or artefact can be studied as part of a sign-making process, as something that signifies something from someone to someone. Applying semiotics to consumer research enables consumption to be viewed as a kind of language enabling the communication and transmission of meanings from one set of people to others. Objects of all kinds, including products, are exchanged and used to symbolize or signify all kinds of meanings within society and it is this *signification* process that is the primary focus when studying consumption semiotically.

Semioticians regard products as commodity signs and it is these signs that are exchanged, used and consumed. For Baudrillard (1981), traditional understandings of consumption as involving material acquisition and material-commodity exchange and use are completely abandoned, and these processes are subsumed under an 'economy of signs'. The symbolic perspective of consumption examines the system of signs and what they signify, or mean, for consumers. This approach has been most widely applied in advertising research (Goldman & Papson, 1996); but as consumer theory moves beyond explanations of consumption in solely economic and utilitarian terms ideas of symbolic consumption, sign consumption and commodity signs have become increasingly applied in consumer research (e.g. Holt, 1995, 1998; Hirschman & Holbrook, 1982).

When products are analysed for their symbolic meaning as portrayed in their images, one problem is that there are several levels of the 'symbolic meaning' involved. This can refer to the product that embodies a meaning, the meaning itself that it carries, and the interpretation of the meaning by the consumer.

The act of consumption need not involve any material exchange. People can consume visually when they watch television, catch adverts, look in shop windows or recognize brand logos (Schroeder, 2002). Because consumer culture relies on images and signs so extensively, the semiotic aspects of consumption are important for marketing management in general and advertising and consumer research in particular.

When Mark & Pearson (2001) argue that Nike is a heroic brand, they are linking these brand meanings to a long history of warrior archetypes that have populated the world's literary canon. Nike's success purportedly derives from consumers' favourable (and inherent) dispositions towards the meanings of strength, bravery, nobility and achievement of the athletic field (i.e. battlefield) encoded in its heroic brand image.
Thompson, 2004

Brands are developed based on images, products are advertised via images, corporate image is critical for management success. Marketing is fundamentally about image management.
Schroeder, 2002

FURTHER READING

Consuming culture

Douglas, M. & Isherwood, B. (1978) *World of Goods*. Allen Lane: London.

Featherstone, M. (1991) *Consumer Culture and Postmodernism*. Sage: Thousand Oaks, CA.

Consuming value

Holbrook, M. (ed.) (1999) *Consumer Value*. Routledge: New York. (See also Marketing Contexts: Marketing values.)

How consumers consume

Holt, D. B. (1995) How consumers consume: a typology of consumption practices. *Journal of Consumer Research*, **22** (June), 1–16.

Consuming labour and work

Illich, I. (1981) *Shadow Work*. Marion Boyars: Salem, NH.

Consuming materials and energy

Kilbourne, W. (1998) Green marketing: a theoretical perspective. *Journal of Marketing Management*, **14**, 641–655.

Visual consumption

Schroeder, J. (2002) *Visual Consumption*. Routledge: London.

Consumption of experiences

Carù, A. & Cova, B. (2007) *Consuming Experiences*. Routledge: London.

Pine, B. J. & Gilmore, J. H. (1999) *The Experience Economy: Work is Theater and Every Business a Stage*. Harvard Business School Press: Boston, MA.

Why Consume? Motivation and Stimulation

Christina Goulding

No act of consumption takes place without some form of stimulation. This may be the result of a basic biological need, such as the pangs of hunger which stimulate the urge to eat, the stimulation of a utility need, such as a washing machine breaking down, or the stimulation of an aspirational need, as in the case of the desire for designer clothing or luxury brands. Most textbooks tend to locate the stimulation of needs within the framework of Maslow's hierarchy of needs, which proposes that we satisfy needs at different levels. At the lowest level are physiological needs such as the need for food, which must be satisfied before we can think about moving on towards more sophisticated needs. The second level deals with basic safety or security needs, while the third is concerned with love and belongingness. Moving higher up, the fourth level focuses on issues of esteem and respect, while the pinnacle, 'self-actualization', is the attainment of total self-fulfilment.

However, this is a rather simplistic analysis of human motivation and, while it offers a basic framework, it has attracted a number of criticisms and so should be looked at in conjunction with other models and theories of motivation. Bernard Weiner (1992) suggests that at the very minimum a general theory of motivation must:

- be based on general laws rather than individual differences
- include the 'self'
- include the full range of cognitive processes
- include the full range of emotions
- include sequential (historical) causal relations
- be able to account for achievement strivings and affiliative goals
- consider some additional common-sense concepts.

This section, while acknowledging that motivation underpins most human behaviour, examines a variety of other influences, including perception and the senses, memory and nostalgia, consumer culture theory (CCT), identity and lifestyle, consumer communities, and fantasy and fiction as stimulants of consumer experiences.

Perception and the five senses

Germane to much of our consumption behaviours is the role of the senses. Perceptual stimulation occurs largely through the five senses of sight, sound, smell, taste and touch. Each of these can be, and is, manipulated to some extent by marketers to create a sense of arousal, curiosity and interest in a particular product or service. As consumers, consider how the following affect you:

- *Sight*. The visual element in communication possibly offers the greatest opportunity for stimulation given the ability to play with colour, shape, size, contrast and distortion.
- *Sound*. Music is probably the most obvious example to provide with regard to the sense of hearing. It can have a positive or negative effect on mood and can be influential in determining such things as the length of stay in a particular retail environment, feelings of relaxation or irritation, and the association of a particular image with a product. However, the overemphasis of particular noises or unexpected delays or silences can also stimulate curiosity.
- *Smell*. Smell can be a powerful stimulant whether pleasant, as in the case of perfume, or repulsive, as with rotten eggs. A common technique used in supermarkets is to deliberately accentuate the smell of baking bread across the store in order to arouse a sense of hunger and want.
- *Taste*. Taste is a sense that can lead to immense pleasure or total disgust. It is also possibly the most powerful of the senses in that it involves a combination of the others. For example, we do not just taste food, we see it, feel it, smell it and even hear it cooking. Naturally enough, however, individual tastes differ. If we consider the Marmite advertisements, the emphasis is on the fact that you will either love it or hate it. Nevertheless, the first step is to get you as the potential consumer to try the product and this can often involve free samples, tasting trials, gourmet evenings and wine tastings.
- *Touch*. Touch can be an immensely sensuous experience. The feel of silk or velvet, for example, may evoke images of luxury, indulgence and even decadence. Consequently, the packaging of certain luxury items can play an important part in communicating the personality of a product. Moreover, a tried-and-tested sales technique is to get the potential customer to handle the product, to become engaged with it, based on the premise that having done so the likelihood of a sale increases.

Subliminal perception

There is, however, a sixth aspect of perception, and that is subliminal perception, or messages and images that are received by the individual below the level of conscious awareness. One area that has received attention and some criticism in recent years is the use of subliminal manipulation – or possibly more accurately *subconscious* manipulation – through product placements and celebrity endorsements in high-exposure films. It is probably true to say that when you watch a film your defences are down, you are relaxed and receptive to the images that you see on screen, you are drawn into the unfolding story and may not consciously notice the products that form part of the backdrop to that story.

However, there seems to be some evidence of subconscious internalization of these images. For example, in the film *The Horse Whisperer*, starring Robert Redford, an internet company 'equisearch.com' used product placement to promote their website. Although the name was only shown for a total duration of 30 seconds throughout, subsequent hits to the site more than doubled. Similarly, AOL were linked to the film *You've Got Mail*, the title of which was a direct soundbite used by the company. On a slightly different note, in Steven Spielberg's *Minority Report*, Tom Cruise is pictured in a futuristic Gap store, which provides an association between the label and the star. However, possibly one of the most convincing indicators of the power of product placement is evident in the fact that the 2002 James Bond movie *Die Another Day* attracted over 160 million dollars in marketing support.

Interpretation

It is a commonly held view within psychology that individuals will look for harmony and closure in images, and will actively seek to fill in any gaps. This is largely based on what we expect to see, hear, smell, taste and feel, and also on our need for continuity. Consequently, there are many techniques used in marketing in order to stimulate a sense of curiosity and interest in the consumer. These may include the use of contrast, where a commercial is shot entirely in black and white with the exception of a single figure shown in colour, as was the case with the Renault advert that featured a little girl in a red coat set against a black and white background, or the placing of advertisements upside down in newspapers in order to engage the viewer and encourage them to find out why. Nonetheless, it must be recognized that perception is selective – that is, as consumers we do not necessarily notice all the details of, for example, the packaging of a product which may include colour, imagery and information. Furthermore, perception and interpretation tend to differ across individuals which complicates the process of ensuring that the message is transmitted in the manner intended by the communicator.

In addition to this, for certain products, particularly those linked to identity expression and self-concepts, the image expressed in the communication should ideally match that of the intended audience. Perfumes are an obvious illustration of developing brand personalities with a distinct market in mind. Chanel has always sought to embody the ultimate in chic sophistication with its subtle and understated numbers – Chanel No. 5, 9, 19 and so on – minimalistic frills-free bottles and the classic, instantly recognizable, intertwined double C. Yves Saint Laurent's Opium, on the other hand, is meant to convey mystery, seduction, and an illicit and dark side to the wearer's personality.

From a marketing perspective, the aim is to ultimately gain a positive response and ensure that the message has a strong appeal to the consumer. Nevertheless, this is not always the case, as the classic example of Strand cigarettes demonstrates. The advert featured a man standing alone on a bridge smoking a Strand cigarette with the strap-line, 'You're never alone with a Strand'. However, this was interpreted as: if you are a loser and you have no friends, console yourself with a Strand – not necessarily a self-concept that most people would want to embrace and project.

The recent ban on cigarette advertising in the UK has highlighted some of the issues concerned with the influences of branding, imagery and the use of celebrities on consumer behaviour. Consider the examples in the past of advertisements which featured film stars, doctors, babies and even the 'health' benefits of cigarettes to promote tobacco. Such adverts may seem laughable in today's society, which is much more media sophisticated and aware, which itself means that communication must be based firmly on a clear understanding of the consumer perceptual process if the message is to be noticed amid the intense competition.

Provocative/offensive advertising as stimulation

It is fair to say that we live in a world of perceptual overload as marketers compete on a daily basis for consumers' attention. This has seen the rise of a more provocative form of communication which Stephen Brown (2001) describes as 'offensive advertising'. He provides numerous examples of advertising campaigns that were deliberately designed to shock. These include French Connection's 'FCUK' (French Connection United Kingdom) strap-line, which featured on billboards proclaiming 'FCUK me', 'FCUK fashion', etc. These adverts had the power to halt traffic and motivate thousands of individuals to write in to complain. However, despite being censored by the Advertising Standards Authority, the campaign helped to double the company's pre-tax profits and propelled them to the cutting edge of cool. Nevertheless, French Connection are by no means the only perpetrators of offensive marketing. Benetton were among the first to upset popular perceptions of what is acceptable with their images of dying Aids victims and prisoners on death row awaiting execution. Others use religion and even disgusting images of bodily fluids to attract attention and stimulate a feeling of revulsion, yet fascination.

As consumers, can you deny that there is an irresistible pull towards the illicit, the repulsive or the offensive when it is wantonly displayed daring you to look? To quote from Brown (2001), offensiveness is effective: it stands out in a world where consumers are bombarded by countless messages, most of them safe and sanitized and serious. Essentially it works because:

* it 'stands out from the crowd'
* it is efficient – it necessitates a second look
* it is cheap and often attracts the attention of a news-hungry media, thus generating more free publicity
* it is easily emulated.

In a parody of the 4Ps, Brown (2001) offers a classification of offensive marketing entitled the '4Cs' which differentiates between the various types of offensive communication:

* *Carnal*. This involves sexually explicit or 'sexploitative' campaigns, such as the shirt maker Van Heuston's proposal that 'a man is not a man without fifteen and a half inches to play with', or even Pot Noodle's campaign which portrays its consumption as something degenerate, disgusting and perverted.
* *Corporeal*. Refers to bodily fluids, faecal matter and unnatural functions, for example Super Noodles' contention that plates should be licked clean rather than washed.
* *Creedal*. This consists of offences against religious beliefs, illustrated in Benetton's nun-kissing-a-priest poster.
* *Cultural*. Images that offend the canons of aesthetic good taste. Stella Artois's campaign which depicted bottles of beer being opened on 'top of the range' durables such as a Gibson semi-acoustic guitar is an example of this.

Of course, there is no suggestion that all advertisements are destined to adopt an offensive stance if they are to fully register in your minds, although the rise in the phenomenon does raise some interesting questions regarding our level of retention and information processing, particularly in relation to what we remember.

Memory

In discussing the perceptual process, it is important to consider the nature of memory and the relationship to perceptual stimulation. As with motivation, there are a number of conceptual descriptions of memory, which range from habit formation and control, Jungian psychoanalytical perspectives of the collective unconscious, to human conditioning associated with the behavioural school. However, the most common interpretation of memory within consumer research is to view it as an information processing mechanism which works on a number of levels (see Figure 3.1).

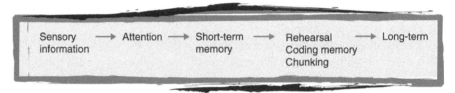

Figure 3.1 Different levels of memory

The first level involves some sort of sensory input or information, which is noticed but may be dismissed instantly. If the information is of interest it passes through into the short-term memory, which has a limited storage capacity and basically deals with the problem in hand. For example, consider going into a shop to purchase a number of items that you have not written down. You may well mentally repeat the list until you have paid for the items, after which time the information is no longer of any use and may be forgotten. However, should the information be of future value, you will employ techniques such as chunking, which involves breaking down information into manageable units, as you possibly do with telephone numbers, and rehearsal or repetition. This allows the information to pass into the long-term memory, where it is retained and retrieved at a later date.

If you consider the process involved in revising for an exam the stages become clearer. For example, the stimulus may be a textbook which is read and the information temporarily stored in the short-term memory. In order to retain information, notes are taken and synthesized using key words, colours or symbols, which are then re-read and rehearsed, allowing them to register in the long-term memory, hopefully to be retrieved during the exam. Obviously, the aim of marketers is to attract attention through the stimulus induced through their communication, provide information and ensure that consumers retain that information for future action. As we have seen, offensive marketing campaigns are one way of doing this. People certainly remember the images, discuss them and, according to the resulting sales figures, act upon the information. Another aspect of memory that is used to stimulate a desire for products is that of nostalgia.

Nostalgia – a subcategory of memory

Memory and nostalgia differ on one fundamental level. When we look back objectively at certain times or events in our lives, we remember both the good things and the bad associated with that particular period. When, however, we reflect nostalgically, we remember only the positive features. Nostalgia therefore is a kind of filter mechanism that acts as a kind of memory without the pain. The nostalgic reaction can also be stimulated through any one of the senses. The sight of a photograph taken on holiday can instantly transport you back to that time. The unexpected smell of a perfume once worn by someone close can conjure up an image from the past, as can the playing of a particular song. The taste of food associated with childhood can summon up scenes of earlier days in the same way that handling a possession that holds fond memories can bring to life images of happy times.

It is little wonder, therefore, given the positive nature of nostalgia, that it has been used in marketing to create favourable product images and consumer experiences. These can range from reinventing popular classics, such as the Volkswagen Beetle in a new turbo-charged form while still retaining a familiar shape reminiscent of the 'flower power' generation, or Coca-Cola's reintroduction of its classic glass bottle (Brown, 2002), to advertisements such as Levi's small-town 1950s American commercials which projected an aura of innocence and safety. There are also a number of retail outlets dedicated to presenting an 'olde worlde' image, such as Laura Ashley and the now-defunct Past Times. In addition, the leisure industry has been quick to recognize the power of the 'untainted' past and acted accordingly. Breweries, for example, have spent millions 'theming' and 'pastiching' hundreds of their public houses, while the heritage industry is busy offering trips back in time to enable visitors to experience anything from Viking settlements to industrial Victorian working towns.

Nostalgia, due to its selective nature, relies heavily on fantasy and to a degree fiction, which are two powerful stimulants for the consumer experience.

Consumer culture theory, identity and lifestyle

So far, this section has focused largely on the psychological processes that influence consumer behaviour. However, in recent years there has been a challenge to the dominant psychological view of consumption which treats consumers as driven predominantly by internal individual needs. This has manifested itself primarily in the school of thought known as consumer culture theory (CCT) (Arnould and Thompson, 2005). In particular, CCT research has questioned the view that consumers are isolated individuals who self-consciously consume to maximize utility. Central to the development of this perspective is the role of consumer identities, not only individual identities but the multiple identities that consumers construct, adopt and shed depending on the context they are in and the influence of peers and other influential members of the various groups they may belong to. Of particular interest are studies of marketplace cultures that explore the many ways that consumers interact with consumable resources to establish emotional and hedonistic social relationships. Such studies lie at the heart of the recent shift in understanding of the value-creation process.

Simply put, companies no longer create and embed value through their ability to design and manufacture goods and services with utility that is then exchanged in the marketplace, with consumers subsequently extracting utility from the market offering. Rather, consumers are now viewed as active co-creators of value and linked with the creation of meaning attributed to brands and goods. This relates strongly to the idea of brands as being highly symbolic expressions of identity and central to an 'appropriate' lifestyle.

Consider the power of television – and not just advertising – on your consumption patterns. You may be able to see certain clues and cues that have created awareness of a lifestyle, a certain 'look' or an image that has aroused a sense of desire for a particular brand. Take for example the popular *Sex and the City* television programme and films. In these you can see the lives and lifestyles of four very different women played out in meticulous detail. The emphasis is on looks, style, careers, romance and, of course, the close-knit relationship between the friends. The programme is basically a reflection of a society where women want it all and are not afraid to strive for it: Carrie, the relationship columnist; Miranda, a partner in a law firm; Charlotte, the romantic debutante; and Samantha, the successful public relations executive. All four are looking for love, albeit of a different nature; all are independent; but most significantly, all surround and adorn themselves with the trappings of a successful contemporary lifestyle. Prada handbags, Chanel earrings and Jimmy Choo shoes form the mainstay of their wardrobes. Manolo Blahnik, although extremely successful prior to the series, has become almost iconized thanks to the constant referencing of his shoes as the ultimate accessory. In one scene, Carrie is mugged in an alley for her watch and purse, yet the things she is most reluctant to give up are her Manolo Blahnik sandals. On the other hand, Samantha, the oldest of the group, talks openly about her Botox injections and the 'impulse purchase' of a facial chemical peel. These programmes are not about advertising but without the brands there would be no believable lifestyle; as a consequence, anyone unfamiliar with Manolo Blahnik before viewing certainly could not claim to be after watching a whole series.

Another successful phenomenon is one that is dedicated to exposing the nation's lack of imagination and creativity in their fondness for wood-chipped walls and magnolia paint – namely, the home improvement programme. Over the last decade there has been a proliferation of these guides to 'a better home', ranging from do-it-yourself make-overs to total house transformations. Interior designers have become the new media stars as they encourage normally sane individuals to hang hammocks in their living rooms, paint their bedrooms scarlet and black to create a decadent theme, or indulge their fantasies for French rural living by distressing their furniture and painting their walls orange. Their popularity has not only changed attitudes and behaviour towards interior décor but has also contributed greatly towards the profits of the numerous DIY stores which cater to all aspects of this new consumer obsession. IKEA, the Swedish furniture store, takes the concept of aspirational living one step further in its adverts, which started off encouraging people to 'chuck out their chintz' and progressed to the idea of 'chucking out your partner' if he or she does not complement the newly modernized and streamlined surroundings. As tongue in cheek as this may appear, lifestyle shopping is a fundamental part of today's consumer society which is increasingly fuelled and stimulated by widening communications, internet access, multi-channel television and, importantly, the influence of others.

Consumer communities

In line with this shift in perspective from the psychological to the social is the notion of communities of consumption. A popular means to describe such micro-communities is 'brand community' – a set of social relationships that are structured around the use of a focal brand. For example, the kind of relationships that exist, whether virtual or real, surrounding the Apple brand where incidents have been reported of people travelling to the area and camping outside in anticipation of the opening of a new Apple store. Such events are accompanied by a welcoming series of 'high fiving' from store assistants and a message of belonging to 'the Apple family'. Members of the Apple community may share many interests and passions surrounding the brand but outside of this may have nothing else in common. It is the brand that binds the community together.

Studies of brand community suggest that the shared use of products and services structures interpersonal connections among likeminded individuals, as well as distinction from non-users of the focal brand. In particular, brand communities generate shared rituals and ways of thinking, and in some cases a religious zeal towards the brand. These characteristics enhance the co-creation of value by consumers and firms by upholding brand values, maintaining appeal, increasing members' affiliation and commitment to the brand, as well as offering managers dialogue with these loyal consumers.

Another form of analysing collective behaviour has been to use the metaphor of the tribe. Consumer tribes differ from brand communities in that tribes may be multiple. Unlike brand communities, tribes rarely dominate consumers' lives.

Rather, they often represent a temporary escape from the stresses and pressures of the working week. Moreover, membership of one kind of tribe does not preclude membership of other tribes or communities. On the contrary, tribal theory stresses the occurrence of flows between different identities under different circumstances. Goulding *et al.* (2009) use the example of clubbing which, unlike many other more permanent subcultures, is a transitory experience where participants congregate at the weekend, engage in a collective, often emotionally charged and highly sensorial experience fuelled by feelings of connectivity and unity, and then disperse to return to their everyday lives of work and other, often-multiple tribe memberships. In this sense, tribal membership offers a means of escape and hedonistic release in a mutually reciprocal environment of high stimulation.

Fantasy and fiction as consumer stimulation

We can characterize consumer experiences and stimulation on the basis of whether individuals seek 'cognition', 'novelty', 'sensation' or 'fantasy' (see Table 3.1). Of course, as complex consumers we may move from one state to another depending upon our situation and context. However, some consumers have a greater or lesser propensity to engage, for example, in fantasy or novelty seeking, while others may be more rational and logical. There is a growing view that certain aspects of consumer behaviour are characterized by hedonism, by fantasy and the quest for romance (Campbell, 1987). Indeed, the power of the romantic fantasy as a stimulant is evident across many consumer product offerings and experiences. If we take, for example, the transformation industry, which may include cosmetics, the anti-ageing industry, gyms, the market for health foods and aesthetic cosmetic surgery, all of which hint at the promise of eternal youth, there is some support for the notion that many of us hold close the desire to become a better, more perfect 'other' (Belk, 2001).

Much of this, however, is a fantasy, based on a propensity to believe the many testimonials which appear in countless infomercials detailing stories of balding

Table 3.1 Characterization of consumer experiences

Novelty seeking	Safari holidays, latest/alternative fashions, exotic foods
Sensation seeking	Skiing, horror films, paragliding, bike/motor racing
Fantasy seeking	Literature, novels, magazines, romantic films
Cognition seeking	Information-seeking consumers, high interest in advertisements, product evaluation reports

men whose hair has grown back after applying a miracle lotion, or the before-and-after pictures of the middle-aged woman whose wrinkles have been dramatically reduced thanks to the latest technology in skin care. Two elements are prevalent in these cases – promise and hope – two ingredients that are found in abundance in popular magazines, especially those aimed at women, and in popular romantic fiction.

According to Stevens *et al.* (2001) the romantic discourse is important, particularly when advertising to women. An analysis of soap operas, romantic fiction and women's magazines shows that they offer a rich source of fantasy and escape that seldom bears any resemblance to the reality of individuals' everyday lives. Indeed, it is often the complete contrast and lack of realism that holds the attraction, allowing them to look, dream and sometimes purchase. The mixture is usually one of showing a different, and better, life while at the same time striking a balance between information and entertainment, and practical realism and escape. Russell Belk (2001) distinguishes between different types of consumption fantasies, classifying them as:

- *Hopeful fantasies*. Here individuals engage in fantasies in the hope that they will translate into reality, for example women who read bridal magazines from an early age in anticipation that one day they will actually be able to consume the products – the dress, reception, hairstyles and so on – depicted in their pages.
- *Hopeless fantasies*. With hopeless fantasies the images shown in magazines may appear totally out of reach of the viewer, evoking in the process more pain than pleasure. This is often the case in beauty magazines where incredibly thin, flawless models are used to promote products aimed at the average person while being in no way representative of them.
- *Enchanted illusions*. Here readers of, for example, specialty magazines are seeking imagination-inspiring consumption in which they can believe. They read to find out about new things they can want, whether they be based on beauty, sport or health.

Stephen Brown takes a slightly different tack in his analysis of contemporary popular novels, and those of Judith Krantz in particular. Krantz is responsible for the 'sex and shopping' novels *Scruples* (1978) and *Scruples Two* (1992). These are basically raunchy, romantic fiction which charts the rise from rags to riches of an ugly duckling who, of course, turns into a beautiful swan, inheriting along the way a fortune that she uses to open a specialty clothes store called Scruples. The books contain the usual mix of highs and lows, misfortunes and fortunes, love and deceit, the obligatory gratuitous sex and, of course, a happy ending. However, Brown makes the interesting observation that, although works of popular fiction are routinely dismissed as atrociously written and mindlessly consumed, on closer analysis it is impossible to ignore the pervasiveness of marketing phenomena and consumption behaviours. National brands, such as Coca-Cola, designer labels and famous celebrity names are present within the pages, along with discussions of specialty retail operations and the intricacies of the mail-order business. However, their main appeal is that they offer an insight into the lives and lifestyles of the impossibly rich, which brings us back to the start of the section which discussed images in the media as stimulants. So whether it is the contemporary *Sex in the City*-style television programme or the popular novel that is consumed, the mix of fantasy, aspirational lifestyles, hedonic consumption and education in the form of showing the viewer what is possible and how to achieve it, are all significant influences in today's consumer society.

Key terms

- *Perception*. Information gained through the stimulation of the five senses.
- *Subliminal perception*. Messages or images received below the level of conscious awareness.
- *Provocative/offensive advertising*. Images used to attract attention and stimulate a strong response through offending socially accepted norms.
- *Memory*. The process through which we internalize and retain information, from sensory input, short-term retention, coding, rehearsing and chunking, through to long-term memory and later retrieval.
- *Fantasy*. The stimulation of the imagination through the use of images, stories and scenes that result in a temporary escape from reality.

FURTHER READING

Motivation

Weiner, B. (1992) *Human Motivation: Metaphors, Theories and Research*. Sage: London.

Sensations and perception

Singer, J.L. (1993) Experimental studies of ongoing conscious experience. In: *Experimental and Theoretical Studies of Consciousness* (G.R. Bock & J. Marsh, eds.), Ciba Foundation Symposium 174. Wiley: Chichester.

Zucherman, M. (1979) *Sensation Seeking*. Lawrence Erlbaum: Hillsdale, NJ.

Experiences and behaviour

Csikszentmihalyi, M. (1992) *Flow: The Psychology of Happiness*. Rider Press: London.

Hirschman, E. (1984) Experience seeking: a subjectivist perspective on consumption. *Journal of Business Research*, **12** (March), 115–136.

Attracting attention

Brown, S. (2002) FCUK consumer research: on disgust, revulsion and other forms of offensive advertising. *European Advances in Consumer Research*, **5**, 61–65.

Memory

Baddeley, A. (1976) *The Psychology of Memory*. Basic Books: London.

Houston, J.P. (1981) *Fundamentals of Learning and Memory*. Academic Press: New York.

Nostalgia

Brown, S. (2001) *Marketing: The Retro Revolution*. Sage: London.

Goulding, C. (1999) Heritage, nostalgia and the 'grey' consumer. *The Journal of Marketing Practice: Applied Marketing Science*, **5** (6/7/8), 177–199.

Goulding, C. (2001) Romancing the past: heritage visiting and the nostalgic consumer. *Psychology and Marketing*, **18** (June), 565–592.

Holbrook, M.B. (1993) Nostalgia and consumption preferences: some emerging patterns of consumer tastes. *Journal of Consumer Research*, **20** (2), 245–256.

Holbrook, M.B. (1998) Rocking the ages. *Journal of Macromarketing*, **18** (Spring), 72–77.

Consumer culture theory

Arnould, E.J. & Price, L.L. (1993) River magic: extraordinary experience and the extended service encounter, *Journal of Consumer Research*, **20** (June), 24–45.

Arnould, E.J. & Thompson, C.J. (2005) Consumer culture theory: twenty years of research. *Journal of Consumer Research*, **31** (4), 841–849.

Kozinets, R.V. (2001) Utopian Enterprise: articulating the meanings of *Star Trek*'s culture of consumption. *Journal of Consumer Research*, **28** (1), 67–88.

Kozinets, R.V. (2002) Can consumers escape the market? Emancipatory illuminations from *Burning Man*. *Journal of Consumer Research*, **29** (1), 20–38.

Consumer communities

Cova, B. & Cova, V. (2002), Tribal marketing: the tribalization of society and its impact on the conduct of marketing. *European Journal of Marketing*, **36** (5/6), 595–620.

Cova, B. & Pace, S. (2006) Brand community of convenience products: new forms of customer empowerment – the case of 'my Nutella The Community'. *European Journal of Marketing*, **40** (9/10), 1087–1105.

Chaney, D. & Goulding, C. (2016) Dress, transformation and conformity in the heavy rock subculture. *Journal of Business Research*, **69**, 115–165.

Goulding, C., Shankar, A. & Elliott, R. (2013) Facilitating the formation of consumer tribes. *European Journal of Marketing*, **47** (5/6), 813–832.

Goulding, C., Shankar, A., Elliott, R. & Canniford, R. (2009) The marketplace management of illicit pleasure. *Journal of Consumer Research*, **35** (February), 759–771.

McAlexander, J.H., Schouten, J.W. & Koenig, H.F. (2002) Building brand community. *Journal of Marketing*, **66** (January), 38–54.

Muñiz, A. & O'Guinn, T.C. (2001) Brand communities. *Journal of Consumer Research*, **27** (March), 412–432.

Role of fantasy

Belk, R. (2001) Speciality magazines and flights of fancy: feeding the desire to desire. *European Advances in Consumer Research*, **5**, 197–202.

Scott, L. (2002) Barbie genesis: play, dress and rebellion among her first owners. *Gender, Marketing and Consumer Behaviour*, **6**, 151–166.

Stevens, L., Brown, S. & Maclaran, P. (2001) The joys of text: women's experiential consumption of magazines. *European Advances in Consumer Research*, **5**, 169–173.

The role of consumers

We are all consumers. Unless we go and live on a desert island we cannot avoid consuming, and we all play an important role, or roles, in the marketing process as consumers. The important thing to note is that the consumer's role is not passive but active.

The role of the 'prosumer' and consumer co-creation

Certain aspects of consumers' activities can actually contribute to production, i.e. they play a role in making things as well as consuming them. Traditionally in marketing, even though one would expect the consumer to occupy a central position, it was generally assumed that a product was something that was produced by the firm and offered to the customer, whose role in the market was then to purchase it (or not) and consume it. A number of writers (e.g. Normann & Ramirez, 1993) now take a contrary view of the marketing process whereby products, or 'market offerings', are *co-created* by the firm and the customer/ consumer.

Alvin Toffler coined the term 'prosumer' in his book *The Third Wave* (1980), where he claimed that due to the information revolution the consumer would be more demanding and more participative. Since then, largely due to the advent of mass information and customization, the consumer has become part of the development, production and delivery of goods and services. By these means consumers co-create and construct value for themselves. Nowadays the communication process is also substantially enriched with the consumer contributing to the firm's message more indirectly via social media.

This has led marketers to implement the idea of looking at the consumer as a co-producer whereby some or all production activities are devolved by suppliers to consumers. A basic example is where some children's toys (and some for adults) are deliberately designed and aimed at engaging the user and stimulating their own entertainment. These might include Meccano kits, which have to be constructed before use, toy soldiers which have to be painted (and imaginatively activated) by the consumer, and self-assembly model railways. At another level, the IKEA phenomenon, which has been so successful in revolutionizing how people shop for furniture, involves the transfer of 'self-service' to the shopper from the retailer, including loading and delivery. In addition, the 'job' of the customer also involves the assembly of the furniture from flat-pack, an operation that would otherwise be performed by the manufacturer.

The consumer's role as part-worker, however, is not confined to the realm of tangible consumption. The recent public obsession with 'reality' television – whereby the audience are not only invited to vicariously view the unfolding events, but actively encouraged to determine the outcome and fate of the 'victims' through telephone voting – is a further example of consumer involvement in the production process of their own and others' so-called entertainment.

Some marketing activities have to be 'prosumed' in the sense that they have to be produced and consumed at the same time, together, and the consumer is therefore involved in their production. This is the case notably for most services, which are characterized by 'inseparability' of production, exchange and consumption. For services such as airlines, hairdressers and restaurants, the interaction between the front-line staff and the customer directly affects the perceived quality of service; the service 'experience' can be enhanced not only by the 'service provider' performing well, but also by customer-input factors such as their knowledge, effort and attention.

A number of writers, such as Normann & Ramirez (1993), take a similar view of the entire value-creation process in marketing, whereby value is co-created through interaction between the firm and the customer, not in 'value chains' but in value '*constellations*'. They see consumers playing a key role in value creation, not just firms, and the role of consumption – i.e. the activities, behaviours and motivations that consumers undertake when making decisions and forming perceptions about products and services – is not just to 'use up' or 'deplete' value but is also more fundamentally one of value creation (see Marketing Contexts: Marketing values).

This idea of the consumer as *co-creator of value* has been enthusiastically adopted by many leading marketing thinkers. This has meant that marketers have had to reassess their understanding and calculation of what constitutes 'value' for their customers and how this value can be produced and delivered. According to Gummesson, the true role of the customer is ignored in the earlier traditional marketing view of value, in which production is viewed as value creation by the supplier whereas consumption is value depletion caused by the customer. If the consumer is the focal point of marketing, however, value creation is only possible when a product or service is consumed: 'An unsold product has no value, and a service provider without customers cannot produce anything' (Gummesson, 1997).

For Grönroos, suppliers only create resources for customers or the means to create value for themselves: 'It is only when suppliers and customers interact, they are engaged in co-creation of value' (Grönroos, 2006: 324). Notably, Lusch

Four characteristics of services are usually given: intangibility (as opposed to tangibility of physical goods), perishability (cannot be stored) and heterogeneity (hard to standardize); it is the fourth characteristic – inseparability (or simultaneity) – that more distinctly captures the essence of services. It states that services are partly produced and marketed at the same time by the same people, that the customer is partly involved in the production and delivery process and that the customer partly consumes the service during its production.
Gummesson, 2000

and Vargo make a core proposition in their 'service logic' that 'value is always uniquely and phenomenologically determined by the beneficiary' and 'the customer is always a co-creator of value' (Lusch & Vargo, 2006: 284).

> *For advanced economies, services now constitute far more value of national output than manufactured products. Vargo and Lusch (2004) proposed a 'new dominant logic' for marketing based on a service-centred perspective. Their key propositions include: 'all economies are service economies', 'the enterprise can only make value propositions' and 'the customer is always the co-producer'. This involves a shift in emphasis from a goods-centred logic, based on tangible resources, embedded value and exchange transactions, to one that focuses on intangible resources, relationships between buyers and sellers, and the co-creation of value.*

The notion of consumer co-creation is not new, however. Forty years ago, von Hippel (1978) identified customers as lead innovators and many innovative firms actively look to consumers as the creative source for new products. The games industry is a good example, where enthusiastic players of board games and computer games generate many ideas for new versions. Similarly, bloggers and vloggers have become the focus for users of various consumer products to articulate suggestions for improvements and completely new ideas (see Moving Space; Social media marketing).

In their seminal paper, Cova and Dalli (2009) describe consumers who co-create value for firms as 'working consumers', whether or not they are aware of being 'workers'. As such they are not merely recipients or even arbiters of value, but members or partners in the production system. In other words, these firms use consumers *as a resource* in a way that is very far removed from the traditional conceptualization of the value-creation process in marketing theory. Working consumers play an important role as producers by providing a resource for firms like labour or finance, except the factor of production that they contribute is *consumer capital*. This is similar to the way in which Baudrillard (1970) regards consumption, not as the conventional 'mirror' opposite production, but as an *integrated part of the production process* – and thus consumers as indistinguishable from workers.

Cova and Dalli (2009) themselves adopt a critical stance in the conclusion of their analysis of this phenomenon. They point out that working consumers increase the value of goods and services, and companies capture this value on the market, but almost none of this value is returned to consumers. Given that consumers contribute to companies' profits through the value of their co-production, they ask the following searing questions about the distribution of this value:

1 Why do they not consider the disparity in the distribution of profits arising from consumers' work?
2 Why do they not receive any 'economic' reward for their labour?
3 Why are the economic benefits of their production still in the hands of 'pro-ducing' companies?
4 If consumers produce goods and services, why do they have to pay to purchase them? (Cova & Dalli 2009: 326)

For firms that benefit from having working consumers engaged in the production process, the term 'consumer lifetime value' refers not to value they create for consumers, but to the value the customers create *for the firm* (Saren & Tzokas, 1998). Furthermore, as Zwick & Cayla (2011) observe, the more consumers are involved in co-production and design, the more they are willing to pay for the products. In this sense, they argue that there is a 'double exploitation of working consumers'.

Collaborative consumption and sharing

There are, however, other types of working consumers engaged in co-creation who are not exploited by commercial organizations. These consumers engage in various forms of 'collaborative consumption' with other consumers, not for regular businesses or companies. These types of consumer/producer networks are one feature of the so-called 'sharing economy'. In these cases, they are sharing with other consumers in loosely formed, often internet-connected peer-to-peer (P2P) or consumer-to-consumer (C2C) collaborative networks.

The rise of various forms of access-based sharing or collaborative consumption has shifted the focus of consumption from ownership to access, and altered the way that value is created by and delivered to customers (Bardhi & Eckhardt, 2012; Botsman & Rogers, 2010; Belk, 2010; Barnes & Mattsson, 2017). Market exchange through consumers collaborating or sharing does not fit neatly into any of the prior categories of market-based exchange. It is not exactly a transactional market exchange nor a gift exchange, and not only a relational exchange – it is partly all of these types. The conceptual issues in positioning sharing and collaborative consumption has been explored most thoroughly by Belk (2007, 2010), whose categorization and definitions on this subject are widely cited by other researchers and authors in marketing.

Belk adopts a particular standpoint in conceptualizing and studying this subject as a consumption phenomenon. There is also, however, a consumer co-production aspect to most forms of collaboration between consumers, even where they also involve some provider input. An alternative approach was adopted by Benkler (2004) who approaches sharing from a production perspective. He proposed sharing as an alternative economic production system that has been enhanced by new digital networking and communication technologies. This form of 'social production' is conducted and controlled by consumers as opposed to being organized by the market, the firm or the state. Scaraboto (2015) views collaborative consumption as an alternative micro-economy created by the efforts of interdependent participants who switch between the roles of consumer and producer as they engage in collective value creation by means of common social and economic activities.

Such schemes apply most easily to shareable goods that have specific characteristics which enable and encourage common ownership, according to Lamberton (2016). This applies even more widely to most types of services where private ownership of a service is not itself transferrable and, as Lovelock (2004) emphasizes, 'non-ownership' is a core characteristic of services. This feature of non-ownership provides the basis for so-called 'access rights consumption', which Rifkin (2000) argues more accurately portrays the sharing economy than the 'right to use'. The passengers of Uber taxis only access the right to ride in the car – the right to use the car remains with the owner.

Although studies of consumer practices of collaboration, sharing, and common ownership and access rights are at an early stage, some authors are already arguing that these trends indicate that the private property system is weakening. Much of the consumer research so far has focused on collaborative sharing of taxi and hotel services, usually Uber and Airbnb (Bardhi & Eckhardt, 2012; Hellwig et al., 2015). These demonstrate another important implication of collaborative consumption of these types: that the distinction between production and consumption has been overturned as consumers can also be providers and providers can become consumers at various times. Furthermore, in these examples, the needs of both owner and consumers can be fulfilled more efficiently, usage of cars and hotel rooms can be maximized for common benefit, and unnecessary idle usage and waste of productive resources can be reduced.

Consumer identity

There are various ways in which consumption is related to identity for consumers.

First, there is the economic and social identity, which everyone has as a consumer in the marketplace. When considering making purchases, then buying, using and evaluating them, we become a consumer – we take on a consumer identity. Playing the 'role' of consumer gives us certain expectations about behaviour and confers on us certain rights and responsibilities. We will discuss this aspect in more detail under Consumption as performance later in this section.

Second, some people use consumption to *display their identity* to others. Such 'conspicuous consumption' behaviours of buying, using and showing off products and brands can be used to 'say something' about the person's identity (see Brand Selection).

Third, at another level, consumers can be doing more than displaying their identity through products; they can be *creating* their own perceived self by *identifying with* the objects and symbols of their consumption, i.e. 'You are what you consume.'

Displaying identity

Consumer goods are used to signify social status as demonstrated through the choice of a particular selection of goods that classifies the consumer according to various socio-economic hierarchies, such as their wealth, knowledge, social position, taste, refinement. It is not simply the display of the material possessions themselves that is important, nor simply economic capability or the price paid. According to Bourdieu (1984), modern consumption is primarily concerned with the establishment and maintenance of 'distinction' or difference between social classes and status groups. The maintenance of difference thus not only implies a competitive relationship between consumers who perceive themselves to inhabit different groups and identities, but also has the effect of 'bonding' consumers more closely within these subcultures and social communities (see subsections on Consumer culture and Consumer subcultures and tribes). By seeking to align themselves with certain group norms, consumers must share with the others in that group such things as their common consumption ambitions and adopting similar behaviours and lifestyles.

The notion that consumer goods are employed to signify social position, and their use by individuals to demonstrate their taste and distinction, is not a particularly modern phenomenon. Several classic anthropological studies have shown that the primary function of material culture is not the satisfaction of 'needs', but the role in social rituals and the establishment of social hierarchies both within and between groups (e.g. Mauss, 1966). It was Veblen (1899) who first detailed the modern 'conspicuous consumption' behaviour of the *nouveaux riches* and the manner in which certain types of goods and services were employed by them as registers of their new social position. The success of early department stores as centres for taste and fashion was largely a consequence of the vast appetite for status symbols among the newly emerging affluent middle class in the nineteenth century (Laermans, 1993).

Creating identity

An important theme within consumer research aims to understand 'the co-constitutive, co-productive ways in which consumers, working with market generated materials, forge a coherent, if diversified and often fragmented sense of self' (Arnould & Thompson, 2005). Consumers are viewed as identity seekers and makers, and it is the marketplace that is the primary source of 'mythic and symbolic resources' through which people construct 'narratives of identity' (Belk, 1988; Holt, 2002).

For Bauman (1988), individual freedom in modern society takes the form of 'consumer freedom' through which the individual is able to invent and create their own self-identity. People are free to use consumer goods to 'become' any of their 'possible selves'; they can be *creating* their own perceived self by *identifying with* the objects and symbols of their consumption. This is one aspect of human behaviour that 'actor–network theory' (Callon, 1999) deals with from a sociological perspective.

People may identify themselves with objects of consumption in many forms in their everyday life. If 'lifestyle' TV programmes and magazines are to be believed, for many people these are often consumer objects such as their home, possessions, decoration, furniture, clothes, garden, car and jewellery. Of course, the most intimate physical manifestation of one's identity is the body, and so in this respect are the use of products and services to make it look better and 'improve' one's 'self-image'. Identity is therefore also often related nowadays to body image and thus to the consumption of particular beauty, health care and cosmetic products. People's identities and 'self-esteem' are so closely associated with their bodies that it can strongly motivate their choice of food consumption, diet, sports, fitness, and medical and surgical products aimed at affecting or changing their body image.

The body is, after all, the site of *all* consumption. There has been a growth in interest on the part of consumer researchers in the nature of the body, identity and symbolic consumption (e.g. Thompson & Hirschman, 1995), and in particular the role of the *'embodied self'* (Featherstone, 2000; Mauss, 1979/1936), which includes body modification such as cosmetic surgery (Schouten, 1991) and body art (Goulding & Follett, 2001; Velliquette & Bamossy, 2001). The field of body modification provides a wealth of possible case studies for understanding the degree of consumer involvement in the production, creation and consumption of a new, highly visible 'identity'.

> *The emotion-laden experiences of the consumer: irrational, incoherent and driven by unconscious desire . . . able to build a DIY self through consumption, yet suffering an expansion of inadequacy through advertising.*
> *Elliot, 1999*

> ### Creating identity: the case of tattoos
>
> *One popular form of body adornment which has a long and well-documented history is that of tattooing. Perhaps as a consequence of celebrity role models sporting tattoos, and shifts in fashion towards body adornment, including body piercing and tattooing, acquiring a tattoo is now seen as part of contemporary popular culture and it is a global multibillion pound industry (DeMello, 2000). However, the tattoo, the 'object' that is purchased, is unique both in its concept and practice, and has very few comparisons, largely due to the permanency of the act. Whilst information search is a key aspect of many service encounters, the nature of tattooing probably provokes a greater degree of investigation, time and involvement. Tattoos are permanent. They are considered by most recipients to be works of art, to be created by 'artists' upon a canvas, the body. They are both public and private statements about the individual's identity, and, significantly, the act involves an often-extended period of pain and potential risk of infection. This brings into question the role of trust due to the very high risk and high degree of involvement by the consumer.*
>
> (Goulding & Follett, 2001)

For some people, whatever personal problems they may face – whether it is loss of community, lack of self-esteem, unhappiness or boredom – they can be 'solved' by adopting a particular consumer lifestyle and constructing a 'better' self through the products and services associated with it (Elliot & Wattanasuwan, 1998). Some argue that the 'freedom' to construct their identity through consumption is in fact quite limited by the 'structuring influence of the marketplace' and that, while consumers can pursue personal goals through the market, they are in fact 'enacting and personalizing' from a choice of 'cultural scripts' or lifestyles, many of which are set by marketers (Arnould & Thompson, 2005).

Consumer culture

In today's consumption society, Featherstone (1991) argues that a new powerful social and professional group has emerged, members of which are engaged in the production and distribution of symbols, taste and ideal lifestyles, and work within the fields of marketing, advertising, fashion and design. Many other researchers and authors have come to regard marketing as one of the key cultural architects of our time. They suggest that marketing since the 1950s has come to play a significant role in the creation and reproduction of taste, dreams and aspirations (Ewen, 1988), needs (Packard, 1957), selves and identities (Elliot, 1999), desires (Bauman, 2001), morality (Grafton-Small & Linstead, 1989), materiality and hedonism (Pollay, 1986). The abundance of marketing messages and signs for which the so-called 'culture industries' are responsible in everyday life may even qualify marketing professionals for the label of the 'ministers of propaganda of the consumer culture'.

Although the power and influence of the marketing profession is undoubtedly very great in creating the cultural language and 'setting the scene' for consumers (Svensson, 2004), one criticism of the argument and observations above is that they *understate the role of the consumer* in determining their own culture. For example, Elliot (1999) pointed out that 'consumers do not passively accept marketing communications but may actively renegotiate the meaning subjectively and construct their own interpretations'. This view of the culturally active consumer has been supported by other studies of 'marketplace' cultures in which consumers are seen as 'culture producers'. Many of these studies use ethnographic methods of research.

Ethnographic studies of consumer cultures

The roots of ethnography lie in cultural anthropology, with its focus on small-scale societies, and the original central concept remains paramount today; that is, a concern with the nature, construction and maintenance of culture. Ethnographers aim to look beyond what people say to understand the shared system of meanings we call 'culture'. Pettigrew (2000) argues that consumption represents a phenomenon that can be effectively addressed with the use of ethnographic techniques, based on the understanding that the social meanings found in material possessions can be viewed as cultural communicators. These include, for example, Arnould & Price's (1993) 'river magic', Hill's (1991) study of homeless women and the meaning of possessions, and Schouten & McAlexander's (1995) longitudinal study of the new 'biker' culture in the US.

(Goulding, 1999)

Warde (2005) notes that the wider practices in which the consumption process is integrated have often been ignored by consumer researchers. He argues that this is an important omission because people consume products and services in order to support the particular conventions of the practice in which they are engaged, such as eating, skiing, motoring etc. The similarities and differences between people in terms of their possessions and consumer behaviour can then be seen less as an outcome of personal choice and more as an outcome of the way in which the practice is organized in their culture.

A very influential approach to studying this topic is the framework of consumer culture theory (CCT), developed by Arnould and Thompson (2005), which maps out the conceptual domain and the theoretical advances in this field of consumer research. CCT recognizes the articulating role of consumption in today's market-mediated societies, and the globalizing – but also simultaneously localizing – dimensions of this consumer culture. The framework combines findings and theories from various disciplines such as economics, political theory, consumer culture, anthropology, sociology and psychology, thus producing a general framework for theory that is inherently interdisciplinary in nature. The authors of CCT distil and integrate these culture-orientated strands of consumer research under one 'umbrella' theory (see Why consume? Motivation and stimulation).

Arnould and Thompson (2015) have defended their theory against a number of criticisms, such as CCT being communist (Cova *et al.*, 2013) and that CCT is not sufficiently theoretical to be labelled a theory (Moisander *et al.*, 2009).

Consumer subcultures and tribes

Our 2005 conceptualization built upon Don Slater's definition . . . of consumer culture as a social arrangement in which the relations between lived culture and social resources, and between meaningful ways of life and the symbolic and material resources on which they depend, are mediated through markets. We further emphasized the importance of market-made commodities, market-mediated social relationships and identity projects, and desire-inducing marketing symbols in the socio-cultural and ideological operations of consumer culture. And consumer culture also encompasses an interconnected system of commercially produced images, texts, and objects that groups use – through the construction of overlapping and even conflicting practices, identities, and meanings – to make collective sense of their environments and to orient their members' experiences and lives.

(Arnould & Thompson, 2015)

As Arnould and Thomson recognize in the above quotation, consumer cultures are not monolithic and homogeneous: they consist of smaller collective groupings of individual consumers known as subcultures. The study of subcultures, their

activities, power relations, hierarchies and constitutent identities has a long tradition of analysis within the discipline of sociology. In the UK, several studies have
focused on youth subcultures as a form of resistance to cultural domination, e.g.
Hall and Jefferson (1976) on youth subcultures in Britain and Hebdidge (1979) on
the mods of the 1960s. Other authors have regarded music-based youth subcultures
as 'the culture industry's commodification of dissent' (Frank & Weiland, 1997).

Beyond 'sites of resistance', subcultures are also a form of consumer culture
at the micro level. They are responsible for the creation of micro-markets and
the products and services to meet these demands. They have opinion leaders,
innovators and imitators of the latest trends in specialized clothing, jewellery
and accessories. Examples of contemporary subcultural groupings include heavy-
metal music fans, gay consumers, motorcycle gangs, white river rafters, skydivers, *Star Trek* followers, the rave music scene, Goths, surfers, freerunners, etc.

Marketing and consumer researchers have more recently begun to focus on the
material artefacts and consumption practices that underpin, support and define
the very existence of many subcultures and the consumption experiences of those
involved. These look at how consumers forge feelings of social solidarity and
create self-selected, sometimes transitory and fragmented (sub)cultural worlds
involving the pursuit of common consumption interests. Much of this work is
based on Maffesoli's (1996) concept of the 'neo-tribe' (see Cova & Cova, 2002).

*Subcultures may be
defined as sites of
praxis, ideologic-
ally, temporally
and socially situ-
ated where fantasy
and experimenta-
tion give way to
the construction,
expression and
maintenance of
particular con-
sumption
identities.
Goulding et al.,
2002*

The concept of the neo-tribe

*Maffesoli (1996) argues that traditional bonds of community between
individuals have been eroded and the free-market ethos promotes a con-
tinual quest for personal autonomy and difference. Consumers, however,
find such conditions lonely and alienating; therefore, they form looser
groupings of shared interests and engage in joint activities and rituals
based on lifestyle choices. The neo-tribe provides affectual bonds between
people based on things such as leisure activities, cultural pursuits, religion
and intellectual interests. The process of feeling emotions together provides an 'emotional glue' that creates a reconnection between people
who are otherwise disparate in today's individualistic society. Members
are bound together by a process called 'proxemics' which develops from
being close to someone because you share the same space/sentiment –
surfing, driving the same car. Marketing has recognized these tribes and
advertising addresses them directly – and tribes recognize themselves in
these messages and images.*

Tribes take the form of *consumer tribes* when members are emotionally connected by similar consumption values and usage, using the social 'linking value' of products and services to create a community and express identity. This is often the case as societies become more consumer orientated. However, tribes are different from 'brand communities' which are formed around a particular brand or product; these are explicitly commercial whereas pure tribes are not. Brand communities are concerned about the relationship between brand and consumer, whereas tribes focus on the *relationship between consumers*.

Brand community

Brand communities are groups of consumers who merge together around brands. They are based on some form of product or label that provides a shared meaning and common interest for that group of people. They are essentially an imagined community whereby physically distanced people are united by their attachment to the brand. The members' use of brand is public and visible and serves as a badge that signifies membership within the community of interest (see Brand Selection). Muñiz & O'Guinn define a brand community as:

> a specialized, non-geographically bound community, based on a structured set of social relationships among admirers of a brand. [They] are legitimate forms of community, but communities of a particular stripe, and of their time. These communities may form around any brand but are most likely to form around brands with a strong image, a rich and lengthy history, and threatening competition.
>
> (Muñiz & O'Guinn, 2001)

Other consumer researchers looking at brand communities and consumer tribes have studied heavy-metal music fans, gay consumers, skydivers, *Star Trek* followers, mountain men, the rave music scene, Goths, surfers and freerunners. There a number of themes that emerge from these studies of different consumer subcultures or tribes:

1 Subcultures are made up of diverse groups of people – not gender or class based. Subcultures provide a platform for the display and construction of alternative consumer activity-based identities.
2 Subcultures are based around product constellations, places, events and services. Businesses emerge to serve the wants and needs of participants.
3 Myth, play and fantasy are important aspects of experiential and 'carnivalesque' consumption.
4 Tribal aspects of consumption are pervasive, fostering collective identifications grounded in shared beliefs, meanings, myths, rituals practices and status hierarchies.

5 There are different levels of commitment which reflect the individual's identity. People can escape from their 'everyday life'. For example, the subculture
enables the bank manager during the week to become a biker at the weekend.

Examples of consumer subculture studies

- *Schouten & McAlexander (1995) – US bikers*
- *Belk & Costa (1998) – mountain men*
- *Miklas & Arnould (1999) – Goths*
- *Kozinets (2001) – Star Trek fans ('Trekkies')*
- *Goulding et al. (2002) – dance culture*
- *Kates (2002) – gay consumers.*

Consumption as performance

In a groundbreaking article, Deighton (1992) pointed out that the word 'performance' often occurs in accounts of consumption but it is seldom brought into
the foreground of the discussion or analysis. He gives examples of several different types of uses:

- Consumers attend performances that are staged for them, such as sports
events, music concerts, religious services, theatre performances, college lectures, circuses.
- Consumers participate in performances that require them to play an active
role. In many service markets consumers have to play their part in the 'performance' of the service operation, such as restaurants, weddings, workshops,
sales demonstrations (see Grove & Fisk, 1983).
- Consumers perform with products such as clothes, using them as props in performances which they enact to influence others – and it is the others who
actually consume the performance.
- Products perform for consumers as they use them. Detergents perform by
cleaning. A product is the 'frozen potential for performance'. The marketer's
purpose in designing and delivering the products is to direct their performance well.

In all these examples performance is the core element in the consumption experience. Deighton (1992) suggests that it might be argued that frequently it is performances, not products, that are the objects of consumption. Many consumer

> *In its concern with performance, marketing reveals itself as an inher-ently dramatistic discipline – it scripts, produces and directs per-formances for and with consumers and manages the motives consum-ers attribute to the decision to perform. From this perspective, con-sumers behave as if they were audi-ences responding to or participating in performances . . . Consumers may be said to choose products, but they consume perform-ances.*
> *Deighton, 1992*

transactions involve performances, not possessions. Yet marketers have in the past tended to study things – products, consumers, adverts, demands, distribution channels – not events (Vargo & Lusch, 2004).

Like other aspects of social interaction, consumption events are improvised around what Schank & Abelson (1977) call 'situational scripts' in which:

- the situation is specified (e.g. eating in a restaurant)
- several players have roles to perform (cook, waiter, customer, cashier, owner)
- the players share an understanding of what is to happen (show to table, give menu, choose items, take order, serve food, eat meal, ask for bill, pay bill, leave tip).

The situational script does not have to be written out word for word; the consumption event is 'scripted' only in the sense that once each 'actor' knows the roles to be played, then they can improvise the performance accordingly. It is a structure that delineates the sequences of events in a particular situation.

The notion of performance is a useful way of looking at consumption because it encompasses and unites many of the concepts inherent within the consumption experience. All performances take place within a setting or on a stage. One of the phenomena associated with consumer communities or subcultures (see subsections on Consumer culture and Consumer subcultures and tribes) is that important places are transformed and resignified, and this may apply equally to the 'rendezvous' of mountain men in the USA (Belk & Costa, 1998) or the annual Gothic festival at Whitby, normally a quiet fishing village in north-east England. For Goths, Whitby has emotional attachments due to its connection with the Dracula myth and a perceived authenticity, resulting from Whitby Abbey, which is a tangible reminder of the vampire's arrival in Britain (Goulding et al., 2002).

> *Performances are imbued with certain characteristics. These include a setting or a stage on which the performance takes place, stories or plays with scripts which are acted out by actors and stars who take on supporting and key roles, props and costumes, and the creation of a spectacle.*

Performances depend on stories, plays, narratives or myth. The vampire myth is the cornerstone of the Gothic movement and is played out and reconstructed during the festival. However, other leisure-based communities are also often predicated on either 'real' or fictitious myth – for instance, the 'mountain men'

(Belk & Costa, 1998), the 'easy rider' myth that feeds the biker culture (Schouten & McAlexander, 1995) or the science fiction-based story that has inspired and seen the *Star Trek* phenomenon develop and grow (Kozinets, 2001). Myths allow for fantasy and escape, which are central to both performance and observation of performance. This performance allows for the construction and enactment of alternative identities through the adoption of temporary roles. Thus, individuals may shed their everyday identities and become 'actors' for a temporary period in time.

Most consumption communities are rooted in material culture whereby the costumes and accessories that support the performance also serve to differentiate the individual. These props convey meaning and are heavily encoded and symbolic. They act to extend the 'self' (Belk, 1988) and imbue the individual with dramatic persona. Finally, performances involve spectacle and can be acted out in a carnivalesque atmosphere (Bakhtin, 1984) that provides the opportunity to reverse the codes and norms of everyday behaviour.

Implications of viewing consumption as performance

1 *The role of place, space and time in consumer experience is reconceptualized and adds depth to our understanding of temporally and spatially situated consumption (see Moving Space).*
2 *The role of myth, play and fantasy and their role in contemporary consumption (Thompson, 2004) offer insights into the complex nature of fantasy construction and alternative realities.*
3 *The idea of the consumer as 'actor' leading to a reformulation of the construction of consumer identities, from 'we are what we have' (Belk, 1988) to 'we are what we do' (Deighton, 1992).*
4 *The role of props and the nature of material culture have the potential to strengthen our understanding about the commodification process.*
5 *The modes of symbolic consumption and the relationship between individual, group and object, which links to the ideas of actor–network theory (Latour, 1987; Appadurai, 1986).*
6 *The nature of spectacular consumption (Peñaloza, 2000), which appears to be growing in importance as society becomes more insatiable for the novel, the thrilling and experiences that are far removed from the everyday.*

Consumer satisfaction

Satisfaction is closely related to the consumption performance and in a sense follows on from it. Following purchase of the product, service or event, the customer will normally evaluate its performance in some way, unless they are completely non-judgemental. In traditional marketing this is what determines the customer's satisfaction or not.

Most of the theory and measures of customer satisfaction come from services marketing, including the famous SERVQUAL scale for rating service quality. This employs a comparison of customer expectations of service performance with their evaluation of its actual performance to indicate confirmation or disconfirmation of expectations. It is this level of dis/confirmation of expectations that is taken as the measure of quality and/or satisfaction.

SERVQUAL rating scale – technique for measuring service quality
- *A multiple-item scale that measures customers' perceptions and expectations so that the size of the gaps can be identified.*
- *Based on five criteria: reliability, responsiveness, courtesy, competence and tangibles.*
- *Respondents indicate the extent of their agreement/disagreement to a series of statements according to a numerical scale (typically a 1–5 or 1–7 Likart scale).*

(Parasuraman et al., 1985)

Despite its roots in service quality, it should be noted that the concept of 'satisfaction' is not exactly the same as 'quality'. Strictly, quality is an attribute of the product/service performance and satisfaction is the customer's perceived gratification from their experience of it.

The similarity nowadays of the measures of product/service quality and customer satisfaction has compounded the difficulty in distinguishing the two concepts, especially since the two are often used interchangeably. For example, Holbrook (1999) writes:

> One admires some object or prizes some experience for its capacity to accomplish some goal or perform some function. Such a utilitarian emphasis on the appreciation of instrumentality relates closely to the *concept of satisfaction*

based on comparison of performance with expectations and appears to constitute the essence of what we mean by quality.

A further confusion is that both quality and satisfaction are related to loyalty and sometimes used synonymously with 'value' (see Marketing Contexts: Marketing values). Another complexity which is noted by Oliver (1997) is that quality is an input to value, but quality is also an input to satisfaction through customers' comparison of performance to expected quality standards. The essential problem is that all these terms are related to each other and 'embedded in a web of consumption constructs'.

Although consumers may accurately be described as 'satisfied' or 'dissatisfied' with a product or company performance, there is considerable confusion as to the meaning and multiple uses of this and related concepts. The use of the term 'consumer satisfaction', therefore, should always be treated with caution, and in particular the measures employed should be scrutinized carefully in order to reveal exactly what the customer is being asked to evaluate. Even when the customer's rating is broken down into key components, their rating of, say, 'how satisfied are you with the delivery service' may be based on various interpretations of 'satisfactory' delivery in terms of different elements of the process and/or outcome which may not be apparent in the questionnaire results, such as on-time delivery, early delivery, order completeness, staff help, ease of packaging, etc.

One of the key points to remember is that both quality and satisfaction are personal judgements about things, events and feelings. Because often it is different 'actors' in the product and consumption performance that are making the evaluation, it is quite possible for the quality ranking of a product or service to diverge significantly from customer satisfaction ratings, for example in the case of high-quality glassware which nevertheless does not meet the consumer's expectations, use requirements nor their aesthetic appreciation. Equally, I am satisfied with the performance of my medium-quality personal computer, which is perfectly adequate for my use of it – and indeed for my ability to use it. An MBA programme may not be rated as high quality, but students are very satisfied with it. These differences are partly due to the fact that quality can be ascribed to a product or service by both producers and consumers, whereas *consumer satisfaction is entirely subjective and evaluated by customers alone.*

Disadvantaged consumers

Along with the rise of consumerism in today's societies, there has been a shift away from values of community and integrity towards those of materialism and competition. This has been problematic for society as a whole since some people

Those who are at a disadvantage in exchange relationships where that disadvantage is attributable to characteristics that are largely uncontrollable by them at the time of the transaction.
Andreasen, 1975

are better equipped to thrive in these conditions and the voice of the customer is louder for some consumers than others.

Even in the USA and Europe there are many people who are unable to fully participate in the consumer society because they have little discretionary spending or choice. Some of this is due to low incomes; however, consumer disadvantage may take several forms, including lack of access to markets, information and education, availability of finance, exploitative practices of business, and other personal factors such as immobility or illness. Marketplace exclusion might result from factors linked to deprivation including poor educational levels, poor levels of communication and support in the home, and poor access to jobs and forms of credit. It can also result from the activities of retailers, marketers and cultural intermediaries in advertising, broadcasting and social media who shape the messages and measures of success and belonging in terms of the market.

The problems faced by poor consumers go beyond the resource scarcity and meagre consumption opportunities. From his extensive studies of the poor and the wider 'culture of poverty' in which they are said to exist, Hill (1991, 2002) found that their plight is exacerbated by living in an inescapable consumer culture. For example, social and mass media all too effectively communicate the standards and opportunities for material accumulation in society through television, movies, celebrity images and social media. For poorer consumers, however, this only highlights the vivid contrast between their conditions of relative disadvantage and the consumer abundance that surrounds them. Not only are they materially deprived but they are also unable to fully participate in the so-called 'semiotic democracy' that Fiske (1987) suggested is provided by television and other mass communications.

A further cause for concern regarding disadvantaged consumers is that participation in the market, and the accompanying rights and responsibilities that allow individuals to be valued as legitimate consumers, is an essential aspect of social cohesion and social relations. Consumers who are unable to fully participate in consumer choice are also potentially further handicapped by their exclusion from the symbolic and cultural aspects of consumption.

Of course, marketing itself cannot liberate all consumers from such deprivations. Many of these problems have wider public policy implications. We have seen earlier in this chapter the importance of consumption in the process of identity, self-esteem and connectedness to other consumers, and therefore the daily activities of the marketing profession affect individuals' sense of wellbeing in these respects. Marketers can attempt to alleviate some of the disadvantages faced by the worse-off consumers, even in small practical ways, by means of policies such as more economical quantities and packaging, advice on economical uses, encouragement of healthy eating by retailers. At a strategic level, marketers can adopt policies of corporate social responsibility, the 'triple bottom line', social marketing, business ethics and consumer education policies (see Marketing Contexts: Marketing values).

FURTHER READING

Prosumers and co-production

Normann, R. & Ramirez, R. (1993) From value chain to value constellation: designing interactive strategy. *Harvard Business Review*, July/August, 65–77.

Vargo, S. L. & Lusch, R. F. (2004) Evolving to a new dominant logic for marketing. *Journal of Marketing*, **68** (January), 1–17.

Wikström, S. (1996) The customer as a co-producer. *European Journal of Marketing*, **30** (4), 6–19.

Consumer identity

Belk, R. W. (1988) Possessions and the extended sense of self. *Journal of Consumer Research*, **15**, 139–168.

Elliot, R. & Wattanasuwan, K. (1998) Brands as resources for the symbolic construction of identity. *International Journal of Advertising*, **17** (2), 131–144.

Goulding, C., Shankar, A. & Elliot, R. (2002) Working weeks, rave weekends: identity fragmentation and the emergence of new communities. *Consumption, Markets and Culture*, **5** (4), 261–284.

Consumer culture, subcultures and tribes

Arnould, E. & Thompson, C. J. (2005) Consumer culture theory: twenty years of research. *Journal of Consumer Research*, **31** (4), 841–849.

Arnould, E. J. & Thompson, C. J. (2015) CCT: ten years gone (and beyond). In: *Research in Consumer Behavior Volume 17* (A. Thyroff, J. B. Murray & R. W. Belk, eds.). Emerald Group Publishing: Bingley, UK.

Belk, R. W. (2010) Sharing. *Journal of Consumer Research*, **36** (February), 715–734.

Cova, B. & Cova, V. (2002) Tribal marketing: the tribalization of society and its impact on the conduct of marketing. *European Journal of Marketing*, **36** (5/6), 595–620.

Goulding, C., Shankar, A. & Canniford, R. (2013) Learning to be tribal: facilitating the formation of consumer tribes. *European Journal of Marketing*, **47** (5/6), 813–832.

Schouten, J. & McAlexander, J. (1995) Subcultures of consumption: an ethnography of the new bikers. *Journal of Consumer Research*, **22** (1), 43–61.

Consumer performance, satisfaction and disadvantage

Deighton, J. (1992) The consumption of performance. *Journal of Consumer Research*, **19** (December), 362–372.

Hill, R.P. (2002) Consumer culture and the culture of poverty: implications for marketing theory and practice. *Marketing Theory*, **2** (3), 273–293.

Oliver, R. (1997) *Satisfaction: A Behavioural Perspective on the Consumer*. McGraw-Hill: New York.

Richins, M.L. (1994) Valuing things: the public and private meanings of possessions. *Journal of Consumer Research*, **21** (3), 522–533.

Collaborative consumption and sharing

Bardhi, F. & Eckhart, G.M. (2012) Access-based consumption: the case of car sharing. *Journal of Consumer Research*, **39** (4), 881–898.

Belk, R.W. (2010) Sharing. *Journal of Consumer Research*, **36** (February), 715–734.

Rifkin, J. (2000) *The Age of Access*. J.P. Tarcher/Putnam: New York.

Scaraboto, D. (2015) Selling, sharing and everything in between: the hybrid economies of collaborative networks. *Journal of Consumer Research*, **42** (4), 152–176.

References

Andreasen, A. (1975) *The Disadvantaged Customer*. The Free Press: New York.

Appadurai, A. (1986) *The Social Life of Things*. Cambridge University Press: Cambridge.

Arnould, E. J. & Price, L. L. (1993) River magic: extraordinary experience and the extended service encounter. *Journal of Consumer Research*, **20** (June), 24–45.

Arnould, E. & Thompson, C. J. (2005) Consumer culture theory: twenty years of research. *Journal of Consumer Research*, **31** (4), 841–849.

Arnould, E. & Thompson, C. J. (2015) CCT: ten years gone (and beyond). In: *Research in Consumer Behavior, Volume 17* (A. Thyroff, J. B. Murray & R. W. Belk, eds.). Emerald Group Publishing: Bingley, UK.

Arnould, E., Price, L. & Zinkhan, G. (2002) *Consumers*. McGraw-Hill: New York.

Bakhtin, M. (1984/1965) *Rabelais and his World* (H. Iswolsky, trans.). Indiana University Press: Bloomingdale.

Bardhi, F. & Eckhart, G. M. (2012) Access-based consumption: the case of car sharing. *Journal of Consumer Research*, **39** (4), 881–898.

Barnes, S. & Mattsson, J. (2017) Understanding collaborative consumption: test of a theoretical model. *Technological Forecasting and Social Change*, **118**, 281–292.

Baudrillard, J. (1970) *The Mirror of Production*. Telos Press: St Louis.

Baudrillard, J. (1981) *For a Critique of the Political Economy of the Sign*. Telos Press: St Louis.

Bauman, Z. (1988) *Freedom*. Open University Press: Milton Keynes.

Bauman, Z. (2001) *Community: Seeking Safety in an Insecure World*. Polity Press: London.

Belk, R. W. (1988) Possessions and the extended sense of self. *Journal of Consumer Research*, **15**, 139–168.

Belk, R. (2001) Speciality magazines and flights of fancy: feeding the desire to desire. *European Advances in Consumer Research*, **5**, 197–202.

Belk, R. W. (2007) Why not share rather than own? *The Annals of the American Academy of Political and Social Science*, **611** (1), 126–140.

Belk, R. W. (2010) Sharing. *Journal of Consumer Research*, **36** (February), 715–734.

Belk, R. W. & Costa, J. A. (1998) The mountain man myth: a contemporary consuming fantasy. *Journal of Consumer Research*, **25** (December), 218–252.

Benkler, Y. (2004) Sharing nicely: on shareable goods and the emergence of sharing as a modality of economic production. *The Yale Law Journal*, **114** (2), 273–358.

Bitner, M. J. (1992) Servicescapes: the impact of physical surroundings on customers and employees. *Journal of Marketing*, **56** (2), 57–71.

Botsman, R. & Rogers, R. (2010) *What's Mine is Yours: The Rise of Collaborative Consumption*. Harper Business: New York.

Bourdieu, P. (1984) *Distinction: A Social Critique of the Judgement of Taste*. Routledge: London.

Brown, S. (2001) *Marketing: The Retro Revolution*. Sage: London.

Brown, S. (2002) FCUK consumer research: on disgust, revulsion and other forms of offensive advertising. *European Advances in Consumer Research*, **5**, 61–65.

Callon, M. (1999) Actor–network theory: the market test. In: *Actor–Network Theory and After* (J. Law & J. Hassard, eds.). Blackwell: Oxford, pp. 181–195.

Campbell, C. (1987) *The Romantic Ethic and the Spirit of Modern Consumerism*. Blackwell: Oxford.

Carù, A. & Cova, B. (2007) *Consuming Experiences*. Routledge: London.

Celsi, R.L., Rose, R. & Leigh, T.W. (1993) An exploration of high-risk leisure consumption through skydiving. *Journal of Consumer Research*, **20** (1), 1–23.

Cova, B. & Cova, V. (2002) Tribal marketing: the tribalization of society and its impact on the conduct of marketing. *European Journal of Marketing*, **36** (5/6), 595–620.

Cova, B. & Dalli, D. (2009) Working consumers: the next step in marketing theory? *Marketing Theory*, **9** (3), 315–339.

Cova, B., Maclaran, P. & Bradshaw, A. (2013) Rethinking consumer culture theory from the postmodern to the communist horizon. *Marketing Theory*, **13** (2), 213–225.

Deighton, J. (1992) The consumption of performance. *Journal of Consumer Research*, **19** (December), 362–372.

DeMello, M. (2000) *Bodies of Inscription; A Cultural History of the Modern Tattoo Community*. Duke University Press: Durham.

Douglas, M. & Isherwood, B. (1978) *World of Goods*. Allen Lane: London.

Elliot, R. (1999) Symbolic meaning. In: *Rethinking Marketing* (D. Brownlie *et al.*, eds.). Sage: London, pp. 112–125.

Elliot, R. & Wattanasuwan, K. (1998) Brands as resources for the symbolic construction of identity. *International Journal of Advertising*, **17** (2), 131–144.

Ewen, S. (1988) *All Consuming Images: The Politics of Style in Contemporary Culture*. Basic Books: New York.

Featherstone, M. (1991) *Consumer Culture and Postmodernism*. Sage: Thousand Oaks, CA.

Featherstone, M. (ed.) (2000) *Body Modification*. Sage: London.

Fiske, J. (1987) *Television Culture*. Routledge: London.

Fiske, J. (1989) *Understanding Popular Culture*. Unwin Hyman: Boston.

Frank, T. & Weiland, M. (eds.) (1997) *Commodify Your Dissent: The Business of Culture in the New Guilded Inn*. Norton: New York.

Goldman, R. & Papson, S. (1996) *Sign Wars: The Cluttered Landscape of Advertising*. Guildford Press: Surrey.

Goulding, C. (1999) Consumer research, interpretive paradigms and methodo-logical ambiguities. *European Journal of Marketing*, **33** (9–10), 859–873.

Goulding, C. & Follett, J. (2001) Subcultures, women and tattoos: an exploratory study. *Gender Marketing and Consumption* (Association for Consumer Research), **6**, 37–54.

Goulding, C., Shankar, A. & Elliot, R. (2002) Working weeks, rave weekends: iden-tity fragmentation and the emergence of new communities. *Consumption, Markets and Culture*, **5** (4), 261–284.

Goulding, C., Shankar, A., Elliott, R. & Canniford, R. (2009) The marketplace management of illicit pleasure. *Journal of Consumer Research*, **35** (February), 759–771.

Grafton-Small, R. & Linstead, S. (1989) Advertisements as artefacts: everyday understanding and the creative consumer. *International Journal of Advertising*, **8** (3), 205–218.

Gronhaug, K. (1999) The sociological basis for marketing. In: *Marketing Theory* (M. Baker, ed.). Thomson Learning: London.

Grönroos, C. (2006) Adopting a service logic for marketing. *Marketing Theory*, **6** (3), 317–334.

Grove, S. J. & Fisk, R. P. (1983) The dramaturgy of service exchange: an analytical framework for services marketing. In: *Emerging Perspectives on Services Marketing* (L. Berry, ed.). American Marketing Association: Chicago, pp. 45–49.

Gummesson, E. (1997) Relationship marketing as a paradigm shift: some conclu-sions from the 30R approach. *Management Decision*, **35** (4), 267–272.

Gummesson, E. (2000) The marketing of services. In: *Marketing Theory* (M. Baker, ed.). Thomson Learning: London, pp. 216–230.

Hall, S. & Jefferson, T. (eds.) (1976) *Resistance through Rituals: Youth Subcultures in Post-War Britain*. Hutchinson: London.

Hebdidge, D. (1997/1979) Subcultures: the meaning of style. In: *The Subcultures Reader* (K. Gelder & S. Thornton, eds.). Routledge: London.

Hellwig, K., Morhart, F. & Girardin, F. (2015) Exploring different types of sharing: a proposed segmentation of the market for 'sharing' businesses. *Psychology & Marketing*, **32** (9), 891–906.

Hill, R. P. (1991) Homeless women, special possessions and the meaning of home: an ethnographic case study. *Journal of Consumer Research*, **18** (December), 298–310.

Hill, R. P. (2002) Consumer culture and the culture of poverty: implications for marketing theory and practice. *Marketing Theory*, **2** (3), 273–293.

von Hippel, E. (1978) Successful industrial products from customer ideas. *Journal of Marketing*, **42** (1), 39–49.

Hirschman, E. C. (2000) *Heroes, Monsters and Messiahs: Movies and Tele-vision Shows as the Mythology of American Culture*. Andrew McMeel: Kansas City, MO.

Hirschman, E.C. & Holbrook, M.B. (1982) The experiential aspects of consumption: consumer fantasies, feelings and fun. *Journal of Consumer Research*, **9** (September), 132–140.

Holbrook, M. (ed.) (1999) *Consumer Value*. Routledge: New York.

Holt, D.B. (1995) How consumers consume: a typology of consumption practices. *Journal of Consumer Research*, **22** (June), 1–16.

Holt, D.B. (1998) Does cultural capital structure American consumption? *Journal of Consumer Research*, **25** (June), 1–25.

Holt, D.B. (2002) Why do brands cause trouble? A dialectical theory of consumer culture and branding. *Journal of Consumer Research*, **29** (June), 70–90.

Illich, I. (1981) *Shadow Work*. Marion Boyars: Salem, NH.

Kates, S. (2002) The protean quality of subcultural consumption: an ethnographic account of gay consumers. *Journal of Consumer Research*, **29** (3), 383–399.

Kotler, P. (1967) *Marketing Management: Analysis, Planning and Control*. Prentice Hall: Englewood Cliffs, NJ.

Kozinets, R.V. (2001) Utopian Enterprise: articulating the meanings of *Star Trek*'s culture of consumption. *Journal of Consumer Research*, **28** (1), 67–88.

Laermans, R. (1993) Learning to consume: early department stores and the shaping of modern consumer culture (1860–1914). *Theory, Culture and Society*, **10**, 79–112.

Lamberton, C. (2016) Collaborative consumption: a goal-based framework. *Current Opinion in Psychology*, **10** (1), 55–59.

Lanier, C.D. & Rader, C.S. (2015) Consumption experience: an expanded view. *Marketing Theory*, **15** (4), 487–508.

Latour, B. (1987) *Science in Action: How to Follow Scientists and Engineers Through Society*. Open University Press: Milton Keynes.

Lovelock, C. (2004) Whither services marketing? In search of a new paradigm and fresh perspectives. *Journal of Service Research*, **7** (1), 20–41.

Lusch, R.F. & Vargo, S.L. (2006) Service-dominant logic as a foundation for general theory. In: *The Service Dominant Logic of Marketing. Dialogue, Debate, and Directions* (R.F. Lusch & S.R. Vargo, eds.). M.E. Sharpe: Armonk, NY.

Maffesoli, M. (1996) *The Time of the Tribes: The Decline of Individualism in Mass Society*. Sage: London.

Mark, M. & Pearson, C. (2001) *The Hero and the Outlaw: Building Extraordinary Brands through the Power of Archetypes*. McGraw-Hill: New York.

Mauss, M. (1966) *The Gift: Forms and Functions of Exchange in Archaic Societies*. Cohen-West: London.

Mauss, M. (1979/1936) *Body Techniques in Sociology and Psychology* (B. Brewster, trans.). Routledge and Kegan Paul: London.

Miklas, S. & Arnould, S. (1999) The extraordinary self: Gothic culture and the construction of the self. *Journal of Marketing Management*, **15** (6), 563–576.

Moisander, J., Valtonen, A. & Histo, H. (2009) Personal interviews in cultural consumer research. *Consumption, Markets and Culture*, **12** (4), 329–348.

Muñiz, A. & O'Guinn, T. C. (2001) Brand communities. *Journal of Consumer Research*, **27** (March), 412–432.

Normann, R. & Ramirez, R. (1993) From value chain to value constellation: designing interactive strategy. *Harvard Business Review*, July/August, 65–77.

Oliver, R. (1997) *Satisfaction: A Behavioural Perspective on the Consumer.* McGraw-Hill: New York.

Packard, V. (1957) *The Hidden Persuaders.* Penguin: New York.

Parasuraman, A., Zeithaml, V. & Berry, L. (1985) A conceptual model of service quality and its implications for future research. *Journal of Marketing*, **49** (4), 41–50.

Peñaloza, L. (2000) The commodification of the American West: marketers' production of cultural meanings at a trade show. *Journal of Marketing*, **64** (October), 82–109.

Pine, B. J. & Gilmore, J. H. (1999) *The Experience Economy: Work is Theater and Every Business a Stage.* Harvard Business School Press: Boston, MA.

Pollay, R. W. (1986) The distorted mirror: reflections on the unintended consequences of advertising. *Journal of Marketing*, **50** (2), 18–36.

Rifkin, J. (2000) *The Age of Access.* J.P. Tarcher/Putnam: New York.

Saren, M. & Tzokas, N. (1998) The nature of the product in market relationships: a pluri-signified product concept. *Journal of Marketing Management*, **14** (5), 445–464.

Saussure, F. de (1959) *Course in General Linguistics.* McGraw-Hill: New York.

Scaraboto, D. (2015) Selling, sharing and everything in between: the hybrid economies of collaborative networks. *Journal of Consumer Research*, **42** (4), 152–176.

Schank, R. & Abelson, R. (1977) *Scripts, Plans, Goals and Understanding: An Inquiry into Human Knowledge Structures.* Lawrence Erlbaum: New Jersey.

Schouten, J. (1991) Selves in transition: symbolic consumption in personal rites of passage and identity reconstruction. *Journal of Consumer Research*, **17** (March), 412–425.

Schouten, J. & McAlexander, J. (1995) Subcultures of consumption: an ethnography of the new bikers. *Journal of Consumer Research*, **22** (1), 43–61.

Schroeder, J. (2002) *Visual Consumption.* Routledge: London.

Schroeder, J. (2003) *Visual Consumption.* Routledge: London.

Stevens, L., Brown, S. & Maclaran, P. (2001) The joys of text: women's experiential consumption of magazines. *European Advances in Consumer Research*, **5**, 169–173.

Svensson, P. (2004) *Setting the Marketing Scene: Reality Production in Everyday Marketing Work*. Lund Business Press: Lund.

Thompson, C. J. (2004) Marketplace mythologies and discourses of power. *Journal of Consumer Research*, **31** (June), 162–180.

Thompson, C. & Hirschman, E. (1995) Understanding the socialized body: a post-structuralist analysis of consumer's self-conceptions, body images and self-care practices. *Journal of Consumer Research*, **32** (September), 139–153.

Toffler, A. (1980) *The Third Wave*. Bantam Books: New York.

Vargo, S. L. & Lusch, R. F. (2004) Evolving to a new dominant logic for marketing. *Journal of Marketing*, **68** (January), 1–17.

Veblen, T. (1899/1995) *The Theory of The Leisure Class: An Economic Study of Institutions*. Penguin: London.

Velliquette, A. & Bamossy, G. (2001) The role of body adornment and the self-reflexive body in life-style cultures and identity. *European Advances in Consumer Research*, **5**, 21.

Walendorf, M. & Arnould, E. J. (1988) My favourite things: a cross-cultural inquiry into object attachment, possessiveness and social linkage. *Journal of Consumer Research*, **14**, 531–547.

Warde, A. (2005) Consumption and theories of practice. *Journal of Consumer Culture*, **5** (2), 131–153.

Weiner, B. (1992) *Human Motivation: Metaphors, Theories and Research*. Sage: London.

Zwick, D. & Cayla, J. (2011) *Inside Marketing: Practices, Ideologies, Devices*. Oxford University Press: Oxford.

creating solutions

Marketing creates solutions by providing products, services and other 'market offerings'. One question is, 'Solutions to what?' It is market offerings *as solutions* that we are concerned with in this chapter – how they are created, what problems or opportunities they solve, how to identify them, how to understand them, how marketers organize for them, and the consumer's role in solutions. Technology, innovation and new product development provide the basis for solutions to many consumer and marketing problems. Here we explain how information technology, organizational processes, and market research and consumer insight help to ensure that the 'voice of the customer' actually contributes to creating solutions.

SoLuTioNs to whaT?

Marketing creates solutions by providing products, services and other 'market offerings'. But then the next question is, 'Solutions to what?' The traditional marketing answer is to 'customer' needs and wants. This is one type of problem that people seek to solve through marketing. In any market exchange, however, with any market offering, there are *two* sets of problems or needs that are relevant – i.e. those of buyers *and sellers*. Both customers and marketers may have problems which they attempt to solve through the market – one by buying an 'offering', the other by making it available and selling it.

We can view market offerings as solutions to customers' problems or marketers' problems, or both. Banks introduced automated teller machines (ATMs) as a 'solution' to customers' need for 24-hour access to cash and less waiting time. But ATMs also solved the banks' problem of the cost of maintaining staff and facilities in high street and other expensive locations. The introduction of ATMs solved both customers' and marketers' problems.

One type of problem can often lead to another. A customer's need for a new product becomes the marketer's problem to find a solution and provide it. A marketer's problem, such as finding customers for a new product, leads to the customer's problem of hearing about it, understanding its use and considering whether to try it. Of course, in the latter case you may say it is less of a problem, more an opportunity for the consumer. But this simply depends on how one looks at it. One customer's opportunity to buy or not to buy may be regarded by another as an evaluation and decision 'problem'; also, one marketer's oppor-

tunity to sell may be a sales 'problem' for others. So problems and opportunities are two sides of the same coin. The term 'problem' is used here to refer to the needs, wants, objectives, targets and requirements that buyers and sellers seek to solve by engaging in an exchange of some market 'offering'.

It is *market offerings as solutions* that we are concerned with in this chapter; how they are created, what problems (or opportunities) they solve, how to identify them, how to understand them, how marketers organize for them and the consumers' role in solutions.

Product solutions

The obvious way in which marketing 'creates solutions' is by making and selling products and services. In marketing we can view products as 'solutions' to customer problems or needs. Products do not normally provide these solutions simply by the act of being purchased; it is only by *using* the car or the bread that the consumer's need for transport or food is satisfied. Indeed, more accurately from the customer's point of view, consumption is essentially an *experience*. How well they enjoyed the 'experience' of using it usually determines how satisfied the consumer is with the product. Many purchases now are not primarily physical products at all – insurance, entertainment, education, health. Therefore, the 'objects of consumption' can be viewed very broadly covering, for example, objects, materials, services, people, places, ideas, information – and even images, identities, cultures and myths (see Consuming Experience).

> *The way in which marketing has dealt with the multiple aspects of 'solutions' that can be created for customers is to consider not only physical products and services, but to think in terms of the 'total market offering'. According to this view, the market offering comprises a 'bundle of attributes' that consists of all of its constituent elements, including benefits, services and expectations, the materials used to make it, its 'intangible' attributes – such as service, guarantees, instructions, image, design, reputation – and functional features – including usability, storage, weight, access, effectiveness, etc. – all of which together make up the 'total offering' to customers.*

One definition of the product is anything that can be offered to a market for attention, acquisition, use or consumption that might satisfy a want or a need. It includes physical objects, services, persons, places, organizations and ideas.
Kotler, 1972

Traditional marketing theory was predicated on the central role of the product in the exchange process and the notion of the 'product concept' as a distinct entity and object of exchange. In the next subsection, we explore what is meant by the idea of a 'product' in order to reach greater understanding of the marketing process. It is important to recognize that marketing theory does not, and never has, regarded the product simply as the *physical object* of exchange and consumption.

In Kotler's view there are five levels of the product (see Figure 4.1). The *core benefit* is defined as the problem-solving capacity that the customer is buying, e.g. 'the purchaser of a drill is really buying holes'. The *generic product* is the basic version of the tool, beyond which are added the 'attributes that buyers normally expect' of the product, such as in this case leads, plug, instructions of use, etc. The *augmented product* provides additional features that distinguish one producer's offer from competitors' versions of the product, a two-speed drill with multiple settings and anti-vibration casing, for instance. The final level is more abstract, the *potential product* which any product represents for future transformation and development – perhaps computerized drill settings or an online drilling-solutions service as part of the product package. So, according to the traditional marketing view, the product can be analysed in terms of these constituent elements, including benefits, services and expectations, which together make up the 'total offering' to consumers.

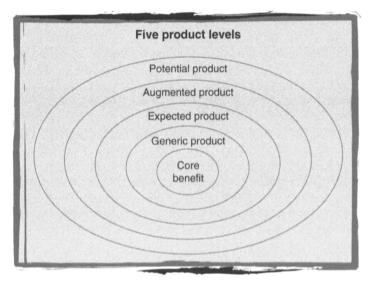

Figure 4.1 Product levels. *Source*: Kotler (1972)

However, products are consumed for many different attributes, not only their functional properties (see Consuming Experience: What is consumed?). Customers do not perceive product value in solely functional, product or any one-dimensional terms. For example, Wilson & Jantrania (1994) separated product-related aspects of value creation from vendor-related types and distinguished economic from non-economic components of value (see Marketing Contexts, Table 1.2).

The field of 'relationship marketing' (see Building Relations) also recognizes that the market exchange process involves much more than the basic exchange of products for money in order to satisfy the parties' needs. Market exchange of products takes place in the context of and encompasses wider social and business relationships and networks. Therefore, the product concept should not be regarded as a separate entity, as 'the object of exchange', which can be broken down into its 'five level' parts.

According to this *relational* view, the product cannot be separated in this fashion from its customer–supplier context and treated as a separate entity that can be deconstructed and understood in terms of its basic elements. On the contrary, the *product itself cannot be separated* from the relationships between the three actors in the market exchange process – i.e. buyers, suppliers and the material objects involved.

The reason for this interlinking of products and people is that people are not distant observers of the world separated by an invisible glass window from other people and material objects. So consumers and producers are not disconnected from the world of objects and products 'out there'. On the contrary, we all exist as part of the world, actively participating *in it*. And by participating in the world, we both influence and are profoundly influenced by other people and objects with whom we interact and create 'inter-experiences'. Thus, the social construction of the market exchange process is created as much by our relations to products as their relations to us (see Consuming Experience).

Figure 4.2 shows how this alternative view of the product regards it as the outcome of a three-way 'signification' process between buyers, sellers and objects. The product does not have any 'core benefit', and any 'expectations' and 'potential' differ widely in place and time. Benefits, expectations and potential are not inherent features of the product, but attributes which consumers and suppliers ascribe or 'read into' it. The product-as-solution is actually the *outcome* of the relationship between the buyer, the supplier and the object during and beyond the market exchange process.

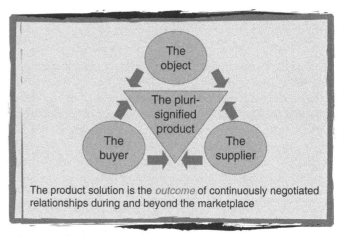

The product solution is the *outcome* of continuously negotiated relationships during and beyond the marketplace

Figure 4.2 The 'signified' nature of the product. *Source*: Saren & Tzokas (1998)

So products do not remain the same, for different parties involved, during their lifetime. According to the product life cycle (PLC) theory, which plots sales of a product over its lifetime, typically products develop through four stages in their life: introduction, growth, maturity and decline (see Figure 4.3). During their life they adapt, are improved and developed, and spread more widely among consumers.

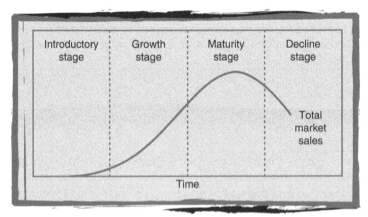

Figure 4.3 The product life cycle

Products are constantly changing as producers adapt and develop them (product innovations) or find better ways of producing them (process innovations), and as different consumers use them in different ways and view them in different ways (signification). Take a product like Scotch whisky, at the mature stage of the PLC. In Britain sales of the traditional spirit are falling, as it is viewed by some young people as 'an older person's drink'. In other parts of the world, such as Spain, Japan and South Africa, it is fashionable among all groups of drinkers. Manufacturers of whisky cannot alter the basic component but are constantly searching for new packaging, labelling, advertising 'innovations' in order to influence the way in which potential and existing customers view the product – i.e. to 're-signify it' (see Brand Selection).

Q. Are diamonds forever?
A. *The PLC suggests all products eventually die.*
Q. Why do products die?
A. *Usually for one or a mixture of the following reasons:*

  1 *Technological advances leading to obsolescence*
  2 *Competition*
  3 *Consumer tastes change*
  4 *Supply of material limited*
  5 *Government regulation.*

Markets therefore require a constant supply of new products in order to replace dying ones and to cater for new needs of customers and suppliers. The degree of 'newness' can vary enormously, however, and the term 'new product' is applied to mean very different things.

New products have different meanings of 'new'

- *New product 1.* A snack manufacturer introduces a new, larger pack size for its best-selling potato chips. Consumer research for the company revealed that a family-size pack would generate additional sales without cannibalizing existing sales of the standard size pack.
- *New product 2.* A consumer electronics company introduces a new miniature drone. The company has further developed its existing larger drone and is now able to offer a much lighter and smaller version.
- *New product 3.* A pharmaceutical company introduces a new prescription drug for the treatment of type 2 diabetes. Following eight years of laboratory research and three years of clinical trials, the company has recently received approval from the government's medical authorities to launch its new anti-diabetic drug.

In order to clarify the multiple uses of the term, one method of classifying new products is by the degrees of newness to the market and newness of the product (Ansoff, 1979). The consulting company Booz Allen Hamilton (1982) divides new products into six convenient categories (see Figure 4.4):

- 'New to the world' products
- New product lines (new to the firm)
- Additions to existing lines
- Revisions to core products
- Improvements to augmented products
- Repositionings.

As already noted, there are always two types of problems being solved with a product offering in a market: those of consumer and producer. Firms need new products too and they face enormous costs and effort in order to develop and market them; all the more so the more 'new to the world' the product. The manufacturing issues in adding new product improvements or achieving cost reductions can also be considerable, e.g. the research and development (R&D) costs in aerospace and pharmaceuticals industries. It follows therefore that firms

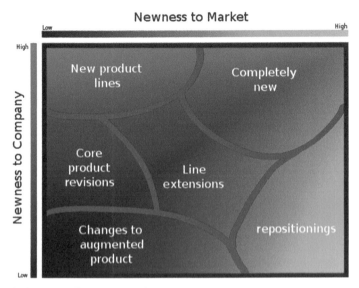

Figure 4.4 'New product' categories

and the business literature tend to adopt a classification of new products which reflects the needs and solutions of the suppliers.

The new product development (NPD) process is normally viewed as comprising a series of activity or decision 'stages' as follows:

1 *Idea generation* – the search for new product ideas to meet company objectives.
2 *Screening* – a quick analysis to determine which ideas are pertinent and merit a more detailed study.
3 *Concept development* – clarification of the product idea, its key features, potential consumer benefits and technology involved.
4 *Business analysis* – the expansion of the idea into a concrete business recommendation including product features and a programme for the product.
5 *Development* – turning the product idea into a ready-made product, demonstrable and reproducible.
6 *Testing* – the technical and market testing necessary to verify earlier business judgements about the product's performance and customer response.
7 *Commercialization* – full-scale production and launching of the product into the marketplace.

This type of linear 'stages' approach to NPD has been criticized for not accurately reflecting firms' existing practices or the ideal methods for organizing and managing the product development process. In particular, it does not allow for, nor illustrate, the following five features which often occur during the NPD process (Saren, 1994):

1 *Recursive processes* – going back and repeating an activity again.
2 *Simultaneous processes* – conducting two or more stages at the same time.
3 *More attention to early stages* – focusing on the initial stimulus, motivation and idea selection.
4 *External activities* – elements conducted outside the firm or with external partners.
5 *Technical and organizational variations* – firm-specific processes and behaviour.

Because the creation of new products is such a major issue for companies, it is entirely logical that the models of the NPD process, whatever sequence they follow, tend to focus on corporate activities, decisions and processes. They help companies to plan and organize their NPD and to identify R&D requirements and the role of technology in developing new product solutions (see The role of technology later in this section). What they also need is to take a products-as-solutions approach *from the customers' perspective*, i.e. to build in the links at each stage to customer problems and the corresponding customer information required in order to develop solutions. The aim should be to permit the 'voice of the customer' to be introduced at key points in the NPD process (Griffin & Hauser, 1995).

Even the conventional categories of product newness fail to take a products-as-solutions approach from the customers' perspective. In the Booz Allen Hamilton classification of newness of products (refer back to Figure 4.4), for example, it is clear that these are predominantly producer issues that are addressed – new lines, additions to lines, cost reductions – with only repositioning being a market issue, and primarily one for the marketer. Although this classification may help point to new product requirements for the company's portfolio, it does not clarify the priorities for the development of new product solutions to customer, as well as producer, problems.

In order to apply the product-as-solution perspective from the consumer point of view, the key questions to ask are, 'what are the customer problems being solved by new products and how can these best be categorized?' In order to answer this the marketer has to understand the nature of the customer problems, to access and 'listen to' the voice of the customer, and to ensure that such information and knowledge drives the innovation structure and not the other way round (see Information for innovative solutions).

Service solutions

In advanced economies, the proportion of economic activity in the service sector is expanding and now far exceeds that of manufacturing or agriculture, with a consequent shift in economic activity away from manufacturing towards services. Fewer businesses in today's advanced economies produce or exchange physical goods; far more now trade in services, produce services and consume services. Therefore, most marketing involves the exchange of services in one form or another, not material products. As the complexity and range of services has grown, scholars studying the marketing of services have identified different types and categories, including consumer services, public services, financial services, retail services, professional services, internal and support services, business-to-business services (Lovelock *et al.*, 1999).

While marketing researchers may find that these different types of services can be considered separately, they all have in common – along with physical products – that they are alternative means of creating and delivering solutions for businesses and customers. However, most services are created at the point of delivery and it is at this 'service nexus' that the quality of the solution is determined by its value as experienced by the customer. Furthermore, technological development means that many services can be delivered remotely, even from distant parts of the world. The emergence of a digital service economy will further alter the ways and places in which firms can create and deliver service solutions to customers in future (Lovelock & Gummesson, 2004).

Partly as result of these developments, there has been a shift in general marketing theory towards services. Until the end of the twentieth century most theory assumed marketing to be about tangible goods and products, reflecting contemporary economic conditions. Services were regarded as the exception and the services-marketing specialist field itself highlighted the 'unique characteristics of services' which set them, and the study of them, apart from the 'normal' marketing, i.e. of physical goods. Hypothetical differences between goods and services were stressed and distilled into the four characteristics of inseparability of production and consumption, heterogeneity, intangibility and perishability (Parasuraman *et al.*, 1985).

More recently, Vargo and Lusch (2004) challenged this view of the key differentiators of services versus goods and proposed a new 'service dominant logic' (SDL) for all marketing that constitutes a general theory of marketing. They present a wider, more abstract definition of 'service' as the application of specific skills and knowledge (i.e. competences) with beneficial consequences for someone. This

definition goes far beyond service as an object of exchange and makes it applicable to *all* marketing practice and theoretically encompasses everything in advanced society. With this over-determination of service theory, by its authors' own admission SDL is posited as the primary organizational principle of society.

The focus of SDL is on marketing as a value co-creation process that is service-based. Vargo and Lusch reject what they regard as the goods-centric nature of traditional marketing which is reflected in the language which dominated the previous era of 'product', 'production', 'goods', 'supplier', 'supply chain', 'value added', 'distribution', 'producer', 'consumer' etc. In the new logic, service, not goods, is the fundamental basis of exchange and goods are merely 'distribution mechanisms for service provision'. According to this view, marketers cannot provide complete solutions, they can only create value propositions embedded in offerings, and their value depends entirely on the experiential evaluation of customers.

Business model solutions

Products and services are not the only means for companies to provide solutions for their own objectives and deliver these to fulfil customers' needs. Some new technologies and so-called 'transformative innovations' are not merely applied by innovating firms to their products and services, but rather require development, innovation and major changes in the firms' *underlying business models* (See Information technology and innovation). Successful business model innovators create or adopt novel solutions that transform traditional existing business practices. These are much more far reaching than innovations in products, services or other specific market offerings for customers, and their effects are manifested in the operations and organization of the innovating firm itself as well as others in the industry and beyond. They are sometimes described as 'disruptive innovations' which reshape industry structures and redefine the bases of competition (Spieth *et al.*, 2014). For example, Apple's new business model around the iPod and the corresponding music download tool iTunes changed the whole music distribution industry. Reshaping industry boundaries and reinventing themselves is especially challenging for established companies (Teece, 2010).

The role of technology

Technology provides the basis for solutions to many consumer and marketing problems. It is used to develop new and improved products, better services, production and delivery methods, and information systems (see Information technology and innovation). Few of these solutions involve great advances in new technologies, however. Many do not require any 'new' technology at all, but new products and solutions are created by *combining* existing 'tried and tested' technologies *in new ways*. Even 'low-tech' products (beer, wine) can be manufactured better by applying high-tech methods, and 'no-tech' services (hairdressing) utilize technology to improve support materials (e.g. hair colouring).

We are often told that technological change is accelerating but not all products or markets are based on 'high-tech' solutions. Some industries face a problem of lack of innovation. This can be either because, like steel, fibres and petrochemicals, they have reached a point of technological maturity, or because they have achieved market saturation with few opportunities for growth or only replacement demand, such as home furnishings, white goods, TV, radio.

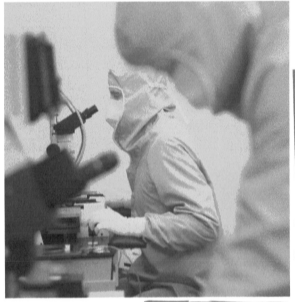

These circumstances encourage firms to restrict their innovation to incremental improvements in the same core technologies. They are unlikely to be able to justify major technological solutions, unless perhaps they can adapt new developments from outside their industry and apply them to their product solutions without the major R&D investment costs and timescales. This, however, requires managers to have the ability to monitor their external environment widely enough to spot technological opportunities; to have the ability to visualize their application in their own business; and to have the organizational skills to adapt the technologies and bring them to fruition.

It is in these tasks that technology and marketing need to combine in order to create market solutions. Professor Lord Alec Broers, president of the Royal Society of Engineers, argued that technology companies should be led by marketers, 'those who understand what customers want' (Broers, 2005).

Ideas about marketing and technology do not fit easily together in most enterprises. Organizing and planning marketing operations assumes that markets are predictable and there exists a set of carefully defined ambitions for the company, normally called 'strategy'. Technological change does not fit comfortably within such a framework – it is unpredictable and can arrive with stunning speed from fields far outside managers' or companies' expertise.

Furthermore, technology is usually described and evaluated from a purely technical perspective which only specialists have the knowledge and language to understand, and it is regarded as the responsibility of R&D specialists in laboratories. The potential offered by a technology and the implications for the company, its products and its customers is less easily demonstrated, understood and implemented than for other marketing opportunities such as exporting, new distributors and advertising.

Technologies are required to develop new solutions and better market offerings, often through new product development, but technology does not fit easily into marketing planning or strategic thinking.

In examining the failure of technology-based products, one of the major reasons seems to be the pioneers' failure to recognize the importance of the social and economic context of the innovation. People do not buy technology; they buy products and services that deliver specific benefits and solve certain problems. The technology is the facilitator that enables the development of the products and services and helps shape customers' needs and wants. Therefore, understanding the social, cultural and economic context in which consumers will use the technology – i.e. how it will be bought, transported, stored, consumed and discarded – is critical to the design of effective new products and services.

> *Technology by itself is rarely a solution. The NPD and innovation field is full of examples of new products that employed exotic technology but failed to achieve customer acceptance.*
> *Wind & Mahajan, 1997*

Defining technology application areas

- What: *the application or need to be solved.*
- How: *the technology required and its potential.*
- Who: *the customer to be served and their perceptions of the technology.*

For example, when a new technology-based product is being developed, the market research should seek to ascertain not only 'what the demand is' and 'how many units will be sold', but more fundamentally how the *consumer* 'understands' the technological function of the say, the iPhone. By analysing common perceptions of how certain technologies work, companies will be able to direct their NPD efforts with a deeper knowledge of how the customer really understands the technology involved.

This may appear unnecessary at the development stage – or even at any stage. How many car drivers understand the technological workings of the vehicle? How many computer users understand the technology involved? Not many, according to Berthon *et al.* (2005), whose investigation into how consumers perceive and use technological products found that companies often 'get it wrong' because, at its most basic, the consumer doesn't understand the technology and the company doesn't understand the consumer. For instance, how well do banks or internet providers understand what the consumer believes is happening, stage by stage, when they give their credit card details online? How does the consumer imagine the information is stored? Who do they believe processes the transaction? What do they visualize when they hear the terms 'secure site' or 'database'? Internet service providers have become a multibillion dollar industry, yet consumers' understanding of the technology and security involved in their operations remains low.

One way in which consumers try to understand the working of technologies they don't understand is to 'picture' it (Schroeder, 2002) through visualization and metaphors. We know that consumers 'use' more than the technical functions of products and that the symbolic meanings they ascribe are important (see Consuming Experience: What is consumed?). Even the technical functions of products are often also understood and expressed by consumers in terms of the symbolic and 'imagery' – e.g. 'building' a website', 'surfing' the internet. These metaphors and images are used and new ones developed by suppliers for the communication of technology to consumers, using terms such as 'the marriage of TV and communications', 'lovable networks' and 'electronic highway' (Dobers & Strannegard, 2001)

The solution is not that the consumer must or should fully understand the technology; it is the responsibility of the firm that employs the technology in products – and specifically marketing researchers – to find how exactly consumers perceive that it works. If they found out how the consumers envisage the operation of the technology then firms would be in a better position to develop service and technical innovations that fit with the consumers' conceptualization of a system that they do not necessarily understand technically. They would also be better able to develop effective marketing communications to directly address any customer concerns about security, reliability and quality with regard to their system.

This market research data should provide a key input to NPD to help design products so that they take into account their 'understandability' or 'user friendliness' for customers in order that they can more easily see the benefits of the new product and make full use of it. This will help both the functional design aspects and the eventual communication of the innovation to customers, both of which have been found to critically affect the rate of acceptance or 'diffusion' of new products in the market (Rogers, 1962).

FURTHER READING

Service solutions

Lovelock, C. & Gummesson, E. (2004) Whither service marketing? In search of a new paradigm and fresh perspectives. *Journal of Service Research*, **7** (1), 20–41.

Lovelock, C., Vandermerwe, S. & Lewis, B. (1999) *Services Marketing: A European Perspective,* Prentice Hall: Harlow.

Vargo, S. L. & Lusch, R. F. (2004) The four service marketing myths: remnants of a goods-based, manufacturing model. *Journal of Services Research*, **6** (4), 324–355.

Vargo, S. L. & Morgan, F. W. (2005) Services in society and academic thought: an historical analysis. *Journal of Macromarketing*, **25** (1), 42–53.

Role of technology

Berthon, P., Hulbert, J. M. & Pitt, L. F. (2005) Consuming technology: why marketers sometimes get it wrong. *California Management Review*, **48** (1), 110–127.

Ford, D. & Saren, M. (2001) *Marketing and Managing Technology*. International Thomson Business Press: London.

Mick, D. G. & Fournier, S. (1998) Paradoxes of technology: consumer cognizance, emotions and coping strategies. *Journal of Consumer Research*, **25** (September), 123–143.

Solutions through innovation

Senge, P. & Carstedt, G. (2001) Innovating our way to the next industrial revolution. *MIT Sloan Management Review*, Winter, 24–37.

Spieth, P., Schneckenberg, D. & Ricart, J. E. (2014) Business model innovation: state of the art and future challenges for the field. *R&D Management*, **44** (3), 237–247.

Teece, D. J. (2010) Business models, business strategy and innovation. *Long Range Planning*, 43 (2–3), 172–194.

Trott, P. (2011) *Innovation Management & New Product Development*. Financial Times/Pearson: London.

Information technology and innovation

Mairead Brady

Introduction

The purpose of this section is to investigate how innovations in information technology (IT), and particularly data and data analytics resulting from IT are changing marketing practice and consumer behaviour. This section focuses on some innovations in how marketing is practiced and discusses how information technology provides marketers with opportunities and challenges never witnessed before. Various technologies including the internet, smart/mobile phones, social media data, 'the internet of things', robotics, virtual and augmented reality and other technological developments have created many technologies, softwares and apps that allow for changes in business models, new products and services (many of which are interactive) and heightened tracking and monitoring of consumers: much of which can be used by marketers for innovative ends.

Big data and innovations in business and business models

There has been much discussion in both the popular press and in business and academic journals in relation to the amount of data flooding into organizations with a speed, frequency and amount never witnessed before. As discussed by Bizer *et al.* (2011: 56), 'information is unbelievably large in scale, scope, distribution, heterogeneity, and supporting technologies'. A term in popular use in the data field is 'big data'. Davenport (2013) suggests that there have already been two eras of big data – what he calls 'BBD' (before big data) and 'ABD' (after big data). He aligns this to Analytics 1.0 – what he calls the era of business intelligence – and Analytics 2.0 – the era of big data starting in about the mid-2000s – and he suggests that we are heading towards Analytics 3.0, an era of data enriched and enhanced solutions and offerings.

This new era can be innovative for marketers and allow them to image the world in different ways. This new era of Analytics 3.0 will be successful for those that can join the dots, competing on analytics innovatively and competently. This means that much of what we know about business could be redrawn. So many

activities online have data trails that can be followed to create new and innovative businesses and business solutions. The term used for this is 'data exhausts', which refers to the data collected as a secondary operation to online engagements and these data sources have now become very powerful data trails that companies can use (Mayer-Schonberger & Cukier, 2013). What we can say is data and data analytics are going mainstream.

It is normal for companies to use data to improve internal operations, but what is new is the use of data to create more valuable products and services and new business models. An example is a UPS case where the scale of the data they have is huge, with over 16 million packages tracked a day from which they receive over 40 million tracking outputs. They have used data internally since the 1980s to track packages but in 2011 they changed their focus and, following the analysis of 46,000 trucks, they were able to cut 85 million miles from the drivers' routes through optimization software (Davenport, 2013). New business models and new companies abound. Companies recently founded and those that have grown or have been built in the last decade do not have the incumbents or traditional company restraints, legacy systems or traditional views of data or information to restrict them. They think differently about data. Think of Uber or traditional taxi firms. Think of TV stations and then think of Netflix. Uber and Netflix have data as central to their organizations, whereas taxi firms and TV stations have a more dated and traditional view. What is clear is that a new way of thinking is needed due to the advent of information technology, data and data analytics. Davenport (2013: 71) suggests that:

> the new capabilities required of both long-established and start-up firms can't be developed using old models for how analytics supported the business . . . Companies that want to prosper in the new data economy must once again fundamentally rethink how the analysis of data can create value for themselves and their customers. Analytics 3.0 is the direction of change and the new model for competing on analytics.

What has to be innovative is how we think about and use the data. How we establish a culture of enquiry – asking questions and looking around corners for different and innovative ways of seeing and finding new answers. Marketers need to be ready to ask questions differently, to attack challenges from different directions, to ask different types of questions and to let analytics answer them. As Hopkins and Brokaw (2011: 36) noted when they were interviewed for 'Matchmaking with math: How analytics beats intuition to win customers':

> the epiphany occurred because we knew that we wanted more . . . and so we put the problem to a different group of people . . . these are data-orientated people so they just simply said – give us everything – all the data you've got . . . they took all the data sets and started crunching it through our statistical modeling.

Hopkins and Brokaw (2011) discuss a case study for an insurance company who changed how they dealt with the customers by using data to ask different and difficult questions of their operations and to move away from the fallacy that increasing operational efficiencies was the most important factor for customer satisfaction and retention. They used state-of-the-art technology and data to change their answer times and to increase their retention rates through a new way of looking at and thinking about data. This discussion aligns with other businesses who have used data to change how they manage customers and therefore change value creation for customers and value appropriation for the company.

So, we can study the business models that no longer work, like the old model of Blockbuster and the video store concept which is being replaced by the Netflix model, which is proactive and aligned with customer needs. The same could be said of WhatsApp and Viber versus the old telecoms model of controlling and charging the customer highly. With the growth in data and data analytics, companies can now understand their customer and react to their needs with new models of business, new practices, new offerings that often align better to customer needs.

So how has this development occurred? One perspective is to understand that the Nolan Stages Theory of IT assimilation has come to be realized. Back in 1988 Harvard Professor Richard Nolan (among others) suggested that businesses would assimilate database information in the following way aligned to organizational learning:

Stage 1 Automation – efficiency – data processing stage
Stage 2 Information – effectiveness
Stage 3 Transformation – the unthinkable – networked stage.

We appear to be very close to or in the third stage now, with major innovations and many developments like Uber cars, dash buttons for purchases, and even apps to track and trace and monitor so many items from cars to household appliances, from baby pampers to running shoes.

In a marketing-related study by Brady, Saren and Tzokas (2002) these three stages were empirically tested and it was clear that in the early 2000s marketers were in the first phase and were struggling to move to the information stage. Over the years many commentators have noted the struggles for marketers in this domain (Brady *et al.*, 2008; Fellenz & Brady, 2010). It has also been noted that marketing is now one of the functions most influenced by technology and data or, as Brinker and McLellan (2014) observe, 'marketing is rapidly becoming the most technology dependent function in business'. This has had a huge impact on the amount of data or information within marketing. Manyika *et al.* (2011) note that as a result of companies' greater access to customer data, data are flooding in to the companies at rates never seen before.

Davenport (2013) suggests ten requirements for 'capitalising on analytics' in this era:

1 Multiple types of data often combined
2 A new set of data management options
3 Faster technologies and methods of analysis
4 Embedded analytics
5 Data discovery
6 Cross-disciplinary data teams
7 Chief analytics officer
8 Prescriptive analytics
9 Analytics on an industrial scale
10 New ways of deciding and managing.

Information technologies in marketing

Table 4.1 categorizes and lists the main ITs currently available within marketing, but there is no full and distinct list of marketing-related ITs as there are so many of them, many of which are multipurpose. We can take two main orientations of the numerous ITs in marketing and they can be classified in relation to their dominant focus as:

- *Information* – focuses include research, analysis and planning (see Moving Space).
- *Interactions* – focuses include communications, channels, communities and connections (see Building Relations).

Of course, it is not so clear-cut and well defined as the table suggests and there are ITs which can and do overlap between the two. For example, an IT can be predominantly for communication but can supply information for research and analysis. There are three major issues.

Table 4.1 Technologies in marketing: an information and interactions perspective

Information (Research, analysis and planning)	Interactions (Communications, connections and collaborations)
Analysis and planning	**Communications**
• Marketing planning systems	• Internet
• Performance tracking software	• Website design software
• Executive support systems	• Website security
• Decision support systems	• Interactive website applications
• Enterprise resource planning (ERP)	• E-commerce applications
• Knowledge management systems	• Social networking
• Pricing software	• Cloud computing
• Project management software	• Intranets
• Promotion tracking software	• Extranets
• Media spend analysis packages	• Electronic data interchange (EDI)
• Logistics systems	• Email
• Geographical information systems	• Video conferencing
• Customer profitability analysis	• Call centres
• PRISM clusters – databases	• Automatic call distribution
• Forecasting software	• Computer telephony integration
• Marketing modelling	• Mobile communication devices
• Enterprise information systems (e.g. SAP, PeopleSoft/i2)	• Instant messaging
• Focused softwares	• Tracking devices
	• Bluetooth
Databases	• SMS (short messaging services)
• Centralized customer database	• Facsimile communications
– integrated with sales	• Tweeting
– integrated with call centre	• Helplines
– integrated with internet	• Voicemail
– integrated with point of sale	• 'Spam' blocking systems
• Data consolidation and display	• Voice activated/recognition software
• Data mining	• Computer links with suppliers
• Data warehousing	• Computer links with customers
• Data profiling	• Web casting
• Data visualization and analysis packages	• Web meetings
• GQL – graphical query language	• Skype
• SQL – standard query language	• Digital imaging software
• Predictive analytics	• Blippar – augmented reality
	• Near-field communication
Research	
• Internet	**Self-service technologies**
• Marketing information systems	• Integrated TV and internet
• Data analysis packages	• Internet technology

(Continued)

Table 4.1 (*Continued*)

Information (Research, analysis and planning)	Interactions (Communications, connections and collaborations)
• Geographic information systems • Demographic online systems • Internet survey – design and application • Online mailing lists • Nielsen information database • Web analytical technologies • Website performance and activity tracking • Monitoring and tracking software • Searchable databases • Interactive databases • Customization technologies	• Automated vending machines (ATMs) • Handheld scanners • Biometrics • Mobile phones • Bluetooth technologies • Monitoring devices • Customization software • Personalization software • Kiosks
Retailing system • Electronic point of sale • Planogram, Spaceman Category Management • Personalization/customizations • Bar codes – scanning	**Sales related** • Customer relationship management • Access databases • Sales reporting software

New product and service development
• Product development and design software
• Simulation technologies
• Idea generation tool: Idea Garden
• Imaginatik's Idea Central
• Statistical tools
• CAD (computer-aided design)
• Interactive products
	Supply chain management
	• Supply chain management software
	• Automated production
	• Internet marketplace
	  – e-marketplace/e-hub
	• Inventory management software
	• Material planning and supply software
	• Electronic data interchange
	• QR/ECR (efficient customer response)
	  software
	• E-procurement systems
	• Online purchasing transactions
	• RFID (radio frequency identification devices)
	• Interactive products
	• Biometric
	• Bluetooth technologies

Metrics • Dashboard	
Others • Training and educational software • Gamification technology	

General underlying and platform technologies
- Hardware: PCs, tablets, smartphones, networked computers, mainframes, laptops, personal palm computers, mobile phones, digital assistants
- Office packages: Word, PowerPoint, Excel, Smart and iWork
- Internal communications: Groupware systems, Lotus Notes, wide/local area networks (WAN/LANs)

Source: developed from Brady *et al.* (2008) and Brady (2006)

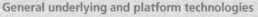

First, many marketing ITs are not specific to the marketing department. So, though consumers may consider that the IT they are utilizing is a consumer IT, this may not be so. Two examples of this clearly indicate the difficulties in this area:

- The ATM machine we utilize was designed to suit the abilities and specification requirements of banking and the IT department, with little or no input from the marketing department.
- The 'killer' application for the mobile phone is text messaging, with several million text messages being sent daily in the UK alone. This application was not designed or even noticed by marketers when they first launched the mobile phone – it was developed as an internal communication line between engineers!

Second, many ITs are industry specific. If we take the example of scanner technology, this is only applicable to products with bar codes. Or we can look at shelf-space technology (see Moving Space) and note that again this is industry specific. Other software needs to be customized for companies. All companies are unique and customization of software for the marketing department was and continues to be very popular, though many off-the-shelf products like Radian 6, Google Analytics, Weebly web design make technology widely available, and many online applications both free and paid for are now in use.

Third, legacy systems are a major issue within companies. As Day (2011: 183) noted, 'Marketers are being challenged by a deluge of data that is well beyond the capacity of their organizations to comprehend and use.' Many businesses have legacy databases dating back to the 1970s which had a dominant finance or production focus. These systems are now being utilized by marketing with varying degrees of success and, with the arrival of social media data, at an amount, type and frequency not experienced before – this has challenged many of these systems. The 'colossal stream of real-time customer-to-customer interchanges' (Larson & Watson, 2011: 10), which are available to companies in huge volumes, can call for really innovative applications to really understand and use them.

Consumer interactions – consumer awareness of ITs

Within the range of ITs available to the consumer, some are very visible (like the internet) while others, though hidden, are part of the consumer's understanding of IT in marketing (like the database) and others are completely hidden from the consumer (dashboard technology, forecasting software). Many of the more information-based IT applications could not operate without consumer input, though consumers are generally not aware of them (see Moving Space), particularly many of the tracking, monitoring and surveillance systems. It must be noted that many consumers understand that companies are collecting data on them which can lead to improved products and services that make their lives easier, educate them and/or help them to save money (Morey *et al.*, 2015). Think of the Nike running app, which tracks runners and can give them all the statistics on their runs along with motivational inputs and ongoing feedback. Many of the interaction ITs are ones that consumers engage with freely. Of interest in this chapter are the self-service technologies. From an interactions perspective we will look at some of the major innovations in this area.

The consumer perspective – self-service technologies

Consumers often want 'right here, right now, tailored to me, given to me the way I want it', and sometimes the only way to do this is through IT. In many ways companies can be seen to be utilizing IT to let consumers satisfy themselves better. But for all the benefits, are self-service technologies better for the consumer?

There is a trade-off for the consumer who self-serves. Rather than the company providing an employee to service consumer requirements, consumers now can do this themselves. So consumers can be seen as virtually an unsalaried staff member for the company. Think about internet banking, booking a holiday online, self-scanners in supermarkets or ATM machines – in all these examples, the consumer does the work. Think of all the searching, researching and decision-making involved in booking a holiday online.

The barriers and the benefits to online shopping have been well articulated in both the academic and business press. One view must be how to capture some of the particular shopping aspects online. How does online shopping cope with squeezing the pan of bread to check that it is fresh? Or how does it cope with impulse shopping, a crucial part of shopping from both the company's and the customer's perspective?

Amazon's dash button

An innovation in shopping is the 'dash button' from Amazon. This is a small button that once pressed allows shoppers to reorder frequently-used products like washing-up liquid, laundry detergent or paper towels which are then delivered by Amazon the next day. So you do not need to shop or, as the promotional video from Amazon says, 'Don't let running out ruin your rhythm.' This innovation links to the vast array of smart technologies in houses aligned to the 'internet of things', with your fridge connected to your online shopping list automatically reordering products you use. The dash button is similar to automatic reordering with companies like Whirlpool designing a washer and dryer that anticipate when laundry supplies are going to be needed and then without checking automatically orders more detergent and dryer sheets. There are also products like water purifiers which could reorder their own filters and printers which can reorder their own ink (Crouch, 2015).

Q. Can you think of any negative aspects to this service?
A. Going shopping can be a very social process. Automatic reordering does not allow for choice or new products to be brought or trailed.

Many services have added online or self-service provision. Some examples are:

- delivery services which allow for tracking of parcels by consumers from the warehouse all the way through the supply chain (for example www.FedEx.com and www.UPS.com)
- online airline ticket booking but also seat selection, or a development by KLM called 'meet and seat' where you can study all the passengers and choose the passenger you would like to sit beside on the plane and connect via social media.

The big worry from the consumer perspective is that the use of technology means a lack of service, no human interaction, that their every action is tracked and that ultimately the technology that was supposed to provide freedom just adds more restrictions and greater control.

Humans are humans and all the technology in the world does not necessarily change behaviour. In our excitement over the benefits of new technologies we run the risk of ceding influence over forces essential to protecting and promoting autonomous decision-making to an industry interested only in activating our buying impulses and a focus on continuous consumption. We have to ask

whether we are controlling the technology or is the technology slowly beginning to control us?

Think about the last time you were without your mobile phone. How did you
feel? Sad, worried, concerned, alone? Are we able to live without our technology and our technology hit? A big innovation in this area is the digital self where
we have our human self and the created digital self online (Belk, 2013).

Enhanced production technology –
the customization option

A major innovation which can be operationalized for a mass market is the
development of production technology in the product area which relates to
the make-to-order or make-to-sell concept. Through the availability and use of
information systems and changing consumer expectations, companies can now
make to order rather than to sell. Gone are the days of inventories and stock-
piling. Do you remember car parks full of new cars at airports waiting for sales
to occur? The policy now is to wait until the consumer orders and then start
to manufacture. Enhanced margins through customization, modularity, intelligence and organization have developed from this technology (Venkatraman &
Henderson, 1998).

The advantage for the customer is customization. You can choose the colour
of your car (from a defined range), you can choose interiors, hubcaps, sunroofs
etc. (see, for example, www.volkswagen.com). There is some level of what
Prahalad *et al.* (2000) refer to as co-creating and personalization of the experience, encouraging choice and flexibility (see Consuming Experience). Within this
development is the digitalized purchase, so instead of books we have digital
books and instead of CDs we have iTunes libraries.

Interactive products

We now have products with which we can interact, products that are in some
ways intelligent products. For example, the car is obviously a product but most
car companies now provide various services which mean that the company can
extend the level of services and have ongoing interactions with the consumer.
Should a consumer lock their keys into their car, with the use of a monitoring
and geographical positioning system the company can remotely unlock the
doors anywhere in the world. GPS systems in cars can also highlight the near-
est petrol station or food outlet. The self-drive car is being tested by Google
but driver-assisted driving is common in many cars, as is self-braking when an

obstacle appears in front of the car. There are cars that stream data back to the manufacturer who can replace and update software within the car without the owners even knowing.

Numerous children's toys have interactive devices, with dolls which can answer questions and toys that utilize voice recognition software and react to a child's voice. As discussed previously with the dash button example, more consumer household products are becoming automated 'assets'.

Remote delivery

We have always had some version of remote delivery – the Sears catalogue was first introduced in the nineteenth century as a mail-order catalogue. But the advent of IT has meant a wider range of products and services can be delivered remotely, or alternatively we can avail ourselves of these services through remote bookings. Products that have an information content can be delivered through IT applications and one of the dominant platforms used is the internet platform. One example is a newspaper which can now have dual delivery of content both in the paper and online versions (see, for example, www.ft.com). Drone technology is a new innovation that could become very popular. Amazon Prime Air suggests that delivery by drone would be within 30 minutes! What an innovation in delivery – but at what cost?

Product and service placements as digital insertions

For a long time marketers have dreamed of targeting specific individuals with customized advertising (see Building Relations). Now IT allows them to do so on a heightened and individualized scale through 'digital insertions' where any content can be uploaded directly to a targeted customer. We see this online when we show an interest in, say, booking a hotel in the Netherlands then for the next few days ads for hotels in the Netherlands appear on your screen whenever you are online. This is also popular offline at, for example, football matches, where the billboard advertising relates to a broadcasting location. If a World Cup match is played between England and Germany, the billboards might display adverts targeting audiences in those countries. But if the match is also being shown live on TV in South Korea, adverts relevant to that location might also be shown around the pitch perimeter, and when it is broadcast in Germany the German commercials can be seen.

Smart, connected products can generate real-time readings that are unprecedented in their variety and volume. Data now stands on par with people, technology, and capital as a core asset of the corporation and in many businesses is perhaps becoming the decisive asset.
Porter and Heppelmann, 2015

The road ahead

The road ahead is full of potentially more-exciting and challenging technologies from robotics to virtual reality, both of which are starting to appear. Search for Paro online and you will find a robotic seal that patients in old folks' homes use as a pet, or look for robotic nurses already working in many hospitals in the US. It is very hard to decide which ITs will be developed and which marketers and consumers will embrace. What we can say is that the technologies that can satisfy a need, or improve a product or service, or create efficiencies and so on, will be the ones utilized. We are still at the early stages of assimilation of IT into marketing practice. A lot of these developments are generational issues. We will be amazed over the next few years at the range and ability of IT.

Remember, though, that all the IT in the world does not make marketers better marketers; what they need to do is to understand and exploit and innovate through IT to improve their marketing practices and to enhance their customers' satisfaction.

FURTHER READING

Belk, R. (2013) Extended self in a digital world. *Journal of Consumer Research*, **40**, October, 477–500.

Brady, M., Fellenz, M. R. & Brookes, R. (2008) Researching the role of information and communication technologies in contemporary marketing. *Journal of Business and Industrial Marketing*, **23** (2), 108–114.

Brady, M., Saren, M. & Tzokas, N. (2002) Integrating information technology into marketing practice: the IT reality of contemporary marketing practice. *Journal of Marketing Management*, **18** (5/6, July), 555–578.

Brinker, S. & McLellan, L. (2014) The rise of the chief marketing technologist. *Harvard Business Review*, **92** (7), 82–85.

Crouch, I. (2015) The horror of Amazon's new dash button. *New Yorker*, April, 2.

Davenport, T. (2013) Analytics 3.0. *Harvard Business Review*, December, 64–71.

Hopkins, M. S. & Brokaw, L. (2011) Matchmaking with math: how analytics beats intuition to win customers. *MIT Sloan Management Review*, **52** (2).

Joshi, A. & Giménez, E. (2014) Decision-driven marketing. *Harvard Business Review*, July–August, 55–63.

Morey, T., Forbath, T. & Schoop, A. (2015) Customer data: designing for transparency and trust. *Harvard Business Review*, May.

Porter, M. & Heppelmann, E. (2015) How smart connected products are transforming companies. *Harvard Business Review*, October, 97–114.

de Swaan Arons, M., van den Driest, F. & Weed, K. (2014) The ultimate marketing machine. *Harvard Business Review*, July–August, 55–63.

Information for innovative solutions

For firms to conform to the traditional marketing concept, they must acquire appropriate information in order to adopt some form of 'market orientation' (see Marketing Contexts). This means that the company's marketing managers have to ensure that they methodically collect and disseminate information about their customers and competitors and take marketing decisions directly based on this information (see Kohli & Jaworski, 1990). In addition, information figures prominently in the new product development literature (e.g. Li & Calantone, 1998) because designing and making innovative solutions requires information. As you would expect, the better the quality of information, the better the potential solutions and the better the innovation. Conversely, creative solutions require innovation, sometimes 'radical', sometimes 'incremental'. Solutions to customer and marketing problems must be based on knowledge and information, and innovation is necessary in order to make new solutions happen.

It is through market research that the building blocks of knowledge are gathered as a key input for innovative solutions in marketing. The term 'market research' covers a wide range of information-gathering techniques and processes, including data gathering, tracking and analysis, consumer research studies and customer insight.

The precise role and use of marketing research by innovative firms is unclear. In some cases it is not employed at all, when competitive pressures to be first-to-market with the latest technology do not allow time for firms to conduct marketing research. Sometimes the cost involved is prohibitive or situations with market and technological uncertainty mean that customers can't articulate their needs and requirements, so marketing research is inappropriate. For highly innovative new products, potential customers often cannot see the benefits, thus cannot 'want' something which they cannot imagine, so less reliance can be placed on conventional market research information. For example, initial market tests for the Sony Walkman indicated little demand for the new product, which was subsequently an enormous market success.

> **The delusion of data**
>
> *If you've got all the data then you've got all the answers. But data is not enough. You need to understand customers – their situations, lifestyles, attitudes, needs.* (Humby, 2004)

Kawakami, Durmusoglu and Barczak (2011) investigated the degree to which technology firms use market research in the new product development process. They found that these companies were using less structured, more qualitative methods (see subsection on Market insight by research) to gather customer information for developing new products, and were disseminating this information and using it to design products and, to a lesser extent, for developing marketing strategies.

Thus, understanding the social–cultural–economic context in which the new product or new technology will be used (as well as bought, transported, stored, consumed and discarded) is critical for the design input for successful innovations (see Solutions to what?, The role of technology). This has significant implications for marketing research and requires the application of various types of qualitative research methods, including those based on anthropology that can produce actionable results.

> *Information for innovation comes from lead users in both business and consumer markets that are encouraged to get 'close to the company' in order that marketers can better hear 'the voice of the customer'.*

An alternative method for gathering information about customers is von Hippel's (1978) proposal that 'thoughtful use of lead users can help to address the problem of market research in areas of new technology'. This highlights the importance of relationship building (see Building Relations) with customers who have bought new products early, in order to gather marketing information to develop solutions for the many customers who, unlike the lead users, are reluctant to commit to technologies they do not properly understand and which have not yet been substantially 'proven' in practice. This can be achieved by building sufficient customer references within an industry or better marketing communication of the innovation, so that the more cautious customers will be willing to risk implementation of what they may regard as an 'immature' new product or service offering.

> *Ultimately, customers exhibit their behaviour through buying. The aim is to understand the different types of behaviour.*

To address some of these issues, Aaker *et al*. (2001) proposed that 'concept' testing is conducted with potential customers as a market research method during the early stage of the product development process. At this stage the product does not yet exist, so the technique involves gathering respondents' reactions to the concept of the new product, which can take the form of pictures, verbal descriptions or a 'mock-up' model of the innovation. This is used extensively by automobile manufacturers who often reveal their 'concept cars' at motor shows and utilize the prototype models for gathering customer reactions. There are, though, several problems associated with this technique:

- Respondents may read the concept statements or see artists' impressions without considering the environment in which the new product will be used.
- Participants are usually presented with only a small amount of information.
- For some new products, consumers prefer to learn through trial and error rather than reading.
- These limitations can be restrictive when testing radical 'new to the world' products because concept statements do not permit the replication of respondents' actual information search and processing.

We must distinguish between information for innovation and scientific knowledge. Scientific knowledge denotes knowledge as 'truth' and represents the output of scientific methods (i.e. experimentation and facts) which cannot be disputed. Market and commercial knowledge does not take the same form, nor can such unequivocal claims be made of it. Demarest (1997) suggested that commercial knowledge is closer to what the French call '*bricolage*': the provisional construction of 'a messy set of rules, tools and guidelines that produce according to the expertise and sensitivity of the craftsman'. This distinction is significant because it explains and allows for different and competing views of market knowledge and information. Thus, information for innovation is necessarily imprecise, imperfect and incomplete.

Commercial knowledge is not truth, but effective performance: not 'what is right' but 'what works' or even 'what works better'.
Demarest, 1997

The design of market research for information and knowledge on innovation needs to address the following questions: *where* to look for knowledge, *what* to look for and *how* to look for it (Tzokas & Saren, 2004). In the next subsection this is considered from the professional market researcher's perspective, based on the work of Andy Barker of Research International.

Market insight by research

The world of commercial qualitative research has undergone significant evolution in recent years. The high degree of competition between research agencies in the UK market in particular has led to unprecedented methodological innovation on the supply (agency) side and innovation in how qualitative information is obtained and used on the client (demand) side. The effect of this has been some blurring of what 'qualitative' means on both sides.

- On the practitioners' side – developments such as an emphasis on ethnography and ethnographic approaches; the gradual shift from the psychological model of qualitative research to a behavioural model; the development in thinking about consumer identity.
- On the clients' side – new trends include the increase in direct consumer experience or immersion; the meteoric rise of the concept of market 'insight'; replacing market 'research, knowledge or intelligence'.

Agency perspective on market research

Anyone who has attended market research industry seminars over the last few years will have noted the increasing reference to ethnographic methods. Commercial qualitative practice has finally caught up with the rhetoric and an ever-greater amount of work with at least an ethnographic flavour is proposed, sold and conducted.

However, we should define our terms here. What the academic reader (or indeed the professional ethnographer or sociologist) might consider to be ethnographic enquiry will involve detailed, painstaking participant observational studies mapping entire subcultures and tribes (see Consuming Experience: The role of consumers). When ethnographic methodology is applied in practice, subject to the pressing commercial constraints of time and budgetary pressures, it often becomes something more like a 'safari into consumerland'. Social scientists might be travellers who immerse themselves in the world of consumer experience, but commercial researchers are more usually required for the reasons above to become tourists visiting consumers in their natural habitat, camcorders and tape recorders in hand, spending a day in their world but back in their comfortable hotel by nightfall.

But in spite of this important distinction between academic and commercial approaches, ethnographic methods, however bastardized, can produce insights into the world and perceptions of consumers which would otherwise be very hard to get from traditional qualitative methodologies such as focus groups.

For example, there are things which consumers might not consider it relevant to talk about in groups but which might be visible even in a relatively short-lived encounter with consumers in their 'real life' context. This is especially true given the low involvement nature of many categories where FMCG (fast-moving consumer goods) brands operate, from washing detergent to ready meals. A further development in qualitative research is the shift in emphasis from getting deeper into consumers' minds and instead getting closer and closer to their lives. This latter approach is a much broader and socially based perspective which has become more popular for a number of reasons.

First, it is a result of a philosophical recognition of a changing conception of the consumer's mind from stable, constant and consistent to fragmented, changing and unstable. Indeed, there is a strong recognition that the consumer 'mind' is really only meaningfully formed at particular fleeting moments of consumption and that these are hard to access/replicate by more and more probing. For this a different methodological approach is required.

Second, at a more pragmatic level, understanding the behavioural context of consumers as well as their psychological motivations is also based on the limitations of consumers' abilities to explain the reasons for their behaviour and attitudes after the purchase or market-based event that researchers are interested in. When called on to reveal their innermost motivations concerning brand choice in a category with very little meaning to them in focus groups or in-depth interviews, respondents tend to resort to some form of 'post-emotionalization' of their behaviour. As a result of the constraints of these research methods, agencies have a pressing commercial imperative to offer something different and more effective to clients.

This shift in focus from market research aimed at understanding what people think to what they do is manifested in methodological terms as a move to the observation of behaviour as a supplement to standard qualitative research activity. Pre-tasking is increasingly common and is often about getting consumers to record their real-life behaviour by means such as paper or video diaries before the face-to-face research activity begins in order to inject a dose of behavioural reality into otherwise 'artificial' focus groups or interview sessions.

Less common is a shift from analysis of the individual consumer as the master/mistress of his/her actions to the provision of an account of the cultural dimensions of consumer behaviour. This can be seen in semiotic analysis (which is, after some years of popularity in theory, enjoying more widespread commercial application) and which, roughly speaking, analyses brands, advertising, packaging, etc. as cultural objects rather than understanding consumers' opinions of them *per se*.

The model of 'the consumer' has changed

As detailed earlier, within the qualitative research world the model of the consumer has largely changed from one where he/she is a passive recipient of marketing, with a stable and constant set of opinions, attitudes and responses, to a model which takes account of consumers' multiple consuming identities (see Consuming Experience). Qualitative methodologies of questioning or analysis have grown up and evolved which deal with this philosophical issue.

Once again there is a practical issue here and it concerns the increasing difficulty of matching messy consumer reality (as reported by consumers or observed by ethnographically orientated researchers) with the ideal world of tidy consumer segmentation. In short, consumers often demonstrably resist pigeon-holing and so it makes sense to develop models and methods that can cope with this.

In the better qualitative research circles it is accepted that consumer identity is – or might as well be, for the purposes of analysis – fragmented, unstable, temporary, context sensitive, and that consumers' needs are correspondingly fragmented, unstable, temporary and context sensitive. The female BC1 social class, 25-year-old working consumer might be a mother, driver, clubber, lover and have widely different needs and indeed consuming identities when operating in those different modes.

Interestingly, in addition to being regarded as schizophrenic, consumers are generally accepted as being 'savvy', i.e. knowledgeable, powerful and able to deconstruct and decode marketing and advertising in order to maintain an active, participatory relationship with brands. This idea is not without its critics and research with consumers has tended to suggest that they might not feel as savvy or 'empowered' as this analysis suggests (see Consuming Experience).

In methodological terms this often translates to changes in the balance of power in the research situation, with consumers no longer ambushed in groups as the real purpose of the session emerges from the camouflage of a general chat about the product category. In addition, respondents are routinely 'given the marketing problem', assuming that they are in a position to solve it directly, which some critics question their knowledge or ability to do.

Client perspective – the demand side

Mirroring these changes on the supply side of the commercial qualitative market, clients' needs and behaviours have also altered the way qualitative market research is defined and used. Market research managers and marketing directors who buy and use the results of professional research agencies are now called 'consumer insight professionals' or something similar. As well as purchasing commercial market research data they are increasing themselves involved in 'consumer immersion', mixing with carefully selected and screened consumers for their dose of authentic consumer reality.

In many respects this is a very positive development because research buyers and users can be out of touch with the consumers they strive to understand and a day spent with the Joneses can be 'worth', in insight gleaned, far more than a $1 million global usage and attitude study. However, the suburban garden path of immersion does not necessarily lead to insight, and research buyers and users are not usually trained in ethnographic methods, or often in how to interact with real people and observe and listen.

Furthermore, once they have gathered their observations these need to be categorized, processed and interpreted in order for these data to be turned into insight that might be useful for the business. It is one thing being able to observe directly that schoolchildren microwave Mars bars until they explode as a snack to keep them going between returning from school and having a 'proper' dinner, but another thing entirely to produce understanding that will be the beginnings of a leverageable opportunity from this.

A further trend in companies buying and using market research has been the move from getting insight from research to the collecting of insights for the business. That move from the singular to the plural is the linguistic signifier of a much bigger shift in research generally, and particularly qualitative research, from data collection to insight generation. This is a result of the need for businesses to innovate and for their innovations to offer solutions to genuine, unmet consumer needs. These needs, in an increasingly crowded and fragmented marketplace (especially in categories with a frightening number of brands, variants, products, etc.), are often relatively niche and can amount to different perspectives (or angles) on a problem rather than entirely new needs. These are expressed in terms of consumer insights, i.e. bite-sized expressions that offer a manageable route into consumers' lives in a particular category.

Thus, 'insights' have now become a valuable commodity in businesses, and research agencies are increasingly charged with providing insights rather than 'truth'. That is not to say that these two concepts are incompatible; rather, there is a difference in emphasis from obtaining a holistic, accurate, objective picture of consumer behaviour, motivations, etc. in a given category to providing useful insights about consumers in that category. In addition, businesses are investing large sums of money in programmes aimed at generating and managing insights in the business, from databases to specif- ically designed methodologies for turning data into insights (see Information technology and innovation).

Mainstream research on the supply side has not yet responded to this shift, which has opened up a lucrative door for para-consultancies to walk through. This has led to the emergence of a new category of super-consultancies who infiltrate client businesses on a multi-platform basis and offer a range of services from design and marketing consultancy to qualitative research. The vacuum left by the wholesale abandoning of the advertising agency planner has also contributed to this. For these reasons, clients' businesses have become adept at buying, generating and in some cases storing insights. However, many are still grappling with the question of what to do with all these insights, i.e. how to turn them into consumer/business propositions. Companies that are better at this have shifted emphasis and structure from the traditional relationship of marketer–researcher– agency planner–research company to an emergent structure of marketer–consumer insight manager–research company partner–planner.

From insights to innovation

We discussed earlier that the need for insight which turned into the rush for insights was driven by the need to innovate in an increasingly crowded global marketplace. However forward looking the practitioner, like it or not, research is inherently backward looking – it can only predict, with any degree of certainty, the past. But within the newly constituted research market there is an increasing emphasis on future solutions. In client businesses this might mean greater use of workshops and systems for generating ideas/propositions or even separate, elite 'futures' units. For agencies it is a new opportunity to stretch the 'qualitative' boundaries into idea-generating products and, indeed, several specialist com- panies or divisions within larger companies offering early stage innovation ser- vices have grown up, which use specially trained consumers in client–consumer workshops to generate, select and refine new product, positioning or communication ideas. In this mode of research, 'respondents' are not asked to 'respond' as such; they are asked to create, they are used as a highly skilled resource – they have one foot in consumer reality but with their heads planted firmly in the clouds. These type of approaches have transferred into more mainstream qualitative work with the often theatrical, exciting and potentially more intensive and therefore expensive methods increasingly requested and incorporated into everyday consumer qualitative research.

Table 4.2 maps the development of qualitative research discourse over time. It shows three phases, from its residual codes of deep exploration to a focus on eclecticism and towards the emergence of a pragmatic set of approaches aimed at gaining insights in partnership with companies.

Table 4.2 Development of the qualitative research discourse

Residual	Dominant	Emergent
Exploring the mind	Exploring the brand	Exploring behaviour
Deeper and deeper	Wilder and wackier	Closer and closer
Academic analysis	Creative presentation	Part of the business
Some rigour	Models of thinking	Pragmatism
Expertise/name	Experience based	Knowledge based
Strong ethics	Loose ethics	Partnership
Guru domination	Boutique domination	Relationships

FURTHER READING

Hauser, W. (2007) Marketing analytics: the evolution of marketing research in the twenty-first century. *Direct Marketing: An International Journal*, **1** (1), 38–54.

von Hippel, E. & Thomke, S. (1999) Creating breakthroughs at 3M. *Harvard Business Review*, **77** (5), 47–57.

Li, T. & Calantone, R. J. (1998) The impact of market knowledge competence on new product advantage: conceptualization and empirical examination. *Journal of Marketing*, **62** (4), 13–29.

Zikmund, W., Ward, S., Winzar, B. & Babin, B. (2011) *Marketing Research*. Cengage Learning: Melbourne.

Organizational processes and capabilities

*Emmanuella Plakoyiannaki and
Georgia Stavraki*

Processes, capabilities and creation of solutions

The purpose of marketing has always been to attract and retain customers, however widely they are defined. This core objective requires that the firm is constantly developing and delivering solutions that not only meet customer needs
and wants but also build strong long-term relationships with them. Under this
core marketing goal, firms increasingly realize that customers are among their
most important assets and view the building of strong customer relationships
as an opportunity for mutually beneficial exchanges that need to be managed
carefully (Plakoyiannaki & Saren, 2006). In order to accomplish this goal, firms
emphasize three important elements that reflect marketing practice – namely,
organizational processes, capabilities and culture.

Organizational processes play a key role in the creation of customer solutions,
since they enable firms to integrate tasks, resources and activities with the purpose of delivering a superior value offering with respect to changing customer
needs. Thus, organizational processes contribute to value creation through the
formation and maintenance of relationships with external marketplace entities
(e.g. consumers, buyers).

Organizational capabilities are deeply embedded into processes and relate to
the capacity of the firm to deploy and combine various resources (e.g. knowledge, relationships, skills and people) in order to deliver superior value offerings
through tailored customer solutions. Capabilities encompass the value chain of
the firm and demonstrate the commitment of the firm to customers.

Organizational culture shapes the focus of organizational processes and capabilities. In other words, the creation of enhanced customer solutions requires an
organizational culture which acknowledges the customer as the focal point of
strategic planning and execution. Viewed in this light, organizational culture contributes to the creation and development of strong customer relationships and, by
doing so, is conceived as an integral part of a relationship-marketing-orientated

company (Iglesias *et al.*, 2011; Plakoyiannaki *et al.*, 2008). Figure 4.5 illustrates the three elements that influence the practice of marketing and the creation of solutions meeting changing customer requirements. It also illustrates the over-arching effect of organizational culture on the deployment of processes and capabilities that engage the firm in the delivery of enhanced customer value.

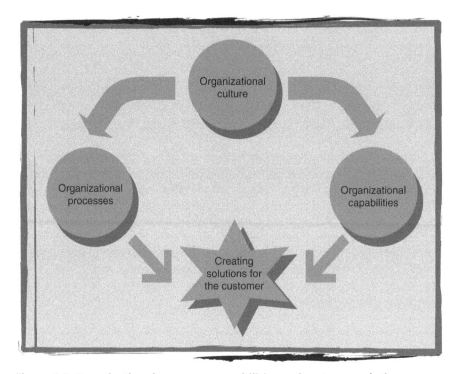

Figure 4.5 Organizational processes, capabilities and customer solutions

This section focuses on the contribution of organizational processes and capabilities to the creation of customer solutions. Specifically, it draws insights from the *customer relationship management* (CRM) process and capabilities, and demonstrates how these elements guide the strategies and practices of organizations towards the satisfaction of customer needs. In the first part, a framework of the CRM process in the organization is proposed and discussed. This framework includes four constructs integrally linked to CRM – the *strategic planning process*, the *information processes*, the *customer value process* and the *performance measurement process*. In the second part of the section, the framework is used as a basis for the identification and analysis of a set of CRM capabilities that may enhance CRM practice in the organization. The section concludes by summarizing the key points of the discussion.

What is CRM?

CRM, as a business practice and as an academic research field, has experienced explosive growth in the past two decades. In the extant literature, a number of scholars have focused on the examination of the concept of CRM, its measurement and the development of successful CRM strategies (e.g. Payne & Frow, 2005; Plakoyiannaki & Saren, 2006; Sin *et al.*, 2005), while more recent studies focus on the investigation of CRM online practices, such as eCRM and social CRM (Choudhury & Harrigan, 2014; Sigala, 2011; Trainor *et al.*, 2014). Despite this increasing prominence of CRM in marketing literature and the general consensus on CRM's aim – namely to create, maintain and manage relations with profitable customers – there is still a lack of agreement about its definition (Lambert, 2009; Plakoyiannaki *et al.*, 2008). Among the different definitions and conceptualizations of CRM that can be found in the marketing literature, CRM is conceived as a strategic and cross-functional organizational process (Coltman, 2007; Lambert, 2009; Plakoyiannaki & Saren, 2006) that 'is enabled through information, technology and applications and integrates processes, people, operations and marketing capabilities' (Payne & Frow, 2005: 168). Further, CRM as an organizational process 'includes all activities that firms undertake in their quest to build durable, profitable, mutually beneficial customer relationships' (Zablah *et al.*, 2004: 477). These conceptions of CRM line up along a continuum, with one extreme referring to a view of CRM as an information technology (IT) solution for data collection and analysis, and the other viewing CRM as a marketing philosophy designed to achieve long-term business gains (see Figure 4.6). In order to enhance our understanding of CRM, it is worthwhile combining these two perspectives so as to benefit from the synergies that the related ideas may generate.

From an information technology point of view, CRM changes the practice of marketing by enabling customer communication and dialogue. According to

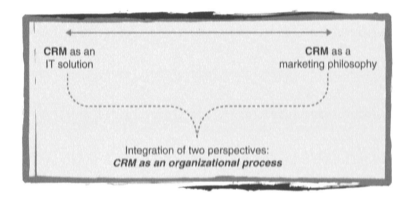

Figure 4.6 The CRM continuum

this perspective, technology is the key driver to profitability since it provides the tools for analysing and understanding customers' behaviours and, as such, it can enhance the performance of customer service processes (Ngai *et al.*, 2009). From a marketing point of view, CRM addresses all aspects of developing interactions between the firm and customers, and shapes customers' perceptions of the organization and its products. It enables the creation and delivery of superior customer service and value. In that sense, the provision of customer value drives profitability and corporate success.

For the purpose of this chapter on creating solutions, CRM can be defined as an *IT-enabled organizational process that places the customer at the heart of the firm's strategy and operations. CRM aims to provide enhanced customer value by establishing a creative dialogue between the firm and the customer.* This empha-sizes the contribution of CRM to the creation of solutions that meet customer needs. It transcends the technological and marketing aspects of the notion in that it develops a view of CRM as an activity that extends to the entire organiza-tion. In other words, the practice of CRM is neither isolated purely in marketing tasks such as planning, development and execution of marketing campaigns, nor is it solely dependent on the launch of customer databases. Instead, it is linked to other practices such as human resource management and financial manage-ment, since these activities reflect on the value delivered to the customer. For example, human resource management practices such as reward initiatives can aim at motivating employees to deliver the essence of CRM, namely customer value (see Marketing Contexts).

The CRM process

This subsection sets out a framework of the CRM process developed by adapting themes from the wider organization, management and relationship marketing literature (e.g. organizational learning, process theory, value creation and per-formance measurement) to the conceptualization of CRM. The framework of the CRM process, depicted in Figure 4.7, integrates four interrelated components (sub-processes):

- the strategic planning process
- the information processes
- the customer value process
- the performance measurement process.

Figure 4.7 shows that successful CRM practice integrates all organizational pro-cesses around a single view of the customer and also shows the purpose of CRM, which is enhancing customer–firm interaction and value. The four sub-processes of CRM are briefly discussed in the following subsections.

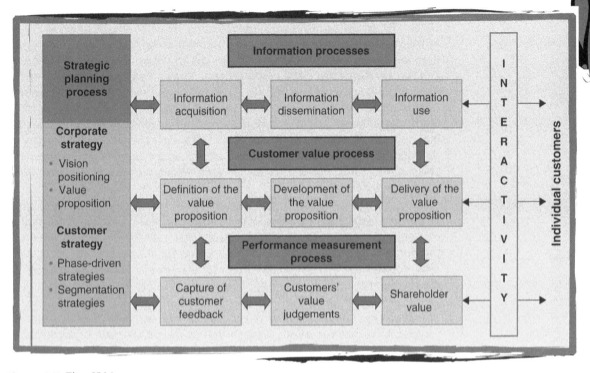

Figure 4.7 The CRM process

The strategic planning process

As demonstrated in Figure 4.7, the central stakeholders in CRM are the customers. However, the development of a continuous customer–firm interaction is the result of a long process that begins with strategic planning activities. In other words, for CRM to thrive there is a need for an organizational strategy that aligns the competencies of the firm and the voice of the customer.

The strategic planning process of CRM provides the direction for the adoption, development, implementation and evaluation of customer-orientated action in the organization. It cultivates a strategic orientation that makes customer relationships a priority (Plakoyiannaki *et al.*, 2008). However, the outcomes of strategic planning are apparent to customers when they experience the total value offering of the firm. The strategic planning process of CRM is comprised of two interrelated components, namely *corporate strategy* and *customer strategy*.

Corporate strategy involves the *vision*, *positioning* and *value proposition* of the business, and ensures that these components are integrated with the *customer*

strategy of the firm and the provision of superior customer value (Payne & Frow, 2005). The *vision* provides an understanding of what the business wants to achieve in comparison with existing and potential competitors. It is an instrument of motivation for employees since it provides the organization with a purpose and focuses the efforts of all organizational participants on the achievement of that purpose. But most importantly, organizational vision influences the perceptions of customers regarding the firm and its products and services. Specifically, it articulates the standards of customer–firm interaction and illustrates what the organization expects to contribute to its customers. The vision of an organization that implements CRM places the customer at the heart of the business and encompasses the concept of *customer value delivery* as the core of the firm's strategy and operations.

The *positioning* of the firm relates to the business vision and the development of a unique competitive advantage, sustainable over time. The positioning of the firm is manifested in the value proposition that customers experience and differentiates the firm (in relation to other market competitors) in the eyes of the customer.

The *value proposition* is central to consumers' interests since it stems from customer criteria and aspirations of value that guide the selection of products/service in specific use situations. The value proposition is linked to both the internal and external environments of the organization. Internally, the value proposition determines the operations of the firm as it is translated into value-generating processes and activities. Externally, the value proposition represents the firm in the eyes of the customer.

In the context of CRM, the selection of the value proposition appears to be based on (1) the customer's needs and activities, and (2) the organization's existing and potential core capabilities. In the context of CRM, two fundamental types of customer strategy can be identified. These are *phase-driven strategies* and *customer segmentation strategies* (see Table 4.3). Phase-driven strategies are related to the relationship life cycle of the customer with the firm and may be classified into three groups – namely, customer acquisition strategy, customer retention strategy and customer recovery strategy. Customer segmentation strategies allow firms to identify, profile, target and reach customer segments based on customer transactional data.

Although many organizations have developed in the market through differentiation and customization strategies, there are still firms that do not differentiate between customers. However, skilful management of customer relationships is usually linked to differentiation and customization strategies since it requires an in-depth understanding of customer differences stemming from heterogeneous preferences, lifestyles, demographics, psychographics and customer profitability variables.

Table 4.3 The strategic planning process of CRM

Vision	Positioning	Value proposition
Corporate strategy		
• What the business wants to achieve – purpose	• Relates to value proposition	• Operationalized by means of processes and activities
• Time horizon	• Facilitates benchmarking with competitors	• Represents the organization in the eyes of the customer
• Performance standards	• Enables identification of opportunities in the market	
Customer strategy		
Customer acquisition strategy: aims to attract new customers to establish a relationship with the firm	*Customer retention strategy*: aims to decrease the customer turnover of the firm	*Customer recovery strategy*: aims to regain lost customers
This is achieved by:	This is achieved by:	This is achieved by:
1 providing appropriate incentives that encourage customers to respond to the organization's initiatives (*stimulation strategy*);	1 providing psychological emotional benefits to customers, such as satisfaction and delight (*solidarity strategy*);	1 amending or improving problematic areas of customer–firm relationships that cause customer defections (*compensation and improvement strategy*)
2 reassuring customers that the supplier is able to satisfy their needs and desires (*persuasion strategy*)	2 setting up barriers to switching providers (*dependence strategy*)	
Customer segmentation strategy: requires the identification of segmentation variables, the methods to form segments, and the appraisal and optimization of existing segmentations		
Non-differentiation of customers	Differentiation of customers	Customization (segment of one)

Source: adapted from Bruhn (2003)

The information processes

The information processes of CRM allow firms to generate customer knowledge, which in turn plays a vital role in the creation and delivery of customer value, satisfaction and retention. These information processes also promote the development of a profit-maximizing portfolio of customer relationships by enabling firms to identify, segment and target the right customers, prioritize relationships and manage interactions with them (Plakoyiannaki *et al.*, 2008). As illustrated in the framework in Figure 4.7, the generation of customer knowledge is based on a series of information processes – namely, *information acquisition*, *information dissemination* and *information use*. For instance, Barclays Bank, as a firm practicing CRM, emphasizes information processes in order to manage multinational contacts and organization data, coordinate customer dialogue and manage key customer knowledge.

Acquisition is the process of gathering primary and secondary (customer) information from internal and external sources and bringing this data within the boundaries of the organization. Specifically, organizations may acquire customer information through customer survey activities and customer research (formal information acquisition), and communication and discussion with customers (informal information acquisition). In the context of CRM, information acquisition facilitates the customer–firm dialogue and provides the means not only to identify customers' characteristics and behaviours but also to better understand the customer. The collected information is stored in the back-office infrastructure of the CRM system and utilized for customer segmentation and targeting purposes.

Dissemination relates to the degree that information is circulated among organizational participants. The dissemination of (customer) information may occur formally through organizational policies, training sessions, presentations of research, cross-departmental teams, company meetings and memoranda, and informally through interaction and conversation between organizational stakeholders. Information dissemination plays a crucial role in the CRM process because it enhances the breadth of organizational and thus customer learning. In other words, when information is broadly distributed in the organization, more varied sources of information exist, making retrieval of information easier and learning more likely to occur. Additionally, dissemination of information contributes to the creation of new information by facilitating the synthesis of several bits of information previously acquired by different units in the organization.

Information *use* is probably the aspect of information processing more relevant to satisfying consumer needs since it demonstrates the response of the firm to the customers based on the acquired information. The use of information may be either direct – referring to the application of information to decision-making purposes and the implementation of customer strategies – or indirect – pertaining to behaviours that organizations deploy in order to elaborate customer information for strategy-related actions.

A central theme illustrated in Table 4.4 is that CRM intensifies customer–firm dialogue as a means of acquiring information. Additionally, it increases the sophistication of information processes with the availability of new technologies. This is demonstrated in the development of customer databases that contain information regarding customer requirements, choices, contact background and unmet

Table 4.4 The information processes of CRM

Information processes	CRM
Information acquisition	• Emphasis on customer–firm dialogue • Emphasis on customer information
Information dissemination	• Dissemination of customer information enhances customer learning • Increased sophistication and intensity of information processes • Customer information tailors products, services and communication efforts • Information processes enable customers to reach the firm
Information use	• Relevant to the interests of the customers • Privacy and security concerns

customer needs. The information processes of CRM enable organizations to tailor products and services according to the profile of customers. But most importantly, information processes help customers to communicate with the firm and express their opinions regarding the value offerings they receive. By processing customer information and linking it to customer behaviour patterns, organizations can generate information that can add value to customer–firm relationships.

Used correctly and ethically, this information can increase the benefits offered to customers. When used inappropriately, though, customers' interests are compromised. For example, mobile phone companies register their users to the network by acquiring personal details. Customers' personal data is used by the marketing team for promotional purposes (e.g. circulation of promotional text messages to the handsets of the customers). Such initiatives constitute bad practice in CRM and cause a number of privacy concerns, such as customer irritation for getting unwanted promotional information and feelings of violation of the customer's personal space. There are also increasing security issues of customer data.

The customer value process

The second group of processes relevant to CRM are customer value activities. Value and customer value activities are crucial sources for the development of competitive advantages. CRM contributes to this value (co-)creation process with the aim of providing superior customer experience and developing long-lasting customer relationships. The central part of the customer value process is the *customers' resulting experiences* that occur when individuals engage in a personal way with the value offering of the organization. The creation of customer experience emphasizes more the relationship that a customer has with the total offering rather than customers' experiences with a given product. Further, it is the customer's appreciation of the experience that determines the worth of the value offering and the survival of the organization.

However, it should be noted that there appears to be a difference between the value offerings of the firm and how customers perceive these value offerings. Moreover, value creation does not reside within firms' boundaries but is co-created through interaction and dialogue developed between customers and suppliers/firms (Nenonen & Storbacka 2010; Payne *et al.*, 2008). The discussion that follows takes into consideration this distinction and focuses on customers' viewpoints of the value process. The three value-generating activities – i.e. the *definition*, *development* and *delivery* of the value proposition – are considered, adopting the customer's frame of reference.

From a customer's point of view, the *definition of the value proposition* entails the benefits sought from the customer under particular circumstances, which are captured in the notion of *desired value*. Desired value is defined as what the customer wants to have from a product or a service in a specific use situation (Töytäri *et al.*, 2011). Desired value can be a multidimensional concept, with each of these dimensions helping individuals to achieve certain goals. In other words, the definition of the value proposition articulates the customers' perceptions of what they want to experience in a specific situation with the help of a product or service offering in order to accomplish a desired purpose or goal. For example, customers might desire speed in the transaction with the firm because this attribute may deliver benefits such as allowing them to concentrate on other activities or be efficient in their professional lives. From a CRM perspective, organizations attempt to understand customers' perceptions of desired value by establishing a customer–firm dialogue capable of revealing the attributes of customer perceptions of value to the firm. This attempt at acquiring knowledge about customers' perceptions of value is closely related to customer loyalty, satisfaction and trust. These concepts (i.e. loyalty, satisfaction and trust) constitute important elements of relationships and facilitate value creation and customer retention (Blocker *et al.*, 2012; Osarenkhoe and Bennani, 2007).

The *development of the value proposition* for customers includes decisions and formation of perceptions about products and services that address customer needs. In the context of CRM, what seems to be important at this stage of the value process is the incorporation of the voice of the customer into the design and production of new products and services, i.e. value co-production. This is because consumers' and firms' interests can be realized through cooperation and interdependence in the customer value process. In particular, the continuity of customer–firm interaction in the development of the value proposition may cultivate trust between the parties involved in the CRM process and offer additional benefits to the customer, such as superior service quality or tailoring of products and services according to the customer's characteristics and preferences.

Furthermore, value co-creation enables firms to 'consider value creation as a process that is dynamic and interactive rather than linear and transitive, and embedded on customer–firm dialogue' (Plakoyiannaki & Saren, 2006: 223). This customer–firm dialogue by providing the opportunity to create value through customized offerings can help firms to identify and better understand customers' needs and wants. The involvement of the customer in the development of the value proposition is evident in the operations of IKEA and Volvo, who advance product and service solutions through experimentation and interaction with their customers. Other examples of firms that collaborate with and learn from their customers in order to create value offering are Toys 'R' Us, The Home Depot, Wal-Mart and FedEx.

From the customer's perspective, *delivery of the value proposition* helps individuals to experience the desired value, which takes on two aspects: value in use or possession value. Value in use pertains to the use of a product or service in a specific situation in order to achieve certain goals. Possession value reflects the inherent meaning of the product or service to the customer. The delivery of the value proposition is linked to the consumption process, which is in fact a value-producing activity in itself. Consumption is often a playful activity which involves hedonism and communicates status and social position. During consumption, customers are autonomous and create value in their own arenas (by competition or collaboration) independent of the constraints that a firm's environment might impose. Consuming goods and services may be used as bases for individuals to compete against one another (e.g. conspicuous consumption) or join desirable groups that share the same aspirations, behaviours and lifestyles. Consequently, an in-depth understanding of the consumption process may enable organizations to appreciate customers' perceptions of value. Table 4.5 summarizes the characteristics of the customer value process in the context of CRM.

The performance measurement process

The performance measurement process relies on continuous monitoring of CRM activities and captures customers' feedback about the success of CRM practice in the firm. It ensures that both customers' and firms' goals are mutually reached through the CRM process (Plakoyiannaki et al., 2008; Plakoyiannaki & Saren, 2006). Particularly, in order to assess the contribution of CRM to the firm, the outcomes of CRM practice are considered in relation to the objectives of CRM practice. Taking into consideration that the purpose of CRM is to develop and maintain customer relationships through value-creation processes, the performance appraisal of CRM initiatives involves the assessment of value that customers have received from the specific products/services of the firm. In other words,

Table 4.5 The customer value process of CRM

Customer value process	CRM
Definition of the value proposition	• Desired value • Resulting customer experiences • Customer–firm dialogue reveals customers' perceptions of value
Development of the value proposition	• Customer–firm co-production • Provision of high-quality products and customer services • Continuity of customer–firm interactions cultivates trust and provides additional benefits to the customer
Delivery of the value proposition	• Possession value or value in use • Consumption

organizations need to assess the value judgements of their customer in order to evaluate whether the CRM has been successful or not. *Value judgements* include consumers' assessments of the value they receive given the trade-offs between all relevant benefits and sacrifices in a specific use situation. Consequently, organizations may enhance CRM performance by increasing the benefits (or decreasing the sacrifices) that customers experience in the use of products and services.

However, the performance measurement of CRM is considered in terms of the firm's responses not only to customer value expectations, but also to shareholder value maximization. In this wider context, performance assessment of CRM ensures that all stakeholders of the firm have mutually reached their goals and acknowledges the role of employee involvement and satisfaction in creating value (Plakoyiannaki *et al.*, 2008; Bohling *et al.*, 2006). For example, HSBC uses CRM in order to build up shareholder value through cross-selling activities, cost reduction, and improved customer acquisition and retention. The linkage between the CRM process and shareholder value highlights the importance of CRM in the organization and provides a valid claim for capital investment in CRM initiatives. The shareholder value (SHV) perspective involves the identification of four value drivers:

1 Acceleration of cash flows – earlier cash flows are preferred because risk and the time adjustments reduce the value of later cash flows.
2 Enhancement of cash flows by increasing revenues and reducing costs, working capital and fixed investments.

3 Reduction in the risk associated with cash flows by decreasing both their volatility and, indirectly, the firm's cost of capital.
4 Augmentation of the long-term value of the business (at the end of the planning horizon) through investments in processes that result in both tangible
and intangible assets.

Table 4.6 illustrates how the CRM process enhances the SHV of the firm. In particular, CRM initiatives contribute to *cash flow acceleration* by facilitating product

Table 4.6 The performance measurement process of CRM – the drivers of shareholder value

Shareholder value drivers	Contribution of CRM to shareholder value
Accelerating cash flows	• Reduces time for market acceptance (i.e. market penetration cycle time) • Minimizes customer solution development cycle time
Enhancing cash flows	• Supports high margins with branded products and superior service • Cross-selling of parts, consumables and complementary services • Up-selling of branded products and services • Maximizes customer value (and revenues) by combining customer solutions (including competitive products and services) • Acquires customers; grows existing customer base • Refines the quality of the customer base • Lowers product launch costs; lowers sales and services costs
Reducing risk (vulnerability and volatility of cash flows)	• Enhances customer retention and loyalty • Increases customer switching costs • Retains excellence in the delivery of customer value and enhances customer experiences with the firm and its products/services • Cross-selling of parts, consumables and complementary services • Implementation of differential pricing and price concessions for long-term and profitable customers • Implementation of customer education and training programmes
Augmentation of the long-term value of the business	• Grows and refines customer base • Cross-selling/up-selling of products and services • Focuses on enhancing customer satisfaction and loyalty (involves customers in the development of the value proposition) • Aligns organizational capabilities to the delivery of customer value

Source: adapted from Srivastava *et al.* (1998)

entry, trial, acceptance and diffusion in the customer base. For instance, Levi Strauss builds upon customer relationships by using consumers' preferences to customize jeans fit for women. At the same time the company attempts to capitalize on its dialogue with the customers by sending them information regarding new products and sizes, lines and styles of jeans. Additionally, the execution of campaign management activities such as advertising and promotion plays a central role in the development of brand awareness, motivates the product trail and minimizes barriers to market.

The practice of CRM *enhances cash flows* through activities such as cross-selling, customer acquisition, and reduction of product, service and sales costs. For example, CRM enables Amazon, the online bookshop, to cross-sell its products and services by matching the profile of its customers with solutions of possible interest in order to generate repeat purchasing behaviour and increased cash flows.

Successful implementation of CRM initiatives contributes to *reduction of vulnerability and volatility of cash flows* by increasing customer switching costs, facilitating loyalty programmes and excellent customer value delivery, and by leveraging market-based assets. For instance, recent studies (e.g. Meyer-Waarden & Benavent, 2009; Meyer-Waarden, 2008) emphasize the importance of CRM in the development of loyalty programmes in order for the firms to create personalized relationships, increase product usage, enhance customers' trust in the firm and facilitate customer maintenance. Thus, CRM contributes to the *augmentation of the long-term value of the business by cultivating customer loyalty and long-term customer relationships*, which minimizes the risk associated with the cash flows, services costs and sales costs, and increases revenues. For example, Sainsbury's UK supermarket, Barclays Bank, BP and Debenhams department store are deploying a CRM programme based on a loyalty scheme with the purpose of achieving financial and strategic growth and establishing a long-term competitive advantage in the market by personalizing offers to customers.

CRM capabilities

The success of cross-functional processes such as CRM is dependent on organizational capabilities that support the major goal of CRM practice, which is the creation and delivery of superior customer value. Capabilities refer to a firm's ability to gather, integrate and organize resources in order to achieve a competitive advantage (Trainor *et al.*, 2014). CRM capabilities are conceived as the 'integration of customer-facing activities, including processes, systems, and technologies to engage customers in collaborative conversations and enhance customer relationships' (Trainor, 2012: 321). This conceptualization of CRM capability acknowledges the combination and integration of human, technological and business capabilities, which positively affect the development and maintenance of customer relationships and organizational performance. Taking into consideration that capabilities are embedded in processes (see Figure 4.7), we can identify five sets of capabilities deriving from the CRM process that enable CRM practice. These are shown in Figure 4.8 as follows:

- learning and market orientation capabilities
- integration capabilities
- analytical capabilities
- operational capabilities
- direction capabilities.

These capabilities are interwoven in the culture of the organization, which has an important role in determining the degree to which employees demonstrate the capabilities that enable the success of CRM initiatives. Based on the discussion at the beginning of the section, it appears to be obvious that, for CRM to thrive, a cultural focus that places the customer at the heart of the business and encourages customer learning appears to be essential.

Learning and market orientation capabilities

Market orientation and learning are closely interrelated organizational capabilities deeply embedded in the CRM process. Market orientation enhances CRM practice by contributing to the development of customer-linking capabilities (e.g. identification of customers' wants, development of durable customer relationships) which in turn may increase customer satisfaction and loyalty as well as firms' sales and profits (Javalgi et al., 2006; Rapp et al., 2010; Wang & Feng, 2012). In particular, market orientation by focusing on creation and maintenance of superior customer value serves to facilitate the essence of CRM, which is maximization of customer value. The creation of customer value is achieved through the activities of the customer value processes of CRM (i.e. the definition, development and delivery of the value proposition) and is further demonstrated in tasks such as customer service, innovative product development, cost-effective manufacturing and quality management.

Market orientation directs the scope of learning towards the customer. In the context of CRM, learning capabilities are embedded in the (1) information processes, (2) the customer value process, and (3) performance measurement processes. First, customer insight generation occurs through learning and requires input of information, which is further used by members of the organization to respond to customer needs. Second, the customer value process of CRM is facilitated by learning capabilities that show the commitment of the organization to listen to customers' requirements and needs and the response to these needs through high-quality and innovative products and services. Third, the performance

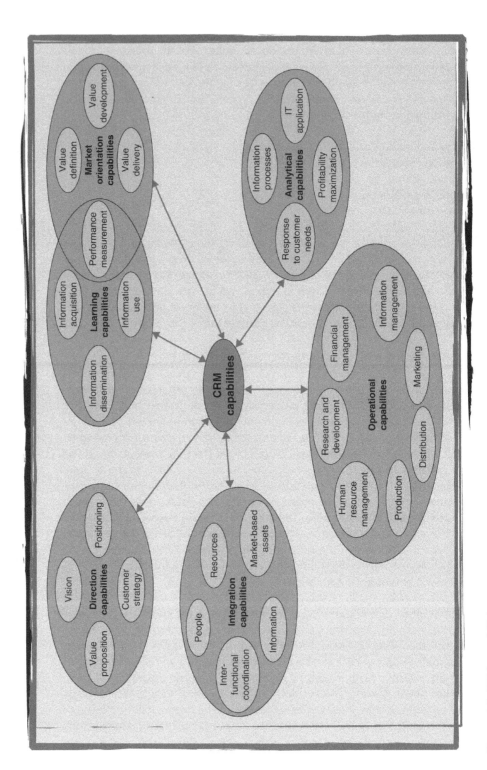

Figure 4.8 CRM capabilities

measurement process of CRM shows an inherent focus on learning, which is illustrated by the capabilities of the organization to measure and improve corporate performance based on customer feedback across all channels and points of interaction.

Generally, it can be argued that companies that practice CRM successfully are *learning organizations* skilled at acquiring, disseminating and using customer information to respond quickly to customer needs and adapt to changing environments. Such organizations modify their behaviour in the market to reflect new knowledge and customer insights gained by means of learning and the CRM process. Studies emphasize the critical role of knowledge competence in implementing successful CRM strategies (e.g. Garrido-Moreno & Padilla-Meléndez, 2011; Shi and Yip, 2007), through which firms can build strong competitive advantages.

Integration capabilities

The CRM process is conceived as cross-functional (Lambert, 2009; Payne & Frow, 2005) since it crosses all departmental boundaries with the purpose of maximizing the value delivered to the customers by establishing a creative customer–firm dialogue. This requires organizations to identify and develop integration capabilities that bring together individuals and organizational units/functions and create synergies that are most able to support successful CRM practice. Lambert (2009: 7) stresses this further by arguing that 'the more business functions that are involved in key customer relationships, the more useful the knowledge that will be generated'.

The coordination of functions and people ensures that organizational actors serve the same goals and place the customer at the centre of the firm's strategy and operations. Furthermore, the alignment of functional areas promotes inter-departmental connections and use of shared resources. Integration capabilities facilitate information processing and align the operations of all business systems, extending from the back-office infrastructure to the front-line systems and channels of interaction. Integration capabilities appear to reflect on the performance measurement of CRM. Specifically, the appreciation of market-based assets that CRM initiatives generate and their link to shareholder value lies in the integration of CRM measures in order to assess the contribution of the CRM process within the firm.

Analytical capabilities

Analytical capabilities are associated with the technological aspects of the CRM process and play an important role in the management of customer relationships for four reasons. First, they assist in the acquisition, dissemination and use of information which supports customer learning, development of clear market segments and consistency in the delivery of service experience across different touch points (Rapp *et al.*, 2010). Second, analytical capabilities refer to the ability of organizations to deploy technological applications and scan for information regarding technological opportunities and threats that may advance CRM practice. Third, analytical capabilities influence the retention process and enhance the ability of an organization to identify and respond to the changing needs of the customer base. Fourth, analytical capabilities enhance maximization of profitability from customer relationships since they enable firms to link investments from customer relationships to the return these relationships generate for the firm.

Operational capabilities

Operational capabilities exploit and enhance resources and relate to the dissemination of information and knowledge at all touch points of the organization and between the organization and its business partners (Keramati *et al.*, 2010). They are skills developed at functional and administrative levels that translate customer insights into value offerings and aim at contributing to the development and reinforcement of customer relationships. Operational capabilities cut across the CRM process and may be relevant in areas such as research and development, production, distribution, marketing (e.g. communication, customer serving), information management, financial management and human resource practices.

Direction capabilities

Direction capabilities are the compass for the course of the CRM process in the organization. They ensure not only that the organization has a clear and well-communicated corporate and customer strategy, but also that the components of these strategies are complementary. As far as *corporate strategy* is concerned, direction capabilities (1) facilitate the development and accomplishment of the corporate vision of CRM that places the customer at the centre of the organization's operations and philosophy; (2) define the positioning of the firm which addresses the development of competitive advantage in the marketplace; and (3) ensure that the value proposition focuses on the customer experience, which truly differentiates the firm in the eyes of the customer.

With reference to *customer strategy*, direction capabilities enhance the organization's ability to focus its resources on its most-valued customers. These capabilities have a significant impact on the development and implementation of strategies for customer acquisition, retention and recovery, as well as customer segmentation.

Summary

This section has described the organizational processes and capabilities that are necessary to manage customer relations so that solutions are created, managed and delivered competitively to the long-term advantage of the firm and its customers. The framework of the CRM process illustrated in Figure 4.7 attempts to provide a holistic understanding of the notion of an organizational process that cuts across business units and departments. The discussion on CRM, in the first part of the section, incorporated the customer's viewpoint of that process. The four sub-processes, i.e. the *strategic planning process*, the *information processes*, the *customer value process* and the *performance measurement process*, are relevant to customers' interests. Table 4.7 provides a summary of the CRM processes and activities discussed in the first part of the section. Furthermore, it puts forward key issues relevant to the practice of CRM and the customer.

Table 4.7 The CRM process, its sub-processes and activities

CRM sub-processes	CRM activities	Key issues emerging from the findings
Strategic planning process	• Corporate strategy • Customer strategy	• Elements of strategy influence the perceptions of customers regarding the firm and its products and services
Information processes	• Information acquisition • Information dissemination • Information use	• Information processes enable customers to reach the firm • Privacy concerns linked to the analysis and use of customer information
Customer value process	• Definition of the value proposition • Development of the value proposition • Delivery of the value proposition	• Desired value • Customers' perceptions of value • Customer–firm co-production • Consumption as a value-generating activity
Performance measurement process	• Use of customer feedback and SHV measures to assess CRM performance	• Need for organizations to capture the value judgements of their customers

The CRM processes outlined in Table 4.7 have been used as a basis for the identification of capabilities critical for the development and delivery of customer solutions. Specifically, the key organizational capabilities required are: *learning* and *market orientation capabilities, integration capabilities, analytical capabilities, operational capabilities* and *direction capabilities* (see Figure 4.8). It also follows that for CRM processes to deliver solutions for the firm and its customers, it is essential for the employees to be committed to these key organizational activities and capabilities. Additionally, management of the firm plays a key role in identifying and acquiring these capabilities, which requires devoting time and resources to organizational development and learning.

FURTHER READING

Customer relationship management

Bohling, T., Bowman, D., LaValle, S., Mittal, V., Narayandas, D., Ramani, G. & Varadarajan, R. (2006) CRM implementation effectiveness issues and insights. *Journal of Service Research*, **9** (2), 184–194.

Bruhn, M. (2003) *Relationship Marketing: Management of Customer Relationships*. Prentice Hall, Financial Times: Harlow, UK.

Lambert, D. M. (2009) Customer relationship management as a business process. *Journal of Business & Industrial Marketing*, **25** (1), 4–17.

Payne, A. & Frow, P. (2005) A strategic framework for customer relationship management. *Journal of Marketing*, **69** (4), 167–176.

Peppers, D. & Rogers, M. (2000) *The One-to-One Future*: *Building Business Relationships One Customer at a Time*, 3rd edition. Piatkus: London.

Plakoyiannaki, E. & Saren, M. (2006) Time and the customer relationship management process: conceptual and methodological insights. *Journal of Business & Industrial Marketing*, **21** (4), 218–230.

Organizational processes and culture

Conduit, J. & Mavondo, F. T. (2001) How critical is internal customer orientation to market orientation? *Journal of Business Research*, **51**, 11–24.

Garrido-Moreno, A. & Padilla-Meléndez, A. (2011) Analyzing the impact of knowledge management on CRM success: the mediating effects of organizational factors. *International Journal of Information Management*, **31** (5), 437–444.

Keramati, A., Mehrabi, H. & Mojir, N. (2010) A process-oriented perspective on customer relationship management and organizational performance: an empirical investigation. *Industrial Marketing Management*, **39** (7), 1170–1185.

Plakoyiannaki, E., Tzokas, N., Dimitratos, P. & Saren, M. (2008) How critical is employee orientation for customer relationship management? Insights from a case study. *Journal of Management Studies*, **45** (2), 268–293.

Rapp, A., Trainor, K. J. & Agnihotri, R. (2010) Performance implications of customer-linking capabilities: examining the complementary role of customer orientation and CRM technology. *Journal of Business Research*, **63** (11), 1229–1236.

Slater, S. F. & Narver, J. C. (1995) Market orientation and the learning organization. *Journal of Marketing*, **59** (3), 63–74.

Organizational strategy and capabilities

Fuchs, P. H., Mifflin, K. E., Miller, D. & Whitney, J. O. (2000) Strategic integration: competing in the age of capabilities. *California Management Review*, **42** (3), 118–147.

Plakoyiannaki, E. & Tzokas, N. (2002) Customer relationship management (CRM): a capability portfolio perspective. *Journal of Database Marketing*, **9** (3), 228–237.

Trainor, K. J. (2012) Relating social media technologies to performance: a capabilities based perspective. *Journal of Personal Selling and Sales Management*, **32** (3), 317–331.

Trainor, K. J., Andzulis, J. M., Rapp, A. & Agnihotri, R. (2014) Social media technology usage and customer relationship performance: a capabilities-based examination of social CRM. *Journal of Business Research*, **67** (6), 1201–1208.

Wang, Y. & Feng, H. (2012) Customer relationship management capabilities: measurement, antecedents and consequences. *Management Decision*, **50** (1), 115–129.

References

Aaker, D., Kumar, V. & Day, G. (2001) *Marketing Research*, 7th edition. Wiley: New York.

Ansoff, I. (1979) *Strategic Management*. Macmillan: London.

Belk, R. (2013) Extended self in a digital world. *Journal of Consumer Research*, **40**, October, 477–500.

Berthon, P., Hulbert, J. M. & Pitt, L. F. (2005) Consuming technology: why marketers sometimes get it wrong. *California Management Review*, **48** (1), 110–127.

Bizer, C., Boncz, P., Brodie, M. & Erling, O. (2011) The meaningful use of big data: four perspectives – four challenges. *ACM Sigmod*, **40** (4), 56–60.

Blocker, C. P., Cannon, J. P., Panagopoulos, N. G. & Sager, J. K. (2012) The role of the sales force in value creation and appropriation: new directions for research. *Journal of Personal Selling & Sales Management*, **32** (1), 15–27.

Bohling, T., Bowman, D., LaValle, S., Mittal, V., Narayandas, D., Ramani, G. & Varadarajan, R. (2006) CRM implementation effectiveness issues and insights. *Journal of Service Research*, **9** (2), 184–194.

Booz Allen Hamilton (1982) *Management of New Products*. BAH Inc.: New York.

Brady, M. (2006) A holistic view of ICT within the marketing domain: challenges and issues. British Academy of Management Conference, Belfast, September.

Brady, M., Fellenz, M. R. & Brookes, R. (2008) Researching the role of information and communication technologies in contemporary marketing. *Journal of Business and Industrial Marketing*, **23** (2), 108–114.

Brady, M., Saren, M. & Tzokas, N. (2002) Integrating information technology into marketing practice: the IT reality of contemporary marketing practice. *Journal of Marketing Management*, **18** (5/6, July), 555–578.

Brinker, S. & McLellan, L. (2014) The rise of the chief marketing technologist. *Harvard Business Review*, July/August, 2–5.

Broers, A. (2005) The triumph of technology. The Reith Lectures, BBC. www.bbc.co.uk/programmes/p00ghv8z, accessed June 2017.

Bruhn, M. (2003) *Relationship Marketing: Management of Customer Relationships*. Prentice Hall, Financial Times: Harlow, UK.

Choudhury, M. M. & Harrigan, P. (2014) CRM to social CRM: the integration of new technologies into customer relationship management. *Journal of Strategic Marketing*, **22** (2), 149–176.

Coltman, T. (2007) Why build a customer relationship management capability? *The Journal of Strategic Information Systems*, **16** (3), 301–320.

Crouch, I. (2015) The horror of Amazon's new dash button. *New Yorker*, April, 2.

Davenport, T. H. (2013) Analytics 3.0. *Harvard Business Review*, December, 64–71.

Day, G. S. (2011) Closing the marketing capabilities gap. *Journal of Marketing*, **75** (4), July, 183–195.

Demarest, M. (1997) Understanding knowledge management. *Long Range Planning*, **30** (3), 374–384.

Dobers, P. & Strannegard, L. (2001) Lovable networks: a story of affection, attraction and treachery. *Journal of Organisational Change*, **14** (1), 8–49.

Fellenz, M. R. & Brady, M. (2010) Managing customer-centric information: the challenges of information and communication technology (ICT) deployment in service environments. In: *Service Science and Logistics Informatics: Innovative Perspectives* (Zongwei Luo, ed.). IGI Global: pp. 46–64.

Garrido-Moreno, A. & Padilla-Meléndez, A. (2011) Analyzing the impact of knowledge management on CRM success: the mediating effects of organizational factors. *International Journal of Information Management*, **31** (5), 437–444.

Griffin, A. & Hauser (1995) The voice of the customer. In: *New Product Development: A Reader* (S. Hart, ed.). Dryden Press: London.

von Hippel, E. (1978) Users as innovators. *Technology Review*, **80** (3), 30–34.

Hopkins, M. S. & Brokaw, L. (2011) Matchmaking with math: how analytics beats intuition to win customers. *MIT Sloan Management Review*, **52** (2).

Humby, C. (2004) *Scoring Points: How Tesco is Winning Customer Loyalty*. Kogan Page: London.

Iglesias, O., Sauquet, A. & Montaña, J. (2011) The role of corporate culture in relationship marketing. *European Journal of Marketing*, **45** (4), 631–650.

Javalgi, R. R. G., Martin, C. L. & Young, R. B. (2006) Marketing research, market orientation and customer relationship management: a framework and implications for service providers. *Journal of Services Marketing*, **20** (1), 12–23.

Kawakami, T., Durmusoglu, S. and Barczak, G. (2011) Factors influencing information technology usage for new product development: the case of Japanese companies. *Journal of Product Innovation Management*, **28**, 833–847.

Keramati, A., Mehrabi, H. & Mojir, N. (2010) A process-orientated perspective on customer relationship management and organizational performance: an empirical investigation. *Industrial Marketing Management*, **39** (7), 1170–1185.

Kohli, A. K. & Jaworski, B. J. (1990) Market orientation: the construct, research propositions and managerial implications. *Journal of Marketing*, **54** (2), 1–18.

Kotler, P. (1972) *Marketing Management: Analysis, Planning and Control*. Prentice Hall: Englewood Cliffs, NJ.

Lambert, D. M. (2009) Customer relationship management as a business process. *Journal of Business & Industrial Marketing*, **25** (1), 4–17.

Larson, K. & Watson, R. (2011) *The Value of Social Media: Toward Measuring Social Media Strategies*. Proceedings of ICIS (International Conference on Information Systems), Shanghai, pp. 1–18.

Levitt, T. (1960) Marketing Myopia. *Harvard Business Review*, **38** (4), 45–56.

Li, T. & Calantone, R. J. (1998) The impact of market knowledge competence on new product advantage: conceptualization and empirical examination. *Journal of Marketing*, **62** (4), 13–29.

Lovelock, C. & Gummesson, E. (2004) Whither service marketing? In search of a new paradigm and fresh perspectives. *Journal of Service Research*, **7** (1), 20–41.

Lovelock, C., Vandermerwe, S. & Lewis, B. (1999) *Services Marketing: A European Perspective*. Prentice Hall: Harlow.

Manyika, J., Chui, M., Brown, B., Bughin, J., Dobbs R., Roxburgh, C. & Hung-Byers, A. (2011) *Big Data: The Next Frontier for Innovation, Competition and Productivity.* McKinsey Global Institute. https://bigdatawg.nist.gov/pdf/MGI_big_data_full_report.pdf, accessed June 2017.

Mayer-Schonberger, V. & Cukier, K. (2013) *Big Data: A Revolution That Will Transform How We Live, Work and Think*. Eamon Dolan/Mariner Books: London.

Meyer-Waarden, L. (2008) The influence of loyalty programme membership on customer purchase behaviour. *European Journal of Marketing*, **42** (1/2), 87–114.

Meyer-Waarden, L. & Benavent, C. (2009) Grocery retail loyalty program effects: self-selection or purchase behavior change? *Journal of the Academy of Marketing Science*, **37** (3), 345–358.

Morey, T., Forbath, T. & Schoop, A. (2015) Customer data: designing for transparency and trust. *Harvard Business Review*, May.

Nenonen, S. & Storbacka, K. (2010) Business model design: conceptualizing networked value co-creation. *International Journal of Quality and Service Sciences*, **2** (1), 43–59.

Ngai, E. W., Xiu, L. & Chau, D.C. (2009) Application of data mining techniques in customer relationship management: a literature review and classification. *Expert Systems with Applications*, 36 (2), 2592–2602.

Osarenkhoe, A. & Bennani, A. E. (2007) An exploratory study of implementation of customer relationship management strategy. *Business Process Management Journal*, **13** (1), 139–164.

Parasuraman, A., Zeithaml, V. & Berry, L. (1985) A conceptual model of service quality and its implications for future research. *Journal of Marketing*, **49** (4), 41–50.

Payne, A. & Frow, P. (2005) A strategic framework for customer relationship management. *Journal of marketing*, **69** (4), 167–176.

Payne, A. F., Storbacka, K. & Frow, P. (2008) Managing the co-creation of value. *Journal of the Academy of Marketing Science*, **36** (1), 83–96.

Plakoyiannaki, E. & Saren, M. (2006) Time and the customer relationship management process: conceptual and methodological insights. *Journal of Business & Industrial Marketing*, **21** (4), 218–230.

Plakoyiannaki, E., Tzokas, N., Dimitratos, P. & Saren, M. (2008) How critical is employee orientation for customer relationship management? Insights from a case study. *Journal of Management Studies*, **45** (2), 268–293.

Porter, M. & Heppelmann, E. (2015) How smart connected products are transforming companies. *Harvard Business Review*, October, 97–114.

Prahalad, C., Ramaswamy, V. & Krishnan, M. (2000) Consumer centricity. *Information Week*, 4 October, **781**, 67–72.

Rapp, A., Trainor, K. J. & Agnihotri, R. (2010) Performance implications of customer-linking capabilities: examining the complementary role of customer orientation and CRM technology. *Journal of Business Research*, **63** (11), 1229–1236.

Rogers, E. (1962) *Diffusion of Innovations*. Free Press: New York.

Saren, M. (1994) Reframing the process of new product development: from 'stages' models to a 'blocks' framework. *Journal of Marketing Management*, 10 (April), 633–643.

Saren, M. & Tzokas, N. (1998) The nature of the product in market relationships. *Journal of Marketing Management*, **14**, 445–464.

Schroeder, J. (2002) *Visual Consumption*. Routledge: London.

Shi, J. & Yip, L. (2007) Driving innovation and improving employee capability: The effect of customer knowledge sharing on CRM. *The Business Review*, **7** (1), 107–112.

Sigala, M. (2011) eCRM 2.0 applications and trends: the use and perceptions of Greek tourism firms of social networks and intelligence. *Computers in Human Behavior*, **27** (2), 655–661.

Sin, L. Y., Tse, A. C. & Yim, F. H. (2005) CRM: conceptualization and scale development. *European Journal of marketing*, **39** (11/12), 1264–1290.

Spieth, P., Schneckenberg, D. & Ricart, J. E. (2014) Business model innovation: state of the art and future challenges for the field. *R&D Management*, **44** (3), 237–247.

Srivastava, R. K., Shrevani, T. A. & Fahey, L. (1998) Market-based assets and shareholder value: a framework for analysis. *Journal of Marketing*, **62** (January), 2–18.

Teece, D. J. (2010) Business models, business strategy and innovation. *Long Range Planning*, **43** (2–3), 172–194.

Töytäri, P., Brashear Alejandro, T., Parvinen, P., Ollila, I. & Rosendahl, N. (2011) Bridging the theory to application gap in value-based selling. *Journal of Business & Industrial Marketing*, **26** (7), 493–502.

Trainor, K. J. (2012) Relating social media technologies to performance: a capabilities based perspective. *Journal of Personal Selling and Sales Management*, **32** (3), 317–331.

Trainor, K. J., Andzulis, J. M., Rapp, A. & Agnihotri, R. (2014) Social media technology usage and customer relationship performance: a capabilities-based examination of social CRM. *Journal of Business Research*, **67** (6), 1201–1208.

Tzokas, N. & Saren, M. (2004) Competitive advantage, knowledge and relationship marketing. Journal of Business and Industrial Marketing, **19** (2), 124–135.

Vargo, S. L. & Lusch, R. F. (2004) The four service marketing myths: remnants of a goods-based, manufacturing model. *Journal of Services Research*, **6** (4), 324–355.

Venkatraman, N. & Henderson, J. C. (1998) Real strategies for virtual organising. *Sloan Management Review*, **40** (1), 33–48.

Wang, Y. & Feng, H. (2012) Customer relationship management capabilities: measurement, antecedents and consequences. *Management Decision*, **50** (1), 115–129.

Wilson, D. T. & Jantrania, S. (1994) Understanding the value of a relationship. *Asia–Australia Marketing Journal*, **2** (1), 55–66.

Wind, Y. & Mahajan, V. (1997) Issues and opportunities in new product development. *Journal of Marketing Research*, **34** (1), 1–12.

Zablah, A. R., Bellenger, D. N. & Johnston, W. J. (2004) An evaluation of divergent perspectives on customer relationship management: towards a common understanding of an emerging phenomenon. *Industrial marketing management*, **33** (6), 475–489.

Brand Selection

The more the world is dominated by mass media, mass production, mass markets, the greater the need for producers to identify their products and services in a way that distinguishes them from others and grabs consumers' attention. This is the original role of 'branding' which, although far from being a new phenomenon, has evolved to such an extent that the word itself has become ubiquitous – you see it everywhere. Consumer brands, high street brands, virtual brands, corporate brands, personal brands, sports brands, celebrity brands, household brands, sub-brands – these are just a few of the various different types of brands. This section reviews these categories and discusses the various roles that branding plays, particularly for corporate identity and 'fast fashion' retailing.

The role of branding

In modern society human beings instinctively want to be unique and identified as individuals. The more our world is dominated by mass media, mass production, mass markets, the greater the desire for individuality. The conventional identification for a person is their 'given' name and surname. Individuality requires making one's own choice, however, and therefore we ascribe different labels of identification to others and ourselves in addition to our formal 'names'. So much so that labels such as nicknames, coats of arms, tattoos, furnishings, language, living spaces, entertainment haunts and the clothes we wear make more statements about who we are than our names and initials do (see Consuming Experience).

> *In a business world of fast impressions, you're only as good as your first impression.*

In the same way, marketers seek to identify their products and services to distinguish them from others and grab our attention. This is the original role of what marketers traditionally call 'branding'. The logic is apparently a simple behavioural one: if the name is catchy, you like it and remember it; if you think the logo is cool, the product looks good and makes you feel great; if it is available in your favourite outlets and is within your price range, you buy it.

What is a brand?

The use of branding is far from being a new phenomenon. It originated in the marking of animals like cattle and sheep in order to identify their owners. Livestock had their owners' particular marks burnt onto their hides. It is thought that the word 'brand' originated from the Anglo-Saxon word 'to burn'. In modern times a brand means a name, sign, symbol or design, or more usually a combination of these, that is intended to identify the goods, services or other market offerings of a

manufacturer or provider organization and to differentiate them from competitors' brands. At one extreme the brand can simply be the name of the company, and at the other end a different brand can be attached to each individual item that they produce.

Today branding has evolved to such an extent that the word itself has become ubiquitous – you see it everywhere. In the marketing literature you can read about consumer brands, high street brands, virtual brands, corporate brands, personal brands, celebrity brands, household brands, sub-brands, brand extensions, fashion brands, luxury brand 'fever', brand communities, own-label brands, diffusion brands, brand stretching and lifestyle brands. In everyday use the term is applied to political parties, movies, TV programmes, footballers, nations, pop stars, military regiments, science, and works of art, artists, cartoons, fictional characters and literary icons.

The benefits of branding can be summarized as:

- Branding provides the potential to attract a loyal and profitable set of customers. Brand loyalty gives sellers some protection from competition and greater control in planning their marketing programme.
- Strong brands help build the corporate image, making it easier to launch new brands and gain acceptance by distributors and consumers.
- Branding enables one firm to meet the specific preferences of consumers in different market segments. Instead of Unilever marketing one detergent, it offers many detergent brands, each formulated differently and aimed at specific benefit-seeking segments.
- The brand name and trademark provide legal protection of unique product features, which prevents competitors from copying these directly and helps the battle against counterfeit goods.
- The brand name makes it easier for the company to process orders and track down problems in the distribution network.
- The brand is a sign of ownership (manufacturers or distributors – i.e. producers or sellers – such as Marks & Spencer).
- The brand is a differentiating device, offering real benefits that mark each brand out from competition.
- Brands can be used as a functional device, i.e. a guarantee of consistent quality to consumers (for example SEAT cars – functional but good value for money).
- Brands are symbolic with a value beyond the functional – the logo, name, brand personality, desired self and match to this (perfume, clothes, beer, wine).
- Brands can also act as risk avoiders – when new brands come to the market the job is to reassure your target audience that they do not want to take the risk of switching brands.

- Brands can also be a shorthand device, conveying a wealth of information symbolically.
- Brands are also a strategic device, helping companies look to augment, carefully position and understand target markets, research target markets, add value and communicate effectively.

Brands are closely linked to consumer behaviour. Today the brand is becoming more important than the product itself. Brands have a life; brands have personalities; brands can be social; brands can be personal.

While these potential benefits may be clear, there is, however, a set of alternative choices for any organization about whether and how to brand their products and services. This involves several major strategic decisions because not all products are suitable for branding. It depends on whether the item in question is a product or a commodity. A *commodity* is the undifferentiated product where one item is the same as another. Typically raw materials like coal, oil, gas and most agricultural produce are commodities that are not easy to differentiate. On the other hand, many processed, packaged consumer goods have similar characteristics and there is a need for companies to brand their products in order for consumers to be able easily to distinguish between those of different manufacturers.

Making your mark – brand categories, types and roles

The implication of Baudrillard's observation (see box) for branding is that if a label can be applied to almost anything, it becomes meaningless as a distinguishing feature. The paradox is that this is exactly what has happened to the use of the concept of branding itself.

> As Baudrillard (1990) starkly illustrates, once a concept gains totality and becomes appropriate to everything and anything, it also becomes appropriate to nothing. An absolute definition is also meaningless.

Nevertheless, there are various different categories of branding. The accompanying parts of this chapter review these and discuss the various roles that branding plays, particularly for corporate image (see Corporate identity and branding) and 'fast fashion' (see Fast fashion branding – from Prada to Primark).

High street brands

These are the successful high street brands that consumers are quick to recognize by their distinct taste, style, packaging, service, technology, innovation, performance or premium pricing. Unlike luxury brands, their prices are not prohibitive and so they are consumed by a larger share of the market. They are the likes of Coca-Cola, Häagen-Dazs, Diesel jeans, Nokia, Hewlett-Packard and Vodafone.

Household brands

Similar to high street brands but most often used as 'household' products. This is largely subjective, of course. The term was used in the 1950s and 1960s in the advertising of food items, detergents and other cleaning materials, what would today be called 'FMCG' brands (fast-moving consumer goods). This category would now include some consumer durables (so-called 'white goods' labels), e.g. Hoover, Bosch, Indesit, Sony.

Sub-brands

These are the results of a strategy known as 'brand stretching'. Aaker (1997) defined a sub-brand as a brand with its own name that uses the name of its parent brand in some capacity to bolster its reputation. A well-known brand from the UK, Richard Branson's Virgin, is now branding over 30 different products and services – from planes, trains, finance, soft drinks, music, mobile phones, holidays, cars, wines, publishing to bridal wear (www.virgin.com).

However, sub-brands do not necessarily include the name of the parent company (i.e. the corporate brand). In the luxury goods industry, any such connection is usually undesirable. Thus, in the case of Rolex, it's less expensive sub-brand trades under the name Tudor. The idea is both to maintain the parent's credibility and prestige regardless of how the sub-brand performs and to protect the original brand from 'cannibalization', a phenomenon where the cheaper brand takes sales away from its more expensive 'parent'.

Luxury brands

These are usually high-profile brands with a history well rooted in fashion, design, superior quality, exclusivity, performance and that are able to command a price premium compared with the equivalent consumer brands which offer the same functionality. For example, while the recording time function for a Swatch watch and a Bulgari is the same, the price tag is quite different because of the prestige, quality and image of the label. Other examples of luxury brands are Chanel, Louis Vuitton, Tiffany & Co., Jimmy Choo, Porsche, Frette (see also Fast fashion branding).

Brand stretching

This refers to the extension of an established brand name, identified with one product in one market, to another type of product in other markets. The similar words 'extension' and 'diffusion' are also used both as adjectives to describe the dynamics that exist within the process of stretching and as nouns to describe the strategy itself (see Fast fashion branding). A number of luxury brands, including Givenchy, Pierre Cardin, YSL and Gucci, adopted this strategy in the 1980s. Their logos and brand names were printed across a wide range of trivial, inexpensive and poor-quality items, such as pens, tie-pins, baseball caps, socks and key rings – there was even a Gucci toilet roll holder. Since then, faced also with the problem of counterfeiting, luxury brand companies have much more carefully limited their product portfolios in an effort to protect their investments in brand building. Most luxury brands now adopt a more discreet approach – small logos, labels and tags, and monograms.

Own-label brands

With increased 'share of spend', turnovers and volumes, the big supermarket chains have themselves become significant 'brand owners', chipping away at consumer brand volumes by competing with their own-label brands. Own-label brands are invariably positioned as being a cheaper option to the equivalent consumer brands, e.g. Wal-Mart/Asda's Smart Price range of foodstuffs and paper products or Tesco's Value brand range.

Advertising of own-label products is limited mostly to in-store promotion and prominent shelf or stand-alone display. Unlike manufacturer brands, there is little emphasis on product origins. We do not see pineapples growing in the Del Monte plantations in South America or Irish farmers milking healthy-looking cows with green, rolling hills in the background as in the Kerrygold advertising. Own labels are more likely to simply state, for instance, that 'these dates are the product of more than one country' (what, all in one pack?).

Supermarkets can now offer a larger range of products and, through what is known as 'category management', a number of different brands for any one product type.

Celebrity brands

These are brands where celebrities endorse the label as the one they use, the best, or simply to impress the audience by wearing the branded sunglasses or dress. Manufacturers pay the music, movie or social media star to use their name and image on or with the brand. Pop music tours are sponsored by Pepsi or Coca-Cola; famous actors advocate brands in advertisements, sometimes with their signature at the end; popular bloggers and vloggers attract big earnings for brand endorsements; there are multimillion-dollar sponsorship deals with sports champions in order to associate the brand with the sport/the champion/ with winning.

Celebrity branding goes much further than paid endorsement. There are many cases now where the celebrity's agents initiate the celebrity brand. They hire the manufacturer to develop and supply the product, and then brand it with the celebrity and launch it onto the market themselves as their own perfume, lingerie collection, clothing, accessory range, cooking sauce etc. (see Brand it like Beckham).

Branding in movies and TV

Branding can take the more subtle form of 'product placement' within the scenes of cinema and TV programmes. Notable examples are Omega, BMW and Vodafone in James Bond movies; or Apple in *Jurassic Park* and *You've Got Mail*. The media can make an unknown brand famous. Manolo Blahnik shoes were incorporated in the TV series *Sex and the City* by the actor Sarah Jessica Parker, also the producer of the series, because they 'fitted' the character of Carrie whom she plays. Manolo Blahnik, a brand previously known only by a few, gained prominence and exposure. In one storyline, Carrie was mugged in a New York alley. After the robber took her wallet and jewellery, the next thing he demanded was her Blahnik high-heeled shoes.

Internet branding

The internet has given a new dimension to branding and more involvement for consumers with brands. Consumers are now only one click away from finding out more about brands and products, whether for further information about the company which produces them, shop locations, looking for job vacancies or even asking for samples. Likewise, companies have direct access to consumers or potential ones, a mine of information which companies can tap into to find out more about the people who buy their brands (see Moving Space). The internet has given a new form of life to the 'total brand experience' that marketers aspire to achieve.

For example, Ferrero (www.ferrero.it) has created a total immersion experience for children with its flagship product Kinder Surprise. In addition to the plastic figurine enclosed in the chocolate egg, children can also find a 'magicode' which gives them access to a unique, interactive game on the internet (www. magickinder.com). The games import characters from the collection series in season at the time. The site is heavily branded with the Kinder Surprise logo and pack shots. Children enter the Kinder world to play with Kinder characters while they munch through the Kinder Surprise chocolate egg, and when all is over they can play with their own Kinder figurine they animated on the internet.

The case of a virtual brand – Opodo

Unlike Kinder Surprise, which also has a physical entity, a number of totally virtual brands exist on the internet. We cannot drink them, eat them, visit their headquarters or offices to buy or make a booking – their existence depends entirely on the internet. An example is Opodo (www.opodo.com), a pan-European travel portal founded in the summer of 2001 by nine of Europe's leading airlines. The brand was developed by the brand consultants, Wolff Olins (www. wolffolins.com), while the online marketing was developed and created by the now-defunct Planetactive, Germany.

The original plan was for Opodo to support the launch of the portal with an aggressive offline advertising campaign, including TV, billboard and print advertising in Germany, scheduled for November 2001. Instead, they cancelled their offline advertising to minimize the risk of their investment and stuck to online marketing instead. The objectives of the online campaign were:

1 To launch the Opodo brand as an online travel portal
2 To increase the online ticket sales
3 To capture respondents' email addresses.

The campaign included banner advertising, microsites created especially for the campaign and online promotions, including a quiz, which had an hourly prize of a flight offered by one of the nine airlines. Participants in the quiz had the chance to increase their chances of winning by communicating the site to a friend. This viral marketing effect generated some 650,000 participants in the quiz in just eight weeks and around half of them registered for the Opodo newsletter, which again enabled more distribution of information. Within three months and for a budget of significantly less than €1 million, Opodo became the second most visited travel portal in Germany behind the national train company's official website. After the online launch and once a stable travel market post-9/11 was restored, Opodo launched an offline campaign.

The internet provides means for potential and actual customers to get involved in the branding of products that they identify with and consume. The Opodo online quiz is an early example of this involvement.

Brand it like Beckham: the case of celebrity as brand

Right from the beginning, I said I wanted to be more famous than Persil Automatic.
Victoria Beckham
(quoted in Beckham, 2003)

The American pop singer and actress Jennifer Lopez rebranded herself as J.Lo – undoubtedly a catchier version. J.Lo is now branding her own clothing collections for toddlers, girls and teens: J.Lo Toddlers, J.Lo Girls and J.Lo Lovelies, which are available for sale on her website. Glow by J.Lo is also a fragrance, which she describes as being very simple. On her website she uses three words to sum up the fragrance: 'fresh, sexy, clean . . . and it describes what I want for myself'. When asked in 2005 how the fragrance represents her, she said:

> It's very much about me, because it represents everything I've loved ever since I was very young – fresh, clean, simple, sensual things. Things like fresh air, the breeze coming in through the window, the ocean, summer sunshine. People might have expected a Jennifer Lopez fragrance to be more musky, more overtly sexy, but Glow is much more the real me, rather than the two-dimensional image you see on screen or in a magazine.
>
> (www.jenniferlopez.com)

So, according to her own story, Jennifer Lopez had interpreted herself in this fragrance. Here we apparently have a product with a soul, not an endorsement. She loves the perfume because she created it herself and it carries her very own name – the personality is the brand.

Celebrity branded products are not all about perfume and handbags. American actor Paul Newman launched his Newman's Own brand of salad dressings and spaghetti sauces in 1982. Its website (www.newmansown.com) claims that the brand reflects Newman's personal ambition to 'create nutritious, all-natural versions of his favourite foods'.

What these examples show is that famous people, as celebrities, have themselves become brands, extending their name to commodities of various and often of unrelated kinds. Their name adds brand recognition, image and glamour to the otherwise indistinguishable commodities (Agrawal & Kamakura, 1995; McCracken, 1989).

Although many celebrities like the Kardashians are 'famous for being famous', celebrity is not the same as fame. It is still possible to be famous in a localized way, such as in a village or a professional community. Evans and Wilson (1999) link the rise of the celebrity with the decline of 'real' heroes and the ascendancy of the media industry which spawns and sustains celebrities. What is remarkable about this phenomenon is the substitution of fantasy for reality. The real heroes of history are played by actors in the movie industry. Media reality substitutes for actual reality, fiction substitutes for fact, or interrelates with it as 'infotainment'. Our present-day versions of celebrity are media ones; at least two-thirds of those we consider famous are actors, musicians, presenters and entertainers in the media world.

Celebrity brands are graded, like other commodities, by quality and price and they are ranked like the celebrities are by hierarchy (A, B, C, D list) and share values. Unlike most other businesses, however, the celebrity industry is invisible, with no tangible products or services in the traditional sense, its manufacturing operations unclear, its backroom personnel anonymous, and its distributors in PR and the media remaining in the background. Only the brand itself is relentlessly drenched in the oxygen of publicity (Harbison, 2004).

Managing brands through consumer tribes

Consumer tribes are a relatively new concept that has wide marketing application in advertising, innovation and branding. As we noted in the section on the role of the consumer (see Consuming Experience), some tribes are *formed by consumers* themselves and these have genuine common interests and connections, shared passions and history and self-developed hierarchies. They exist independent of companies, products and brands. Such tribes are often conceived of as unmanageable, relatively autonomous consumer zones that elude and even resist organizational or managerial intervention and control (Cova & Dalli, 2007).

Celebrities are brands. They are defined by what people think about them, they have competitive positioning relative to other celebrities. Unlike the people behind them, celebrities exist in the minds of their audience precisely the same way that corporate or FMCG brands do.
Grannell & Jayarwardena, 2004

The identification and targeting of consumer tribes by companies has had a remarkable impact on marketing in youth and heavily branded consumer markets, like Ducati's consumer tribe 'The Ducasti', Red Bull's 'Energy Tribe', Apple's 'Creative Tribe', Nike's 'Running Tribe', 'Imaginative Tribe' and Wii's 'Playful Tribe'. These are examples of tribes that are specifically *manufactured by marketers*, with artificially created interests and passions, manipulated needs and desires. This type of tribe exists because of the brand, providing significant opportunities and advantages for the company.

By encouraging the creation of consumer tribes brand managers can, among other things, communicate directly with lead customers, foster brand loyalty and erect powerful barriers to exit (Goulding *et al.*, 2013).

Marketers' traditional segmentation methods segregate consumers into groups according to their differences and categories and label them accordingly. The deliberate creation of consumer tribes by marketers goes far beyond this, however, by proactively constructing, reinforcing and delineating consumers' collective group identities around a particular brand. This has become a popular strategy because traditional demographic or psychographic means of segmenting markets have become less useful because of lifestyle changes and the loosening of links between consumer behaviour and social class.

> *This [creating tribes] involves finding the brand's 'true believers' and getting them to spread the word, provide charismatic leadership, create tribal culture and most important, create a sense of tribal identity.*
> *Pankraz, 2009*

One alternative to traditional segmentation put forward for the electronic age is for marketers to focus on individual customers directly through CRM, digital or mobile technologies (see Creating Solutions); however, this omits the *key social influence* on consumer behaviour regarding branded products. Consumers' preference for a brand is not simply an individual activity – they like to compare, declare, show off and share their brand choice with others. No matter how smart the technology, the tracking or the contact points with the customer, individualized one-to-one marketing misses out the key aspect of consumers' social behaviour with brands which is evidenced through reference groups, peer confirmation, aspirational figures, conspicuous consumption and word of mouth (see Consuming Experience).

This is why consumer tribes have become a popular way of understanding brand behaviour, identifying target markets and assisting communication about brands with and *between* customers. Tribal marketing is most suited to consumer and service offerings where tribes can be built around the brand. The focus is not on the individual, it is on the communal or tribal and as such an alternative marketing approach for brands is needed. The framework shown in Figure 5.1 categorizes consumer tribes as four main types based on how they were formed and the extent of their members' commitment.

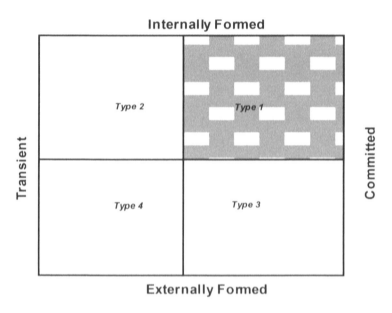

Figure 5.1 Four types of consumer tribes

Figure 5.1 shows four types of tribes grouped by two key features. First, consumer tribes can *be internally or externally created*. Those which are formed by members have genuine common interests and connections, shared passions and self-developed hierarchies. They exist independent of brands or companies. Tribal leadership is based on commitment, experience and place in the hierarchy.

Externally formed tribes are created by outside organizations, companies, brand managers, advertising agencies, whose motivation is usually commercial. The tribe exists because of the brand – they want to be different so marketers give them a story. They have externally stimulated identities and interests and their creators seek to manage members' activities and even their needs and desires. To become members, people have to be true believers in the brand and they have to be led and need 'charismatic' leaders.

Second, tribes can have long-lasting *commitment* or transient short-term affiliation. Tribes with the former are enduring, often linked closely to members' identity and have well-established hierarchies, rituals, rites of passage and codes of practice. Transient tribes are formed by members with shared passions but for whom tribes rarely dominate their everyday life.

People may be members of several transient tribes simultaneously and, since there is less commitment required of them, they are easier to join and leave. Transient tribes tend to take themselves less seriously and permit more playful behaviour by members and are also more receptive to innovation in brands.

The consumer tribe has become a powerful symbolic social phenomenon for consumers and a badge of identity that occurs across all brand categories. Marketers must accept the limitations of their ability to manage the actual use of their brands by consumer tribes. In reality the brands are not 'theirs' at all – they belong to their consumers, whether collectively in tribes or not. The existence of a self-empowered consumer tribe itself fosters brand loyalty, enables marketers to communicate directly with lead customers and erects barriers to exit through powerful forces of tribal identity.

The meanings of tribal symbols do not exist in isolation but are constructed within the tribal culture, negotiated and interpreted by individuals in that specific context. From a managerial perspective, the maintenance of consumer tribes requires that brand marketers connect and collaborate with members of a tribe by fully taking account of its socio-cultural characteristics. They must understand how the tribal community interacts with their brands – through communications, events, services, etc. – in order to facilitate learning experiences that generate and sustain the tribal community. This is uncomfortable for some businesses according to Cova and Dalli (2007) because it requires firms to relinquish part of their power to control the brand – it takes companies outside the market sphere and involves them in societal efforts. Being intimate with tribal enthusiasts requires firms to act more like 'voluntary organizations'.

Tribes are not easy to identify. They are fuzzy: more societal sparkles than socioeconomic certainty. They are shifting aggregations of emotionally bonded people, open systems to which a person belongs and yet doesn't quite belong. Their underlying logic is made up of shared experience, interpretations and representations.
Pierre Le Quéau, 1998 (quoted in Cova et al., 2007)

Tribes need a story, myth or narrative around which they can unite and it is the marketer's challenge to enable them to connect easily with each other. This involves finding the brand's 'true believers' and getting them to spread the word, provide charismatic leadership, create tribal culture and most important, create a sense of tribal identity.
Pankraz, 2009

FURTHER READING

Role of branding

de Chernatony, L. & Riley, F.D. (1998) Defining a brand: beyond the literature with experts' interpretations. *Journal of Marketing Management*, **14** (5), 417–443.

Edelman, D.C. (2010) Branding in the digital age. *Harvard Business Review*, **88** (12, December), 62–69.

Hatch, M. J. & Schultz, M. (2010) Toward a theory of brand co-creation with implications for brand governance. *Journal of Brand Management*, **17** (8), 590–604.

Keller, K. L. (2013) *Strategic Brand Management: Building, Measuring and Managing Brand Equity*. Pearson: London.

Brand building

Aaker, D. (1996) *Building Strong Brands*. Free Press: New York.

Berthon, P., Hulbert, J. & Pitt, F. (1999) Brand management prognostications. *Sloan Management Review*, **40** (2), 53–65.

de Chernatony, L. & McDonald, M. (1993) *Creating Powerful Brands*. Butterworth-Heinemann: Oxford.

Keller, K. L. (2002) Branding and brand equity. In: *Handbook of Marketing* (B. Weitz & R. Wensley, eds.). Sage: London, pp. 151–178.

Murray, W. (2000) *Brand Storm*. Prentice Hall/Financial Times: London.

Celebrity branding

Evans, A. & Wilson, G. (1999) *Fame: The Psychology of Stardom*. Bath Press: Bath.

Grannell, C. & Jayarwardena, R. (2004) Celebrity branding: not as glamorous as it looks. 19 January 2004, www.brandchannel.com

McCracken, G. (1989) Who is the celebrity endorser? Cultural foundations of the endorsement process. *Journal of Consumer Research*, **16**, 310–320.

corporate identity and branding

Cláudia Simões

Companies are not isolated. As we have seen earlier, they belong to external networks of suppliers, customers and other audiences (see Building Relations: A network perspective to business relationships). Companies have to 'introduce themselves' and their offers to customers and other stakeholders and they also have to deal with complex external environmental conditions. For example, the globalization of markets and the reach of social media can make it difficult to survive as business environments become more complex and demanding. Possible ways to handle these dynamics are through creating the sense of individuality of the organization and developing instruments, such as corporate brands, that will make them distinguishable among their audiences.

Organizations generally last longer than products, and the market perceptions of the business are usually more difficult for competitors to imitate than perceptions of a product brand. It is, for example, hard to emulate companies that are perceived as having the highest quality and best-qualified personnel or the most clearly defined and relevant mission. Stakeholders have been increasingly interested in interacting with companies as opposed to with the individual product brands. Managing the perceptions of an organization may, thus, provide an important basis for a more sustainable, long-term advantage. This section presents insights into the realm of corporate identity and its connection to corporate branding and brand management.

What is corporate identity?

To understand the notion of identity, try to answer the following questions. How do I define myself? What distinguishes me from other human beings? How do I want to be perceived by others? Your answers to these questions will be founded on a wide variety of dimensions, such as personality and character traits, personal history, cultural background, physical appearance, etc. The outcome is the portrait of a unique human being and nobody else will fit that exact description. Identity is what makes you distinct and different from others. Identity entails traits that allow one person or object to be distinguished from another.

The term *identity* has been referred to in various contexts. Expressions such as group identity, social identity, national identity, individual identity and corporate identity are frequently used in both scientific and non-scientific settings. If we transpose the concept of identity to organizations, we can say that identity may be seen as an abstract idea, suggesting that every organization has its own personality, uniqueness and character (Simões *et al.*, 2015). Corporate identity is *'what the organization "is"'* and *'seeks to be'* (Abratt & Kleyn, 2012: 1051). Generally, corporate identity is what distinguishes one company from another.

Insights from four core disciplines have contributed to the evolution and study of Corporate Identity: *graphic design, marketing, organizational* and *interdisciplinary* studies. The *graphic design* perspective encompasses all forms of visual identity presentation of the company, such as the management of corporate symbols (e.g. logos and signage) (Olins, 1991), and sensory dimensions (e.g. auditory and olfactory features) (Bartholmé & Melewar, 2011). The *marketing* studies build on brand management and integrated communications research (e.g. Kapferer, 2008; Kitchen *et al.*, 2008). The o*rganizational* studies analyse the concept of organizational identity and are mainly concerned with members' feelings towards their organization (Dutton *et al.*, 1994). Finally, a holistic perspective in *interdisciplinary* studies acknowledges the overlap in different areas of knowledge and advocates an eclectic view of corporate identity. Since identity is shaped according to what the company stands for, it articulates and is articulated in the business philosophy through the company's mission and values. It further entails the visual symbols that capture the company's essence.

Look, for example, at Nike, the sports footwear, apparel and equipment producer. The company partly grounds its identity on the company's experience in the sports-and-fitness business and its evolution as a global company. As a company known worldwide, Nike shapes its identity based on the core purpose and mission 'to bring inspiration and innovation to every athlete* in the world. *If you have a body, you are an athlete' (Nike, 2016). The asterisk emphasizes the company's interest in reaching each individual in the marketplace. Throughout its history Nike has been through ups and downs in public opinion and building a strong identity has been a powerful instrument to handle adverse times and create a unique position in the market. The company 'fosters a culture of invention. We create products, services and experiences for today's athlete while solving problems for the next generation' (Nike, 2016).

Identity is 'the characteristics, feelings or beliefs that distinguish people from others'.
Oxford Advanced Learner's Dictionary

Corporate identity is what helps an organization, or part of it, feel that it truly exists and that it is a coherent and unique being, with a history and a place of its own, different from others.
Kapferer, 1996

Perspectives on corporate identity

1 Graphic design/visual identity

The graphic design/visual identity perspective centres on the management of corporate symbols that transmit the strategic visual dimensions of corporate identity to internal and external audiences. It is concerned with all forms of visual presentation of the company that stakeholders come into contact with. Accordingly, a firm's identity is expressed through name, symbols, logos, colours and rites of passage, premises, packaging, stationary, vehicles (Olins, 1991, 2003). This perspective has expanded to include all sensory dimensions (e.g. auditory and olfactory features) into its constitution (Bartholmé & Melewar, 2011). You may have noticed that retailers often have a particular physical setting and layout/colours. Some also add a distinct scent to their stores. Have you ever been attracted to enter a store because you smelt a nice scent when walking down the street? The handmade cosmetics brand Lush has a strong scent in the stores to easily identify the brand and to attract customers to enter and experience the store's environment.

The visual identity perspective is strongly linked to practitioners' work on visual design systems. Although the field has evolved into a wider approach to the area of corporate identity, there are specialized consulting companies addressing corporate identity by essentially focusing on visual identity dimensions (e.g. logo design, business cards, visual identity manuals, website design, package design, etc.). See, for example, details about the offer from the agency Boundless Technologies on their website (http://boundlesstech.net).

2 Marketing: integrated communications and brand management

The desire for consistency in corporate communications has fuelled interest in integrated marketing communications. The integrated communications approach advocates that it is critical to consistently develop and manage the impressions that customers and other stakeholders hold of the organization. Integrated marketing communications entails 'the strategic coordination of all messages and media used by an organization to influence its perceived brand value' (Duncan and Everett, 1993: 33). Integrating communication strategies aligns, optimizes and creates synergies among the various forms of communication (e.g. advertising, public relations) (Kitchen et al., 2008).

There are agencies that devote part of their work to the development of integrated communication programmes for companies. It is worthwhile browsing some of the agencies' websites to get an idea about

the type of work that they develop and check samples of their output. As a starting point you may check the following agencies offering a full integrated communications service:

- *Saatchi and Saatchi – http://saatchi.co.uk/en-gb/work*
- *Havas – www.havas.com/work*
- *EMA – www.mower.com*

3 Organizational identity

The concept of organizational identity captures the internal aspects of identity, emphasizing the feelings of members towards their organization (Albert et al., 2000; Dutton et al., 1994). In creating identity, businesses internalize a cognitive structure of what the organization stands for and where it intends to go. A frequently used definition of organizational identity suggests it is what is central, enduring and distinctive about an organization (Albert & Whetten, 1985).

Employees' views/perceptions of the organization's identity and external image affect how they behave towards their institution. In general, organizational identification occurs when the images they receive are favourable, distinct and enduring (Dutton et al., 1994). Companies constantly try to enhance their employees' identification with the company and their sense of belonging. For example, when describing the company's culture, the internet software company Google states, 'It's really the people that make Google the kind of company it is' (Google, 2016).

4 Bringing it all together: the interdisciplinary perspective

Interdisciplinary studies support a holistic view based on multiple backgrounds, acknowledging an overlap in various areas of knowledge and advocating a more eclectic view of corporate identity (Riel & Balmer, 1997). The interdisciplinary view of corporate identity is visible in agencies assisting companies in the development of their corporate identity. For example, Wolff Olins, a corporate brand consultancy, undertakes a comprehensive approach to corporate identity. On the firm's website (www.wolffolins.com), you can read interesting case histories based on work developed about very diverse companies. This company develops work that entails dimensions such as design, communications and strategy.

A strong corporate identity may act as a facilitator in the establishment of a close relationship with stakeholders, encouraging identification. As a result, customer loyalty and goodwill among relevant stakeholders is more likely to occur. Ultimately, corporate identity underpins differentiation and enhances market

reputation and relationships. The linkages between brand and corporate identity are revealed when the branding concept is applied at the corporate level.

The corporate brand

When considering brands as hierarchical, the corporate or company brand represents the highest level in the ranking (Keller, 2013, 2014). According to Ind (1997), the corporate brand is 'more than just the outward manifestation of an organization, its name, logo, visual presentation. Rather it is the core of values that define it. The communication of those values is of course an important part of what an organization is.' Hence, corporate branding entails the way companies decide to differentiate and articulate the expression of their company. Ultimately the corporate brand involves the corporate expression, being part of the corporate identity, and is also related to market images and perceptions (Abratt & Kleyn, 2012).

Hence, the idea of identity may be considered when addressing brands. Aaker (1996: 68) defines brand identity as 'a *unique set of brand associations that the brand strategist aspires to create or maintain*'. The core component of this identity is the so-called '*essence*' of the brand – the values and beliefs underpinning it and with which it is associated. Identity also has a number of dimensions that complete and give texture to the brand, such as symbols, logos and brand design.

You may find examples of companies operating in very different industries that clearly present and articulate their corporate brands with an identity. In the travel industry, for instance, British Airways presents the corporate brand and its offers as a brand with history in the vanguard of 'innovation in aviation', committed to focusing on the customer experience (Superbrands, 2016). In the fashion accessories industry, the brand Parfois is presented as an 'ode to every woman' making affordable exceptional fashion accessories (Parfois, 2016).

Corporate identity enables organizations to differentiate themselves in their markets by developing their way of being through their mission, service features, symbols, corporate communications, etc. Each company's unique identity can be expressed via the corporate brand. Coca-Cola and PepsiCo try to differentiate their offer by establishing distinct brand features in their markets. As an exercise, you may try to identify the main traits that distinguish these two corporate brands operating in very similar markets. (Find more information on www.coca-cola.com and www.pepsico.com.)

The brand image

The notion of image reports the audiences' (e.g. customers, competitors, communities) overall perception of a brand – the *brand image* (Kapferer, 2008) – or the company – *corporate image*. The idea is that a strong corporate and brand identity assist image formulation.

Companies cultivate distinct images in order to be taken as unique by their markets and stakeholders. Benetton, the Italian clothing producer and retailer, created a global brand image based on the overall idea of overcoming cultural and racial barriers. Benetton's sometimes controversial advertising campaigns depicted people and accessories allusive to different racial, national, cultural, religious and political backgrounds (Mantle, 1999). According to the company website:

> Benetton Group is focused in the future. Its story is built on innovation and seeing where others fail to see. The Group has always been at the cutting edge . . . with a universal form of communication, which created both a phenomenon and cultural debate.
>
> (Benetton, 2016)

Log on to www.benetton.com and you will find examples of previous campaigns by the company.

Connecting identity and image

Stakeholders such as consumers are increasingly involved with brands, having an impact on the way managers develop and manage their brands and identities. This phenomenon has called for participative brand management models, taking into account the way external stakeholders experience the brand and how they connect with the internal stakeholders (employees) and the brand. The repercussion is that managers start developing networks with employees (internal stakeholders) and consumers/other stakeholders (external stakeholders) accounting for the different perspectives (Ind, 2014). Taking the idea that identity relates to the way managers define their brands and image the audience's overall perceptions, a participative (co-created) brand management approach increasingly intertwines identity and image.

Such dynamics bring a new logic to brand management and existence. Management may develop the core values of the brand, yet consumers continuously interpret and reshape those values (Kay, 2006). To capture such market

[Corporate image is] the consumer associations to the company or corporation making the product or providing the service.
Keller, 2013: 399

dynamics, the notion of brand identity has been revisited to entail consistency and dynamic connections to the market. As da Silveira *et al.* (2013: 33) explain:

> brand identity is a dynamic concept that originates among brand managers, and that further develops through mutually influencing inputs from managers and other social constituents (e.g. consumers); this development involves distinguishing, central, and enduring attributes, where enduring takes a dynamic meaning – core values maintain consistency over time while other dimensions vary, when needed, to adjust to the environmental context.

The involvement of stakeholders in brand management is visible in various companies' strategies, for example the toy company Lego. The company encourages consumers to be involved in the creation of their products. The Lego Ideas online community invites members to submit their own creations and/or vote for other members' creations. Successful ideas are then developed and sold by the company. The author makes the final approval of the product and earns a sales percentage. (You can find details about the process on https://ideas.lego.com/howitworks.)

Brands and consumers

Consumers want to simplify their decision process and brands aid the endeavour. In a complex world of numerous offers, brands reduce search costs, making the identification of the product easier. Brands reduce the time and effort consumers spend finding out about an array of alternative products to meet a particular need and further reduce the perception of risk, such as monetary, social and safety risks (Kapferer, 2008).

Sometimes confusion occurs as products and services are similar and individual brand names abundant. Increasingly organizations link their corporate brand name to individual products and/or make the company's name visible. The corporate brand conveys values and features that are consistent across the company's products. When considered at a corporate level, a strong corporate brand simplifies the consumer buying decision process as it differentiates and creates confidence in consumers' minds. For example, Boots, the UK-based manufacturer and retailer of consumer healthcare products, conveys an image of a reliable company with heritage but a modern feel. Consumers frequently buy products from the company's brand, relying on the trust they have in the company. (For further details on the company and its identity background, check www.boots-uk.com/about-boots-uk/company-information/boots-heritage/).

Kellogg's, the breakfast cereals manufacturer, noted how it was becoming harder for consumers to differentiate among competing brands. In 2000, Kellogg's launched an overall new design on its packages and since then you will have found that Kellogg's product packages have the company 'K' logo highlighted and/or the company name incorporated. The company's 2015/2016 corporate responsibility report said: 'Today's consumers want to know more about their food: where it comes from, who grows it and who makes it' (Kellogg's, 2016: 3). The branding means that consumers can easily see that Kellogg's is the company behind the individual brands.

The consumer connection

Connections between brands and markets go beyond functional aspects. Brands influence markets because the way consumers relate to brands affects their attitudes and behaviour. From a consumer point of view, Batra et al. (2012: 1) define brands as:

> the totality of perceptions and feelings that consumers have about any item identified by a brand name, including its identity (e.g. its packaging and logos), quality and performance, familiarity, trust, perceptions about the emotions and values the brand symbolizes, and user imagery.

Hence, the brand is more than a name given to a product; it embodies a whole set of physical and socio-psychological attributes and beliefs (see Creating Solutions).

What consumers own is often a reflection of the individual's identity (Belk, 1988). Consumption may entail symbolic idiosyncratic or shared meanings. In order to build and maintain their identity, consumers may use the symbolic meanings of consumer goods and brands. Brands may, therefore, play a role in the construction and expression of consumer identity. Consumption is increasingly grounded on the sharing of a symbolic identification (see Consuming Experience); brands may instil identification with the brand and its identity and/or involve emotional connections. In fact, we 'navigate our world using symbols and visual expressions that signal our personality and our values. And strong brands are one of the means by which we do this' (Fog et al., 2010: 20). Some consumers buy organic food because it conveys their healthy lifestyle and 'care for the environment and animal rights'.

Often consumers want to identify with product or service providers. They want to view a company as an entire entity and make sure that they identify with the company's values and that they trust their overall business approach and attitude. In the marketplace, there are numerous opportunities for consumers to make connections between organizations and particular products. For example, many consumers are concerned with environmental issues and companies often create environmentally friendly brands. The Body Shop, the cosmetic and retail company, conveys the core of the company via a mission statement which implies protecting the environment and balancing stakeholders' interests. The following three pillars express the company's identity: 'enrich our people', 'enrich our products' and 'enrich our planet' (Body Shop, 2016). (You can learn more about how the company articulates the link between company values and market if you log on to www.thebodyshop.com.)

Loyalty and brand love

In developing the connection with the brand, the marketing literature emphasizes building strong relationships between customers and brands. Relationship marketing suggests that businesses should be retaining customers and building loyalty (see Building Relations). Brand loyalty is 'a deeply held commitment to re-buy or re-patronize a preferred product or service consistently in the future, despite situational influences and marketing efforts having the potential to cause switching behaviour' (Oliver, 1997: 392).

Identity and image are relevant variables in the relationship between consumers and companies. Consumers' identification with a company's values and self-images are important determinants of the strength of their commitment to a particular brand (Pritchard et al., 1999). Eventually, customer brand responses lead to loyalty as the customer builds 'emotional' links with the company and the brand.

There are numerous examples of companies developing consumer loyalty programmes or schemes. Normally, these schemes establish a link between the corporate brand/company and customers. This leads to mutually beneficial and continuous relationships. For example, the airline company TAP Portugal developed the Victoria loyalty programme for frequent flyers. Members earn miles that can be exchanged for flights and may benefit from TAP's partnerships with hotels, car rental and other businesses. With this programme the link between the customer and the organization goes beyond the company's core service (TAP, 2016).

Loyal consumers may develop a strong emotional attachment to brands. When consumers feel strongly attached and connected to the brand they develop love and passion for the brand (Keller, 2013). The phenomenon of strong emotional bonds and attitudes between consumers and brands has been labelled 'brand love' (Batra et al., 2012). Practitioners use the term 'lovemarks', describing the fact that consumers may love brands 'beyond reason'. The following excerpt about lovemarks is from Saatchi and Saatchi (2016):

> Lovemarks transcend brands. They deliver beyond your expectations of great performance. Like great brands, they sit on top of high levels of respect – but there the similarities end. Lovemarks reach your heart as well as your mind, creating an intimate, emotional connection that you just can't live without. Ever. Take a brand away and people will find a replacement. Take a Lovemark away and people will protest its absence. Lovemarks are a relationship, not a mere transaction . . . Put simply, Lovemarks inspire: Loyalty Beyond Reason.

There have been attempts to specify the scope and components of brand love. Thomson et al. (2005) developed a scale measuring the emotional attachment to brands entailing the following three dimensions: affection, passion and connection. Batra et al. (2012: 12–13) propose a conceptualization for brand love entailing seven elements:

> (1) passion-driven behaviors reflecting strong desires to use it, to invest resources into it, and a history of having done so; (2) self–brand integration, including a brand's ability to express consumers' actual and desired identities, its ability to connect to life's deeper meanings and provide intrinsic rewards, and frequent thoughts about it; (3) positive emotional connection that is broader than just positive feelings, including a sense of positive attachment and having an intuitive feeling of 'rightness'; (4) anticipated separation distress if the brand were to go away; (5) long-term relationship, which includes predicting extensive future use and a long-term commitment to it; (6) positive attitude valence; and (7) attitudes held with high certainty and confidence.

Possessions that consumers 'love' have a role in constructing or expressing the individual's identity (Ahuvia, 2005; Belk, 2008, 2013). Table 5.1 shows examples of how consumers refer to brands they love. You may see the personal, passionate and emotional words consumers use to describe their loved brands. Loved brands may include products, services, TV shows, people, etc.

Table 5.1 Expressions of brand love

Brand	Consumers' expressions
Guinness (Beer)	• 'Love at first sight. I enjoy being able to use all my senses in a delightful way every time I have a Guinness in my hand.' • 'Guinness beer has always been the main choice in our family for generations at family gatherings or celebrations. I think it is a very sensational taste of beer. Guinness beer is always in the hearts of my family members.' *Source*: www.lovemarks.com/ lovemark/guinness/
Moleskine (Family of notebooks, diaries, etc.)	• 'A creative person's best friend, for a quick sketch or a note. A really handy lovemark.' • 'The perfect combination of form and function. A convenient little packet to capture your thoughts and imagination. I love these notebooks for creating art and keeping my life on track. Moleskines are awesome.' *Source*: www.lovemarks.com/ lovemark/moleskine/
Friends (award-winning television series originally broadcast from 1994–2004)	• 'I literally can't imagine living without watching this series. They make me forget about all things that make me blue. *Friends* is the first thing that comes into my mind whenever I want to have a laugh.' • 'I really love this show. Every episode triggers beautiful memories and never fails to make me smile. I have never missed a single episode and have been watching it over and over again for the past 10 years. This is the greatest TV show ever made.' *Source*: www.lovemarks.com/ lovemark/friends/

Brand communities – the corporate view

Brand communities emerge when consumers who share the admiration for a brand socially interact with each other in physical or digital contexts (see Consuming Experience) These are similar to consumer tribes discussed earlier but one difference is that relationships in brand communities have been extended beyond the customer–brand–customer triad to encompass relationships between the customer and their branded possessions, marketing agents, brand organization managers and owners (McAlexander *et al.*, 2002)

Companies can benefit from brand communities in terms of consumer engagement and impact on the brand's equity as they affect, for instance, consumers' loyalty and lead to enthusiastic brand recommendations. Communities are also a relevant source of ideas (see the earlier example from Lego) and in establishing relevant consumer emotional connections (Brodie *et al.*, 2013). In contexts where co-creation is encouraged, brand communities may be a source of consumer involvement and participation in the brand development. Throughout time, consumers develop trust and commitment towards the community and tend to participate more in the issues related to the brand (Ind *et al.*, 2013).

The stronger the brand identity, the more likely these communities are to develop. There are many examples of online and offline brand communities for products from chocolate bars (e.g. Cadbury's) to computers (e.g. Apple). Companies often offer the platform or moderate the interactions of such groups. It is important that when building a community, companies understand the social and individual needs of members. The company should be guided by the community as opposed to trying to control it (Fournier & Lee, 2009). For example, Harley-Davidson, the motorcycle company, developed a strong identity based on the company's charisma and overall style. Harley-Davidson is a legend. If you log onto Harley-Davidson's website you will find a link to Harley Owners Group (HOG). The idea is clear: 'An inside pass to the ride of your life.' Here you can get information about all Harley-Davidson's communities around the world, events and social gatherings, etc. As the group states, 'Nothing is stronger than the bond of two wheels' (HOG, 2016).

Challenges in brand dynamics

Although the pervasive role of brands in markets is unquestionable, the way markets evolve brings challenges to both companies and consumers. In particular, technology and the digitalization of markets have implications for consumer behaviour (Belk, 2013) and for companies' strategies. In a world where customers are technology savvy and information is widely available through expanding social and mobile technologies, managing relationships between consumers

and brands demands new business approaches. For example, it is important to facilitate the decision process through simpler and personalized paths. The hair-care brand Herbal Essences' website is organized to allow the consumer to easily select the product based on hair type, and then further selection options appear based on the consumer's desired result (Spenner & Freeman, 2012).

Social media brings together communities that are geographically dispersed. Such global connections allow individuals from all over the world to increasingly collaborate with each other, having a cultural influence in the way brands are used and practiced. Holt (2016: 43) labels these communities as 'crowdcultures' that 'come in two flavours: subcultures, which incubate new ideologies and practices, and art worlds, which break new ground in entertainment.' There are communities to virtually every product/brand. Such subcultures have participants interacting through digital, physical and traditional media. Members share and 'discuss' new ideas. The art worlds bring together entrepreneurs that exchange ideas and compete in producing new hits.

This context brings new forms of brand exposure and practice that go beyond the traditional brand sponsorship and branded content. For example, PewDiePie, a video games commentator, has a YouTube channel with a global reach. It all started with a subculture around videogames where participants commented and shared their views. This subculture was transposed to social media. PewDiePie (and others) improvised on this idea and made it a comedy. Some of them are now global stars driven by the crowdculture. These new and emerging crowdculture dynamics need to be accounted for in brand development and management (Holt, 2016).

Key points

- *Corporate identity emerges from a company's capacity to understand and manage internal and external reality, its history and decisions, and its overall business attitude.*
- *The expression of an identity is dynamic and identity itself may evolve over time.*
- *Consumers are increasingly involved in brand development, intertwining identity and image.*
- *Emotions are a relevant factor to consider when addressing the way consumers relate with brands.*

FURTHER READING

Albert, N., Merunka, D. & Valette-Florence, P. (2008) When consumers love their brands: exploring the concept and its dimensions. *Journal of Business Research*, **61** (2008), 1062–1075.

Brakus, J.J., Schmitt, B. & Zarantonello, L. (2014) The current state and future of brand experience. *Journal of Brand Management*, **21**, 727–733.

Hewett, K., Rand, W., Rust, R. & van Heerde, H. (2016) Brand buzz in the echoverse. *Journal of Marketing*, **80** (3), 1–24.

Kähr, A., Nyffenegger, B., Krohmer, H. & Hoyer, W. (2016) When hostile consumers wreak havoc on your brand: the phenomenon of consumer brand sabotage. *Journal of Marketing*, **80** (3), 25–41.

Kim, Y. & Slotegraaf, R. (2016) Brand-embedded interaction: a dynamic and personalized interaction for co-creation. *Marketing Letters*, **27** (1), 183–193.

Langner, T., Bruns, D., Fischer, A. & Rossiter, J. (2016) Falling in love with brands: a dynamic analysis of the trajectories of brand love. *Marketing Letters*, **27** (1), 15–26.

Liu, Y. & Lopez, R. (2016) The impact of social media conversations on consumer brand choices. *Marketing Letters*, **27** (1), 1–13.

Park, C., MacInnis, D., Priester, J., Eisingerich, A. & Iacobucci, D. (2010) Brand attachment and brand attitude strength: conceptual and empirical differentiation of two critical brand equity drivers. *Journal of Marketing*, **74**, 1–17.

Fast Fashion branding – from Prada to Primark

Christopher Moore

When in December 2001 the luxury Italian fashion brand Prada opened a new store on the site of a former Guggenheim museum on Broadway in New York, the stakes for fashion marketing were raised to a new level. Various press reports suggested that this store cost between $30 and $140 million. None of these figures have been verified but it is safe to assume that this store did not come cheap. With the blend of the very latest in technology, the use of luxury materials and the creation of computer-managed changing rooms, the brand's owners were making a statement to the world about what Prada stood for and what Prada's customers believed in. The merchandise is presented on hanging cages that glide on ceiling tracks. At the flick of a switch, the products can be transported away and the area can then be used as a performance, exhibition or meeting space.

It is an interesting juxtaposition that the new store of one of the world's leading brands should be a former Guggenheim museum. For just as the former use of the space was based upon experience and engagement, the architect for the Prada Guggenheim, Rem Koolhaas, explained that Prada's use of the space is likewise to deliver an experience; this time, an experience of luxury that is derived from the products and their presentation, the staff, the store environment. Consequently, the Prada Guggenheim is a new take on the museum experience – only this time, if you have the dollars, you can take the artefacts home with you.

> *To discover more about Rem Koolhaas and the ideas surrounding the Prada Guggenheim in New York, see* Harvard Design School Guide to Shopping *by Chung et al. (2001a).*

The notion of 'fashion experience' is now a defining feature of fashion branding. For many companies, creating the correct atmosphere, the right feeling in the store, matters as much as the products themselves. More on *fashion experiences* later in this section.

Prada is one of the world's most successful fashion brands. The brand is important to fashion marketers – it is what they create, manage, nurture, love, protect and what makes them huge amounts of money. The importance of the brand to fashion marketing was brought home to me whenever I was commissioned to undertake research for a Japanese luxury fashion brand. When talking to young men, having the right brand was crucial to them since they believed it radically improved their chance of having sex with the person of their choice. Even for children, brands are enormously important. Having the right brand means that you can be part of the group, you are accepted – indeed, having the wrong brand is worse than having no brand at all. In the boardroom, for company directors, having the right brand matters, too, because it serves as a sign of success. Given the importance of fashion brands to the whole fashion marketing effort, further consideration will also be given to the *process of creating a fashion brand* – with a little help from an interview with two fashion marketing gurus.

According to the eminent fashion historian Colin McDowell, Ralph Lauren is the very master of fashion marketing and, after a visit to his flagship store,[1] the Rhinelander Building on Madison Avenue in New York, it is easy to see why Lauren is deserving of this title. The store does not have the feel of a store. With the clever use of furniture, paintings and other artefacts, it has the feel of an English baronial mansion. The success of the Ralph Lauren store on Madison Avenue is evidenced by McDowell (2003), who noted that in its first year, the store attracted an average of 15,000 visitors each day and exceeded first-year forecasts with sales of more than $30 million.

> *For more details about the origins of the Ralph Lauren marketing phenomenon, read Colin McDowell's (2003) account of Lauren the man, the vision and the style. See Further reading for details.*

However, what is especially interesting about Lauren's store in Madison Avenue is that it sells more than just fashion. The Polo Ralph Lauren label now extends to underwear, perfumes and cosmetics, candles and home fragrance, cutlery and crockery, bed linen, and even wallpaper and paint. It would seem that there is no product category that is not eligible for the Ralph Lauren treatment. As such,

---

[1] A flagship store is a major outlet, normally located in a capital city, which retails a fashion brand's full merchandise range. These stores typically enjoy significant financial investment in areas such as store design and fixtures and fittings.

Ralph Lauren could arguably be described as one of the world's most successful fashion lifestyle brands. Given the importance of *lifestyle brand extension* to fashion marketing, this area will also be considered later in this section.

These three dimensions of fashion experience, fashion branding and lifestyle brand extension are arguably the defining features of fashion marketing. There is also one other dimension that serves to define fashion marketing and that relates to the *speed* of fashion marketing.

Fast fashion is a term that is now commonly used to describe fashion marketing. Fast fashion refers to the timescale that exists between the emergence of a new fashion trend and the time it takes for a company to respond to that trend by having the product available in the market for sale. Fashion retailers, such as Top Shop and Zara, have invested heavily in manufacturing, information technology and distribution systems which enable them to respond to new fashion trends within a seven- to ten-day period. A commitment to fast fashion puts considerable strain on an organization. It requires that they are totally up to date with consumer trends and developments as these emerge, and that they be fully prepared to respond to these developments with new product ranges in advance of their competition. As a result of the shift towards fast fashion, the product life cycle of fashion products has declined considerably. Within the UK, the average life cycle for a product range is approximately eight weeks, while for those leaders of fast fashion, such as Top Shop and Zara, the life cycle span has decreased to around three weeks.

It is the sheer speed of change within the fashion sector that distinguishes fashion marketing from the marketing of products and services in other sectors. It is difficult to imagine any other situation where as many as 500 products are launched onto the market at any one time, only to be superseded by 500 others within a period of less than two months.

Product life cycle (PLC) *refers to the time period from when a product is initially introduced into the market to when it is withdrawn because of a lack of customer demand (see Creating Solutions). Fast fashion shrinks the time that elapses between the launch of a product and its withdrawal from the market. In other words, the faster the 'time to market', the shorter the PLC.*

The difference between clothing and fashion

As a preliminary to any review of the nature of fashion marketing, it is important to first distinguish between *fashion* and *clothing*. Clothing is, by its essential nature, functional. Clothing is boring and dull because clothing is about utility. It is the generic term for those garments that provide us with warmth, modesty and tedium. Clothing is above all about function, performance and visits to the laundry.

Fashion is about something else; it is something other and something greater. Fashion is about escape – an escape from who we really are to who we aspire to be. Fashion is transient. The least fashionable thing in the world today was the most fashionable thing in the world yesterday. Fashion is about meaning and symbol; it deals with representation and also sensation. Clothing is of the mind; fashion is of the heart. OK – that distinction is clear. Clothing is rational, while fashion is emotional.

So if clothing is concerned with function, then fashion is concerned with symbols and belonging and self-esteem. This distinction has important implications for the marketing of fashion since it must by necessity be concerned above all with generating images, signs and meanings (see Consuming Experience).

Psychologists tell us that our 'need' for fashion arises from a primary desire to construct, augment and communicate our self-image. We use fashion as a language to invent a personal image. Different fashion identities afford us the opportunity to possess a portfolio of many self-identities, each of which is relevant to the context in which we find ourselves.

Sociologists also recognize the importance of fashion within society. Fashion acts as a form of 'social glue'. It communicates group identity and membership; it contributes to group cohesion. In addition to defining group membership, fashion simultaneously denotes social group distance, distinctions and difference (see Consuming Experience). See also Horn & Gurel (1981) for a seminal review of the meaning and function of fashion in society.

The brand serves as the mechanism that transforms clothing into fashion. The next section will consider how fashion brands are created. The process of brand creation is discussed in the following excerpt in the form of a light-hearted interview with two Paris-based fashion marketing aficionados, Lulu and Fabian.

Interview transcript: creating the fashion brand

Interviewer: Lulu – I love the brand Fendi. Can you tell me what makes Fendi Fendi?

Lulu: It is a recipe. It is a formula. Each brand is different and it requires a different set of ingredients. But the process is the same every time. It begins the same way. You think of a way of living, a lifestyle, a view of the world that you want your brand to represent. Define the features of that world view – whether it is Burberry, which is essentially English, or The Gap, which is the American dream. Define the values of the lifestyle and isolate these. You make a list. You now have the values that your brand will represent.

Fabian: Fashion brands that fail are the ones that do not mean anything. You say the name and nothing happens, nothing springs to mind, nothing falls out from it. That is a brand failure; a brand in need of therapy.

Lulu: With my list of brand values, I now think of how I can get a link between my brand and these values. I have to make sure that when people see my brand they automatically think about certain attitudes; a certain way of life; a certain view of the world. They think of these values.

Fabian: He is right you know. I start off by insisting that the garments represent the values of the brand. It cannot be that the brand image is about luxury and the collection is not about luxury fabrics, good design, wonderful craftsmanship. Gorgeous. Gorgeous. Gorgeous.

Lulu: Next, we must communicate. *Advertising* is important for fashion. People are lazy sometimes. They need to be shown that this brand means these things. An advertisement for Hermes will be constructed differently from one for PUMA. Hermes will have references to luxury, serenity, elegance, tradition, craftsmanship, France. PUMA's references will be urban, the mood will be modern, technical, energetic. Not only will the advertisements differ, but where these appear will also differ. So I would expect to see Hermes in *Vogue*, but perhaps to see PUMA in *GQ* – because it is essentially still a male brand.

Fabian: Advertisements are not the only communication method. Fashion brands also get their message across through *public relations and media management*. It is as important for a brand to be mentioned in the editorial of the fashion and lifestyle magazines and to get press coverage in the right newspapers. If I can get the editor of *Vogue* or *Tatler* to even mention us, then we see the benefit immediately. Expert endorsement is very important and it is something that the most successful fashion brands court. In fact, there is a growing consensus of opinion that editorial coverage is more effective than advertisements, particularly among younger people. They are sceptical when it comes to advertising. They do not always believe the message or subscribe to the hype. Instead, they value the views of their experts. If one of these magazines says the brand is cool, that is much more effective than any number of advertisements. Who would accept our advertisements if we declared that we were cool? No brand is born cool. Coolness is thrust upon it.

> *Media management involves the development of relationships between the brand and those individuals from the world of television, magazines and newspapers who are felt to influence public opinion.*

Lulu: For those brands with money to spend, then *events sponsorship*, like tennis matches or awards ceremonies, is a powerful way of creating an association between the brand and a particular lifestyle. Brands are built upon connections and associations. Sponsoring the right event puts the brand in view of the customer. Many fashion marketers believe that people are more likely to remember a brand's sponsorship of an event that they are interested in than they would an advertisement. The problem with an advertisement is that it often comes at the wrong time. The person's mind may be on something else. They may be in a bad mood; they may be sleepy. They do not notice your great advertisement that cost millions to think up.

But, if you are associated with an event that was enjoyable and memorable, then there is the chance that the person will remember the brand's association with the event. Better still, the positive feelings that they had about the event may transfer to the brand.

> *Event sponsorship typically involves the provision of some form of financial support or gifts in kind (such as champagne at a reception) in exchange for publicity that recognizes the company's sponsorship of the event. Event sponsorship is used when a brand seeks to establish in the minds of consumers a relationship between a particular activity or event and their product. For example, leading sportswear brands compete to be able to sponsor important events such as the World Cup.*

Fabian: There is no better example of connection building than the whole process of *celebrity endorsement*. When Givenchy dressed Audrey Hepburn he was associating himself with someone famous, glamorous and beautiful. He made Audrey Hepburn even more beautiful and she made him known throughout the world.

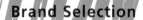

> *For more on the role of celebrities, see the section earlier in this chapter on* Celebrity branding.

Lulu: Whether it is Elizabeth Hurley and the Versace dress, Victoria Beckham wearing Gucci or Madonna wearing Camper shoes, the process is the same. By wearing the brand, the celebrity becomes the face of the brand. They become the personification of the values, attitudes and the lifestyle associations of the brand. The celebrity can bring glamour to the brand and sometimes the brand can bring benefits to the celebrity. We all know that the Versace safety-pin dress gave Elizabeth Hurley more media coverage than her acting success had up to that point.

Fabian: Yes, yes that is all true. But equally as important to the fashion brand is *location, location, location.* The great fashion houses of the world make sure that they are represented in all of the great world centres: London, Tokyo, New York, Milan and, of course, Paris. And not only do they locate in these important locations, they also locate in the most prestigious shopping districts: Bond Street in London or Fifth Avenue in New York. These locations all add to the allure, the prestige, the overall standing of the brand both locally and globally.

> *The 'New York, London, Paris syndrome' was coined by Hollander (1970), who recognized that a retail presence within these world centres was a crucial ingredient in the development of a prestigious, luxury brand identity.*

Distribution decisions have a huge impact upon how a brand is perceived by consumers. For example, if I want to generate and maintain an allure of exclusivity for a brand, I must limit its distribution. I must make sure that it is not over-exposed, make it difficult to find. I make sure that the retailers who stock our brand have similar values to us and attract a similar target customer segment. They must enjoy a positive reputation in the market. If the stockists are wrong, then they will undermine the integrity and standing of the brand. It is for this reason that the owners of prestigious fashion brands carefully manage and control their distribution channels.

You know, one of the greatest threats to fashion brands is not so much the actions of the competition, but the dangers of the grey market and parallel distribution.

> *The* grey market *and* parallel distribution *refer to the unauthorized distribution of fashion brands to unauthorized dealers. The stock is made available as a result of unauthorized over-production by manufacturers; the availability of excess stock as a result of poor sales performance; or as a result of the actions of unscrupulous but authorized agents, distributors or stockists who sell the stock on to unauthorized dealers.*

Our French fashion brands are masters of brand control. How often do you see Chanel in your local discount store or market? Never. We French realize that in order to protect the brand you must protect who gets their hands on the brand. The American brands are the worst for it. The Americans source their ranges from every corner of the globe. They manufacture under complex licensing agreements. None of them actually make anything for themselves. This makes it impossible for the American brands to control where their brand ends up. When it ends up in the local discount store, it does not do much for the standing of the brand. From a customer's perspective, why risk buying a brand at full price when everyone will think that you were smart and paid a third of the price in the local discounter.

Lulu: Yes, I agree that location and distribution management are important. But I say this to you – *experience, experience, experience.* Fashion is about sensation, memories, feeling better about yourself, feeling better about the world. Branding in fashion is as much about branding the experience as it is branding the product. Branding the experience is when the experience of acquiring the brand is managed so that it matches and reflects the values of the brand. The experience of the brand is where all of the attributes of the brand are brought together and are brought to life. It is about living the brand and experiencing the brand.

The capital investment that many fashion brands make in their stores is significant. This investment underlines the importance of the experiential dimension of fashion branding. In some cases, the experience matters almost as much as the product. It is the added value element. It is the factor that justifies the price premium that successful fashion brands can generate.

Interviewer: What are the signs of a successful fashion brand, then?

Fabian: One that has consistent demand, that can consistently attract a premium price. One that celebrities want to wear and the fashion press want to write about. It does not have to continually reinvent, redefine itself. It knows what it stands for and remains true to its values. Of course, it updates itself with new images, new products and new ideas. But it is also sufficiently different from its competition. It is not a me-too, look-alike brand.

Lulu: Yes, it is all of these elements. But a successful fashion brand is one that can credibly be extended into new product areas – but without, at any time, undermining the integrity of the brand and its values. It moves into new product areas but without the customer thinking: 'This is stupid. This is exploitation.' Yes, a strong brand is one that can be extended into other product areas.

Fabian: The brand is really what fashion marketing is all about. But we must go now and lie in a darkened room. We are exhausted with all this explaining, explaining. You are too cruel to us, you know.

End of interview

Creating a fashion brand experience

As was noted in the interview with Lulu and Fabian, a crucial dimension of the process of building a powerful fashion brand is through the creation of a brand experience in store that both augments and enhances the core values of the brand. The recognition of the contribution of positive brand environments to competitive advantages is not confined to luxury fashion brands. In the early 1980s George Davies, the founder of the British fashion chain Next, developed a store brand formula which he replicated in all of the Next stores. The Next brand experience sought to generate an up-market boutique feel within the British high street through the use of expensive, bright and attractive store fittings. Next invested in state-of-the-art lighting and their changing rooms were larger and more comfortable than those of their competitors.

A number of studies have shown how the design of a store can enhance the mood of the consumer and alter their perception of a brand.

Peter McGoldrick's chapter on 'the selling environment' in Retail Marketing *(see Further reading) provides some interesting insights into how brand atmospherics can influence customer behaviour in store.*

There are a variety of ways in which a brand experience can be generated. The store branding process begins before the customer even comes into the store. The very street, the part of town in which the store is located, says something about the brand and what it stands for in the market.

The Comme des Garcons shop in Paris is located in a very prestigious shopping district but it is positioned off-centre and is quite difficult to find. The store exterior is discreet and, to the uninitiated, it does not initially look like a fashion store. These features reflect the characteristics of the Comme des Garcons brand positioning. It is brand that is subtle, that in fashion terms is likewise positioned off-centre. Only those 'in the fashion know' would recognize the brand from these very discreet cues. It is for the discerning consumer. The placement and the entrance into the store clearly evoke and define these core brand values. Even the signage for the store is discreetly positioned on a side wall. This is not a brand that wants to scream about itself. Everything is carefully managed, carefully executed, even down to the colour of the signage which is in the classic red and white signature colours of the Comme des Garcons brand.

Comme des Garcons, Paris

Not all stores adopt the understatement of the Comme des Garcons store in Paris. For their flagship store in New York's Soho district, the Italian fashion brand Max Mara has adopted a radical store exterior that is architecturally stimulating and which draws the attention of the passer-by to the brand. Through the mixed use of traditional materials, such as solid wood, with the latest in window and lighting technology, the new store serves as a potent emblem of the defining elements of the Max Mara brand.

The store windows also serve as an important device for communicating the values of the brand to prospective customers. The primary purpose of a fashion retailer's store windows is to generate brand awareness and interest. High street fashion retailers, such as USC, adopt large-scale graphics for their store window presentations and integrate these with products in order to communicate the latest fashion trends to passing consumers. It is interesting to note that male consumers, in particular, use window displays for guidance when they select their fashion products. Often, the sales of particular styles rise dramatically as a result of their inclusion within a window display.

The development of an in-store brand identity is dependent upon the integration of visual images, fixtures and fittings, and the careful arrangement of merchandise. These elements serve as visual cues that communicate the attitudes and values of the brand to prospective customers. The findings of many empirical research studies indicate that these visual dimensions can serve to change the mood of the customer and may even alter how they engage with the brand.

In contrast, the presentation of men's jeanswear labels, such as Diesel, relies on more masculine colours and the merchandise is presented in a more straightforward manner – evidently in order not to confuse or confound men who may be reluctant shoppers!

Diesel display

Alternatively, some brands deliberately upturn traditional approaches to merchandising and display as a means of communicating their idiosyncratic brand identity. For example, the cult Spanish footwear brand, Camper of Spain, defy the age-old superstition of not putting new shoes on a table by doing just that as a method of merchandise presentation. Within their London store, shoes are attached with Velcro to the wall. Customers pull down their choice of shoe from the walls to try on and return them to the wall once they have made their mind up.

All these various activities of fashion marketers attempt to generate and develop a distinctive identity for their brands. These various activities invariably require significant capital investment and this expenditure is justified on the basis that it serves to enrich and enhance the brand-purchasing experience. The development of a credible and attractive brand image may also allow the company to charge a premium price for their products. The creation of an interesting brand shopping experience contributes significantly to the development of a premium brand image.

Camper display

Lifestyle brand extension

As was indicated earlier, brands such as Ralph Lauren have evolved to become more than just a label on a set of garments. Instead, they now operate as lifestyle brands. A lifestyle brand is typically associated with a particular way of life. For example, the Ralph Lauren lifestyle is ostensibly an American interpretation of the life of an English aristocrat. The images that are used in Ralph Lauren advertisements and the merchandising props that are used in his flagship stores all evoke the lifestyle of the English gentleman and gentlewoman. Ralph Lauren's deliberate association with this very specific lifestyle has provided a platform for the company to extend its participation into other product sectors that are also associated with this lifestyle. Ralph Lauren-branded products now extend into areas such as soft furnishings, crockery, wallpapers and paints, and bathroom accessories, which helps their customers live their dreams. That is what makes Ralph Lauren a lifestyle brand.

The products that Ralph Lauren offers as part of its branded lifestyle are manufactured under licence agreements by specialist suppliers. This strategy has enabled Ralph Lauren to rapidly extend the breadth of its product range without the risk and costs associated with producing products outside its area of immediate expertise.

> A licence agreement *is when a brand owner delegates the responsibility for designing, manufacturing and distributing a branded product range to a specialist supplier. The third party must pay an initial fee in order to obtain the brand licence, as well as an annual fee and a percentage of sales as a royalty. In return, they enjoy the benefits of selling a range that is supported by a brand with international appeal.*

It should be noted, however, that licence agreements do not always provide fashion retailers with a range of positive benefits. While it may be difficult to believe now that the ultra-hip Gucci brand was ever associated with anything other than equally ultra-hip products, in the 1970s and 1980s the company entered into a number of licence agreements that saw the Gucci name emblazoned on mass-market products, such as disposable cigarette lighters. This strategy undermined the luxury brand positioning of Gucci and contributed to their fall from grace in the early 1990s. A key element of the turnaround strategy masterminded by Tom Ford, then Gucci's design director, now turned movie director, was to cancel scores of these inappropriate licence agreements. While recognizing that licence agreements are an important source of revenue, Ford also recognized that these extensions can tarnish the brand's reputation and therefore must be tightly controlled. A brand can never be viewed as a luxury brand when it is available on a cigarette lighter in every tobacconist shop in sight.

Not only do fashion companies extend the breath of products that they market under their brand name, many extend the number of brands that they operate. This activity is usually called brand diffusion (see The role of branding).

> Brand diffusion *is when a company develops other brands in order to target specific customer groups. These brands are typically targeted towards younger customers and they are generally less expensive than the main brand.*

Successful brand diffusion is built upon the strength of the reputation of the original brand. For example, the reputation enjoyed by the Giorgio Armani brand served as the basis for the development of a range of Armani diffusion brands.

Armani diffusion brands

- Emporio Armani – *an upper mid-priced, ready-to-wear range of tailoring and casualwear targeted towards men and women aged between 18 and 45 years. Sold in Emporio Armani stand-alone stores across the world.*
- Armani Exchange – *a lower mid-priced range of casualwear. Targeted towards a younger customer group. Sold in stand-alone stores, principally in the Far East.*
- Armani Jeans – *a premium-priced jeanswear and casualwear brand. Sold in stand-alone stores, department stores and independent stores.*
- Armani Perfumes – *fragrance manufactured under licence and sold in perfumeries and department stores the world over.*

Diffusion brands provide for brand democracy in that they allow a wider range of customers to access the brand. Brand diffusion is a lucrative strategy for many fashion firms, and for most firms these diffusion brands provide the highest profit contribution by virtue of the fact that these tend to generate higher net margins and higher sales levels.

As a word of caution, it is important to note that brand diffusion can undermine the standing of the brand by virtue of its over-availability. Some American fashion brands have been criticized for over-extending their brand diffusion strategies. This has often meant that the availability of the brand has exceeded demand. As a result, much of the stock for these diffusion brands has ended up being reduced and sold in discount stores.

Summary

While fashion may appear to some people to be frivolous, the marketing that supports the fashion system is, in reality, very sophisticated. This section has examined some of the key dimensions of fashion marketing activity. In particular, consideration was given to the processes that support fashion brand development and the dimensions that contribute to the creation of a fashion brand experience. The democratization of luxury fashion brands has been a defining point of the past generation and this has been achieved through the development of lifestyle marketing and the creation of diffusion fashion brands.

FURTHER READING

Chung, C. J., Inaba, J. & Koolhaas, R. (2001) *Harvard Design School Guide to Shopping*. Taschen: New York.

Fernie, J., Hallsworth, A., Moore, C. & Lawrie, A. (1997) The place of high fashion retailing. *Journal of Product and Brand Management*, **6** (3), 151–163.

Goworek H. & McGoldrick, P. (2015) *Retail Marketing Management: Principles and Practice*. Pearson: London.

Hines, T. & Bruce, M. (2007) 2nd Edn *Fashion Marketing: Contemporary Issues*. Butterworth-Heinemann: Oxford.

McDowell, C. (2003) *Ralph Lauren: The Man, The Vision, The Style*. Cassell Illustrated: London.

Moore, C.M. (1998) *L'internationalisation du Pret a Porter*: the case of Kookai and Morgan's entry into the UK fashion market. *Journal of Fashion Marketing and Management*, **2** (2), 153–159.

Moore, C., Fernie, J. & Burt, S. (2000) Brands without boundaries: the internationalisation of the designer retailer's brand. *European Journal of Marketing*, **34** (8), 919–938.

References

Aaker, D. (1996) *Building Strong Brands*. Free Press: New York.

Aaker, D. (1997) Should you take your brand to where the action is? *Harvard Business Review*, **75** (5, September/October), 135–139.

Abratt, R. & Kleyn, N. (2012) Corporate identity, corporate branding and corporate reputations, reconciliation and integration. *European Journal of Marketing*, **46** (7/8), 1048–1063.

Agrawal, J. & Kamakura, W. (1995) The economic worth of celebrity endorsers. *Journal of Marketing*, **59**, 56–68.

Ahuvia, A. (2005) Beyond the extended self: loved objects and consumers' identity narratives. *Journal of Consumer Research*, **32** (1), 171–184.

Albert, S. & Whetten, D. (1985) Organisational identity. In: *Research in Organisational Behaviour* (C. Cummings & B. Straw, eds.). JAI Press: Greenwich, CT, pp. 263–295.

Albert, S., Ashforth, B. & Dutton, J. (2000) Organisational identity and identification: charting new waters and building new bridges. *Academy of Management Review*, **25** (1), 13–17.

Bartholmé, R. H. & Melewar, T. C. (2011) Remodeling the corporate visual identity construct: a reference to the sensory and auditory dimension. *Corporate Communications: An International Journal*, **16** (1), 53–64.

Batra, R., Ahuvia, A. & Bagozzi, R. (2012) Brand love. *Journal of Marketing*, **76** (2), 1–16.

Baudrillard, J. (1990) *Fatal Strategies*. Semiotext(e): New York.

Beckham, D. (2003) *My Side*. Collins Willow: London.

Belk, R. W. (1988) Possessions and the extended self. *Journal of Consumer Research*, **15** (2), 139–168.

Belk, R. W. (2013) Extended self in a digital world. *Journal of Consumer Research*, **40** (2), 477–513.

Benetton (2016) Profile. www.benettongroup.com/the-group/profile/company-vision/, accessed September 2016.

Body Shop, The (2016) The Body Shop. www.thebodyshop.co.uk/commitment/index.aspx, accessed September 2016.

Brodie, R. J., Ilic, A., Juric, B. & Hollebeek, L. (2013) Consumer engagement in a virtual brand community: an exploratory analysis. *Journal of Business Research*, **66** (1), 105–114.

Chung, C. J., Inaba, J. & Koolhaas, R. (2001a) *Harvard Design School Guide to Shopping*. Taschen: New York.

Cova, B. & Dalli, D. (2007) Community made: from consumer resistance to tribal entrepreneurship. In: *European Advances in Consumer Research 8* (M. A. McGrath, S. Borghini & C. Otnes, eds.). Association for Consumer Research: Duluth, MN, pp. 461.

Cova, B., Kozinets, R. & Shankar, A. (2007) Tribes INC: the new world of consumer tribalism. In: *Consumer Tribes* (B. Cova, R. Kozinets & A. Shankar, eds.). Elsevier: Burlington, MA, pp. 3–26.

Duncan, T. & Everett, S. (1993) Client perceptions of integrated marketing communications. *Journal of Advertising Research*, May/June, 30–39.

Dutton, J., Dukerich, J. & Harquail, C. (1994) Organisational images and member identification. *Administrative Science Quarterly*, **39**, 239–263.

Evans, A. & Wilson, G. (1999) *Fame: The Psychology of Stardom*. Bath Press: Bath.

Fog, K., Budtz, C., Munch, P. & Blanchette, S. (2010) *Storytelling: Branding in Practice*, 2nd edition. Springer: London.

Fournier, S. & Lee, L. (2009) Getting brand communities right. *Harvard Business Review*, April, 105–111.

Google (2016) Our culture. www.google.co.uk/about/company/facts/culture/, accessed September 2016.

Goulding, C., Shankar, A. & Canniford, R. (2013) Learning to be tribal: facilitating the formation of consumer tribes. *European Journal of Marketing*, **47** (5/6), 813–832.

Grannell, C. & Jayarwardena, R. (2004) Celebrity branding: not as glamorous as it looks. 19 January 20004, www.brandchannel.com

Harbison, A. (2004) Brand it like Beckham: an investigation into the cult of $ellebrity branding. Unpublished BA marketing dissertation, University of Strathclyde, Glasgow.

HOG (2016) An inside pass to the ride of your life. https://members.hog.com/website/

Hollander, S. (1970) *Multinational Retailing*. Michigan State University: East Lancing, MI.

Holt, D. (2016) Branding in the age of social media. *Harvard Business Review*, March, 40–50.

Horn, M. & Gurel, L. (1981) *The Second Skin*. Houghton: Boston.

Ind, N. (1997) *The Corporate Brand*. Macmillan Press: London.

Ind, N. (2014) How participation is changing the practice of managing brands. *Journal of Brand Management*, **21** (9), 734–742.

Ind, N., Iglesias, O. & Schultz, M. (2013) Building brands together: emergence and outcomes of co-creation. *California Management Review*, **55** (3), 5–26.

Kapferer, J. (1996) *Strategic Brand Management*. Kogan Page: London.

Kapferer, J. (2008) *New Strategic Brand Management: Creating and Sustaining Brand Equity Long Term*. Kogan Page: London.

Kay, M. (2006) Strong brands and corporate brands. *European Journal of Marketing*, **4** (7–8), 742–776.

Keller, K. (2013) *Strategic Brand Management*, 4th edition. Pearson/Prentice Hall: Upper Saddle River, NJ.

Keller, K. (2014) Designing and implementing brand architecture strategies. *Journal of Brand Management*, **21** (9), 702–715.

Kellogg's (2016) *Kellogg's 2015/2016 Corporate Responsibility Update: Nourishing Families so They Can Flourish and Thrive*. www.kelloggcompany.com/content/dam/kelloggcompanyus/corporate_responsibility/pdf/2016/Kelloggs_CRR_2015%20FINAL.pdf, accessed September 2016.

Kitchen, P. J., Kim, I. & Schultz, D. (2008) Integrated marketing communications: practice leads theory. *Journal of Advertising Research*, **48** (4), 531–546.

Le Quéau, P. (1998) *La Tentation Bouddhiste: Les Fleurs Mystiques de Babylone*. Desclée de Brouwer.

McAlexander, J., Schouten, J. & Koenig, H. (2002) Building brand community. *Journal of Marketing*, **66** (January), 38–54.

McCracken, G. (1989) Who is the celebrity endorser? Cultural foundations of the endorsement process. *Journal of Consumer Research*, **16**, 310–320.

McDowell, C. (2003) *Ralph Lauren: The Man, The Vision, The Style*. Cassell Illustrated: London.

McGoldrick, P. (2002) *Retail Marketing*, 2nd edition. McGraw-Hill: London.

Mantle, J. (1999) *Benetton: The Family, the Business and the Brand*. Little, Brown: London.

Nike (2016) About Nike. http://about.nike.com, accessed September 2016.

Olins, W. (1991) *Corporate Identity*. Thames and Hudson: Toledo, Spain.

Olins, W. (2003) Corporate identity: the myth and the reality. In: J. Balmer & S. Greyser (eds.), *Revealing the Corporation*. Routledge: London, pp. 53–65.

Oliver, R. (1997) *Satisfaction: A Behavioural Perspective on the Consumer*. McGraw-Hill: New York.

Pankraz, D. (2009) Youth Want Tribal Ideas: Tips on How to Create a Movement Around Your Brand. http://danpankraz.wordpress.com/2009/06/07/youth-are-tribal-tips-on-how-to-create-a-movement-around-your-brand, accessed 27 May 2011.

Parfois (2016), http://www.parfois.com/en/corporate/?id=25#, accessed September 2016.

Pritchard, M., Havitz, M. & Howard, D. (1999) Analysing the commitment–loyalty link in service contexts. *Journal of the Academy of Marketing Science*, **27** (3), 333–348.

Riel, C. & Balmer, J. (1997) Corporate identity: the concept, its measurement and management. *European Journal of Marketing*, **31** (5/6), 340–355.

Saatchi and Saatchi (2016) About lovemarks. www.lovemarks.com/learn/about/, accessed September 2016.

da Silveira, C., Lages, C. & Simões, C. (2013) Reconceptualizing brand identity in a dynamic environment. *Journal of Business Research*, **66** (1), 28–36.

Simões, C., Singh, J. & Perin, M. (2015) Corporate brand expressions in business-to-business companies' websites: evidence from Brazil and India. *Industrial Marketing Management*, **51**, 59–68.

Spenner, P. & Freeman, K. (2012) To keep your customers keep it simple. *Harvard Business Review*, May, 108–114.

Strauss, A. (1969) *Mirrors and Masks*. Sociology Press: San Francisco.

Superbrands (2016) An insight into Britain's strongest brands: British Airways. www.superbrands.uk.com/british-airways, accessed September 2016.

TAP (2016) Victoria: Tap's Loyalty Programme. www.flytap.com/UnitedKingdom/en/Victoria/promotions-and-highlights?29, accessed September 2016.

Thomson, M., MacInnis, D. & Park C. (2005) The ties that bind: measuring the strength of consumers' emotional attachments to brands. *Journal of Consumer Psychology*, **15** (1), 77–91.

moving Space

Marketing involves the transfer of something from one person to another, from one place to another, bringing it to the marketplace. This chapter looks at the role of logistics and technology in marketing channels which enable goods to be brought to consumers; not the other way around with consumers having to travel far. It goes further to show how the exchanges in markets nowadays are much more than just a process of delivery, moving things from place to place; it also matters where things come from (location, location, location) and where they are purchased. We see how retailing and shopping are essentially spatial practices, and how these activities alter spaces through the architecture of retailing – the mall, the window displays, the arcades. This chapter also illustrates the effect of the internet and social media marketing in taking markets into 'virtual' spaces.

How markets move space

Marketing involves exchange between sellers and buyers (see Marketing Contexts). It involves a transfer of something from one person to another, from one place to another, bringing it *to the marketplace*. It enables goods to be brought to consumers, not the other way around, with suppliers taking products and services to consumers so they do not have to travel to sources of supply. Without a market distribution system consumers in the UK would have to go to Kent or Somerset to buy apples, to France to get wine. Place is very important for marketing of course (location, location, location), but the exchanges that occur in the marketing system

nowadays are much more than just a process of delivery, distribution or logistics, moving things from place to place. Marketing now is 'moving space'.

And it matters where things come from. The 'country of origin' label provides a quality assurance for customers which applies to manufacturers and is particularly influential for agricultural produce. Indeed, the geographical source of farm and mineral products is part of the brand (see Brand Selection), with the labels being the name of the region of origin, e.g. cheeses, milk, bottled water, wine. French wine is defined and controlled by its regional source: the *appellation d'origine controlée* (AOC) labelling system protects the famous wine-growing area boundaries such as Bordeaux, Macon, Alsace, Burgundy and Beaujolais. The AOC is the legal expression of *terroir*, a concept of geographical source of the grape that

Traditional marketing models describe the exchange and distribution process in terms of movement through supply chains, distribution channels, logistics organization, transportation networks, inventories, retail outlets, delivery systems, intermediaries and agents for assortment, conveyancing, consignment and shipment. Indeed, this is where marketing as an academic discipline began (see Marketing Contexts: Marketing values).

The spaces in which exchanges take place in marketing are all these things and more.

Baudrillardians
never make it past
the shopping mall.
Massumi, 1992

Shopping is expanding into every program imaginable: airports, churches, train stations, libraries, schools, universities, hospitals. Airports and malls are starting to look indistinguishable. The experience of the mall is becoming increasingly seamless with that of the department store. Even the city is being configured according to the mall.
Koolhaas, in Chung et al., 2001

goes way beyond territorial origin, embodying the soil, climate, history, folklore, *savoir faire* and emotional attachment of the region in which it is grown.

Giddens (1990) explains this ability of markets to move space as a consequence of the institution of money, which permits exchange to occur across large time–space distances. In contrast, barter, exchange without money, is limited in distance by the requirement for the concurrent transfer of commodities between parties. The institution of money as a medium of exchange is a key feature of 'modernity', he argues, which enables socio-economic activity to be transformed beyond the particular circumstances of local places and practices.

The most obvious illustration of this is the effect that the internet has had on consumer buying and market delivery. When shopping, looking or buying through company websites, the interaction between the buyer and seller does not just move things from place to place; the space in which it occurs is changed. The retailing aspects regarding physical space, architecture, layout, design, store atmospherics, colour schemes, displays, etc. (see Brand Selection: Fast fashion branding) that have been found to affect customer responses are all changed by internet shopping. Of course, here the 'space' is virtual, the customer can be anywhere and the 'shop' can be nowhere. Internet marketing has altered the space in which exchange takes place. Clarke and Purvis (1994) argue that the advent of this 'hyperspace', with its simulations, and 'hyper-reality' (Baudrillard, 1983) will have radical effects on the retailing system.

Many marketers would accept that the internet changes space, but they would also point out that 90 per cent of the products and services that are still exchanged in terrestrial markets must be moved from place to place, perhaps by new and faster means but nevertheless by the same essential processes. This is true. However, these marketing processes are themselves changing the use of spaces – turning more of them into retail outlets. Retailing and shopping space is turning cities into gigantic shopping malls, according to Rem Koolhaas, who designed the new Prada store in New York, which has taken over the site of the Soho Guggenheim art gallery (see Brand Selection: Fast fashion branding). In the *Harvard Design School Guide to Shopping*, he paints an apocalyptic picture of the spread of what he calls this 'junk-space', the shoppingization of urban life, in which cities of the future are consumed by the mass of their own buildings and road signs and advertising hoardings (Koolhaas, in Chung *et al.*, 2001).

The continued accumulation of commodities and the physical speed of market-places can be expected to produce more 'junkspace' of this kind. Indeed, it may be that such spatial entropy in the city, in the marketplace and everywhere else *is inevitable*.

Spatial and territorial affiliations are powerful social influences on consumers, as they are for society generally. The role of proximity in creating tactile and affectual affiliations is well documented. For example, Mafessoli (1996) suggests that spatial 'proxemics' reinforce feelings of belonging to a group or a 'tribe' and that 'co-presence' is central to the customers, ethics and aesthetics of society. So too in marketing activities, the 'sites of consumption' bring into spatial presence consumers with other consumers, sellers, commodities and a network of supporting artefacts (see Consuming Experience).

'Terrestrial' shopping is essentially a spatial practice, and its activities alter spaces. The shopping mall, the window displays, the arcades and the galleries all utilize glass constructions enabling shoppers to be in and see through both the public street and the shopping space simultaneously. This is what Benjamin (1955: 174) described as the 'porosity' of the nineteenth century arcades of Paris and Naples – the transparency between boundaries of the public and private domains in apparently open spaces that are 'harnessed' to the needs of the market.

The capacity of porosity in city spaces is illustrated nowadays by the activity/sport of 'freerunning', where athletes/artists utilize the architecture and spaces of the built environment in cities to create athletic runs, jumps and moves. Their elite exponents have been recruited for several advertisements and marketing events worldwide to create a visual spectacle of movement and space, such as for the Toyota Aygo car launch at the motor shows in Barcelona and Geneva in February 2005. (For more on freerunning, see http://urbanfreeflow.com.)

FURTHER READING

Moving shopping space

Chung, C. J., Inaba, J. & Koolhaas, R. (2001) *Harvard Design School Guide to Shopping*. Taschen: New York.

Clarke, D. & Purvis, M. (1994) Dialectics, difference and the geographies of consumption. *Environment and Planning A*, **26**, 1091–1109.

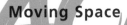

Virtual spaces

Arefi, M. (1999) Non-place and placelessness as narratives of loss: rethinking the notion of place. *Journal of Urban Design*, **4** (2), 179–193.

Lefebre, H. (1991) *The Production of Space* (D. Nicholson-Smith, trans.). Verso: London.

Morley, D. & Robbins, K. (1995) *Spaces of Identity: Global Media, Electronic Landscapes and Cultural Boundaries*. Routledge: London.

Moving materials through market space

his section looks at how marketing involves moving materials through various channels in order to make them available to consumers. This also involves a transfer of information and some form of payment, usually money (see Figure 6.1)

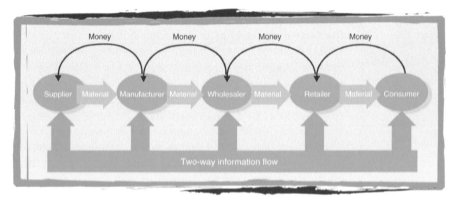

Figure 6.1 Material, money and information flow

The definition of materials has changed

Materials in marketing are traditionally *tangible* items – furniture, bottles of wine, paper, food – but nowadays we must add *intangible* materials to this list. Hitherto, the term 'intangible materials' would have been a contradiction in terms, but now many market offerings constitute intangible materials – for instance e-tickets for air travel, email messages, mobile phone apps. Marketers have had to rethink our definition of 'materials' to include intangibles.

Not only is the environment made up of materials – houses, shops, trees, etc. – today it is materials that are determining the shape and form of our environment. In the past, the goal of the marketing distribution function was to provide the 'right material items at the right time in the right space', i.e. finding the market niche and delivering the product to the place where the customer wants it. This transfer process does not necessarily apply today, as this chapter will show.

Consumers' environmental influences

The idea of providing the right environment to enhance your product or service goes beyond the traditional marketing principle of *promotion*. Companies still need to advertise and deliver products, but marketers must also understand the environment and context in which they will be used (see Consuming Experience). If the environment is not conducive to its use, then it is the marketers' role to improve the environment so their product will be more attractive. In services marketing this is referred to, not as the landscape, but as the 'servicescape'.

A prime example where the environment is at least as important as the actual product is a family restaurant. For instance, the restaurant's service or the food quality is not the only critical factor for a young family frequenting the restaurant because quality and service are assumed to be good by customers or they would not go there. Other critical aspects are the environmental elements, such as: parking, hours of operation, facilities for families (high chairs for toddlers, changing facilities for infants, safe environment for children with no stairs or candles, etc.). Families select restaurants primarily based on the restaurant's environment that supports their lifestyles – in this example, having young children.

A comparable situation can be found in the airline business. What differentiates one airline from another? Many travellers will say 'service'. However, we have accepted the fact that there are many low-cost, 'no-frills' local and national flights which don't provide much service at all – just the seat. What is happening is that the airlines are now competing to provide the right environment and the right materials. In the low-cost airline market, such materials include:

- parking
- choice of arrival and departure airports
- frequency of flights
- number of destinations
- ground transportation
- ease of purchasing a ticket (e-ticketing).

With international travel, in addition to all of the above materials, the in-flight services will be more important due to the length of the journey. The airline must think of materials that make up the environment to win customers. Providing a cheap seat is not enough as competitive prices can be researched on the internet in minutes. For travellers, their purchasing decision includes all the related materials; therefore, marketers must consider *all* the materials that make up the environment that will enhance and promote their offering.

Such 'holistic' considerations have led marketers to offer 'bundles' of materials to consumers. Indeed, bundling was traditionally regarded as one of the functions of the distributor or retailer, who combines several items from different sources into convenient packages. This saves customers time and effort in putting these items together themselves and even saves them thinking about what combinations are possible because the options are presented for them.

Example of bundling

Consider how the menu is displayed in fast-food restaurants today. Often, the menu listing single items is difficult to locate – it's posted on the side wall in smaller print without any pictures or illumination. Behind the staff member taking your order is the glossy, well-lit picture menu of the bundled options. This is because customers have come to expect bundled services and products. By providing 'bundled meals', fast-food restaurants are no longer competing on price. The products are being bundled and fast-food connoisseurs no longer know the price of each food item.

Availability – materials must be ubiquitous

The two trends of *'being available any time and almost anywhere'* have now become norms within many consumer and business markets. This demonstrates how, over the last two decades, the requirements for supplying materials have changed and constant availability is expected.

In order to explore why this has occurred, consider the example of the building materials 'DIY' store, Home Depot. Home Depot is a US-based multinational company that has expanded its retail opening to 24 hours a day, seven days a week. These stores sell building materials, hardware items, seasonal products, tools, houseplants, paint, doors, windows, etc. They service residential customers, large and small contractors, and commercial trades services.

Unless you are an insomniac homeowner, you may ask yourself, 'Who would ever want to buy planks of wood at 3.00 a.m. on a Tuesday morning?' However, the pilot project of being open all hours was so successful that Home Depot extended it to all of their North American stores in 2001. Contractors and delivery couriers have enthusiastically embraced the concept. They have discovered there are numerous cost savings of purchasing their materials at night. First, they avoid the traffic congestion during the day. Second, there is no downtime at the job site since the materials are available immediately in the morning when the workers arrive. Third, if any subsequent items are required they can be picked up by mid-morning delivery without impacting the production schedule. For Home Depot they are maximizing their sales and serving these larger and more dependable buyers. It is a 'win–win' outcome for both the seller (Home Depot) and the buyers (mainly contractors).

This example illustrates how availability of materials has changed the operating and purchasing practices of the construction business. It also reflects how marketing has shifted the way materials are bought and sold, with the customers' needs coming first. This illustrates the way in which marketing practices have moved materials, spaces and time in the marketplace.

Marketing channels

Moving products from place to place through marketing channels involves activities that make products available to customers when and where they want to purchase them, by transferring products from their place of manufacture to the marketplace where customers are located. It is marketing channels that enable goods to be brought to consumers, not the other way around. In the absence of such marketing distribution systems it would be the customers who had to travel to the place of production or source of supply in order to buy. Developing optimal marketing channels of distribution was the main subject of marketing as an academic discipline in the early twentieth century. Traditional marketing models describe the exchange and distribution process in terms of movement through supply chains, distribution channels, logistics organization, transportation networks, inventories, retail outlets, delivery systems, intermediaries and agents for assortment, conveyance, consignment and shipment.

Exchanges in marketing channels now are much more than just a process of delivery, distribution or logistics, moving things from place to place. One reason why it is more than about transport and logistics is because it often matters enormously to customers where things come from. The 'place of origin' label can provide a form of quality assurance for buyers which applies to raw materials (Portland stone), manufactures (Harris tweed) and is particularly influential for agricultural produce (Cheddar cheese; French wine). The geographical source of farm and mineral products can be the key element of the brand with the labels incorporating the name the region of origin, e.g. for milk, water, wine. Indeed, French wine is defined and controlled by its regional source of the grape

embodying the soil, climate, history, folklore and emotional attachment of the place where it is grown.

Another reason why distribution involves much more than the delivery of goods and services is because choosing which marketing channels of distribution to operate in is such a major decision in the formulation of marketing strategy. This is particularly crucial nowadays as the range of traditional, social and online retail options has expanded enormously.

Shaping markets

Brennan (2006: 832) argues that 'firms are not simply passive victims of their environment but strive to alter competitive market conditions in their favour'. But how can firms shape the markets that they engage in? Storbacka and Nenonen (2011) regard this as the key strategic question: how firms influence the shape of the markets that they choose to engage in and through which mechanisms these market conditions can be altered. They propose a framework for understanding how markets are formed and shaped, and use this to identify what they call 'market scripting' activities that firms can engage in to actively develop markets to their advantage. They make their key assumptions about markets which reflect this proactive view of firms' roles: (1) markets consist of networks of market actors; (2) market actors co-create value by integrating their resource with the resources of other actors participating in the market; and (3) markets are social constructions co-created by market actors as they engage in market practices. Based on these core assumptions, there are two important implications for our conceptualization of space and place in marketing distribution channel theory.

One implication is the necessity for a comprehensive mapping of the various 'paths to market' that a firm could follow for their range of products, services and potential customers. This spatial route map would indicate the likely places where each might meet customers and the boundaries of the various spaces within the entire field of possible distribution channels. This would then enable marketers to seek out complementary and alternative routes to market to those which they have adopted. If this mapping can be successfully accomplished, then marketers will have a better understanding of how they can develop their distributions networks – and thus shape their markets.

The other implication of this view for channel strategy follows from the three key assumptions above, which *do not focus* on product flows, channel structures or transport logistics. On the contrary, they emphasize the relationships between market actors, how they deploy resources and their type of operations or 'practices'. According to the market-shaping approach, it is through these activities and interactions that the distribution network is formed and also importantly how value is created by firms and other actors within it.

Storbacka and Nenonen's (2011) approach to shaping and making markets reflects the so-called 'Nordic school' of marketing researchers whose key focus is on relationships between market actors. This is very different from the original view of distribution systems in the early days of the marketing discipline, which included geography-related regional approaches to marketing channels such as Reilly's (1931) *The Law of Retail Gravitation*. Geography was an underlying influence on the development of distribution theories and, furthermore, the concept itself tended to be defined in terms specific to the context of the USA where it was developed. One issue for geographically based theories is that various countries' markets and territories are significantly different in terms of market structure, transport, logistics, competition, infrastructure, etc. As Grönroos (1989) points out, the North American marketing environment is quite specific in many respects, with a huge domestic market, a unique geographical structure and a non-oligopolistic, highly competitive distribution system.

So the geographical sites and global territories in which distribution occurs influence the form of marketing channels which evolved, and this in turn accounts for the particular emphasis of early channel theory on transport, logistics, competition and infrastructure as opposed to channel participants, relationships, perceptions and space.

Design of alternative channels

The primary role of marketing channels is the performance of some basic distribution functions, such as reducing complexity and increasing value and service delivery. These tasks are common to all types of marketing channels and, as we have seen, the movement of physical goods is not the only type of task involved; for example, promotion flows down distribution channels, orders and payment flow back to suppliers, and negotiation and finance can flow both ways. This is illustrated in Figure 6.2 showing the product and information flows which are critical in achieving 'quick response' logistics in the US garment supply. Quick response is measured by the speed at which information about changing market demands can be communicated back up the channel and products manufactured and transported down the chain in response to those demands.

This quick response capability is critical for the clothing textile industry in the era of 'fast fashion' (see Fast fashion branding). This is illustrated by the Spanish clothing company Zara whose core competence has been based on the implementation of rapid-reaction, just-in-time principles and systems and processes which allow customer demand for up-to-date fashions to be brought to the market with lead times dramatically shorter than the industry norm.

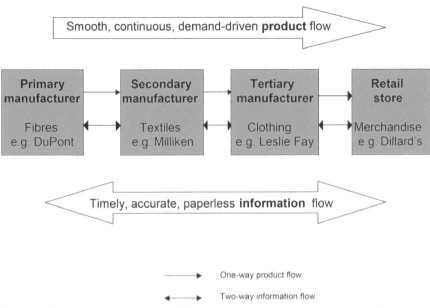

Figure 6.2 Quick response in the US garment industry *Source*: adapted from Christopher (2000)

The Zara brand was launched in May 1975, and Zara opened their first store in La Coruna with a product range incorporating women's fashion, menswear and children's clothes. By 2004 they had 792 international stores in more than 40 countries. They have a commercial team at HQ comprising designers, market specialists and buyers operating on a multi-tasking basis to ensure that design, sales and production considerations are integrated at an early stage. Design ideas observed by company representatives on the catwalk and by co-opted scouts in 'youth' arenas, such as university campuses and discos, are brought back to La Coruna and interpreted by the commercial team. The design, production and distribution 'time to market' has been reduced to 22–30 days in an industry where nine months was the traditional lead-time.

To reduce supplier dependency, Zara employs a network of over 500 subcontractors in Spain and Portugal to assemble pre-cut material sourced from a wide supplier base on a global level. This network of subcontractors, allied to daily feedback from store managers on how ranges are performing, maximizes flexibility in the supply and distribution system. At the retail stores, continuous replenishment on a staggered three-day cycle and the regular introduction of new lines encourages customers to return to the stores and increases footfall. This flexibility in supply and their 'fast fashion' quick-response strategy also provides some protection against other suppliers copying Zara products, because by the time competitors respond the item may have already been taken out of their stores and replaced by the next range.

This example illustrates how time reduction is one crucial element in the design of distribution systems. Christopher (1997) identifies three aspects of time that must be managed in the distribution system:

- *Time to market* – how long it takes the organization to recognize a market opportunity and to translate this into a product/service, and to bring it to the market.
- *Time to serve* – how long it takes to capture a customer's order and to deliver or install the product to the customer's satisfaction.
- *Time to react* – how long it takes to adjust the output of the business in response to volatile demand.

According to marketing theory, buyers' needs and behaviour should be the most important concern of channel members. Channel design decisions are critical because they determine a product's market presence and how and where customers buy the product. They also influence customers' overall satisfaction with the product, manufacturer or service. There are a number of key decisions to be taken over channel design, such as those concerning how many and which channels to select, the intensity and coverage required of the channel(s), and the optimal channel configuration. Their choice will be determined by many factors including the degrees of flexibility, centralization and voluntary cooperation that are best in order to reach and serve their specific markets and segments. Their options may be further limited by the extent to which the individual firm has the power to make such decisions. For example, their choice may be limited because in their sector or market it is the retailers, not the manufacturers, who have power over the channel decisions. Nevertheless, it is the service provided to final consumers that should be the key consideration in all marketing channel decisions.

One option for the distribution system is to use a direct marketing channel from the producer to the customer through courier or mail delivery, mobile download, factory outlet or customer collection. In order to serve customers best and find the best distribution space, most channels of distribution are indirect with one or several marketing intermediaries. There are two main forms of intermediary: merchants (or agents) and functional middlemen (or brokers). The difference is that merchants buy and own the products and resell them, whereas functional middlemen do not own products but sell them on behalf of the supplier for a fee or commission. Retailers are also intermediaries who purchase products and sell them to final consumers, making their profit by a price 'mark-up'.

Supply chain management

Whatever the form or structure of the distribution system, all channel members perform distinct but complimentary roles and therefore they must co-operate closely. This joint effort of all channel members to deliver products to the market quickly and efficiently is often called a 'supply chain'. Supply chain management (SCM) refers to long-term partnerships between channel members that aim to reduce inefficiencies, costs and delays in a coordinated way that builds on the combined strengths of the channel members.

The key elements of SCM include: waste reduction, time saving, flexible response, unit cost reduction. Firms adopting an SCM approach seek to redesign their supply chains in ways that make them more effective and efficient, thus providing improved customer service while at the same time reducing costs and delivery time, often when faced with fluctuating demand. The capacity for flexible response to demand changes requires the ability to switch perspective and 'see' from one point of the supply chain to the other. Some firms specialize in providing IT software for managing and integrating total supply chain processes. This is one example of the contribution of IT to marketing channels, which is the subject of Moving information – the role of IT.

Role of information in SCM

Information is the key to finding the right marketing space. The organization and operations for supplying customers, involving distribution, transportation, logistics, materials flows, order processes, retail outlets, etc. have become more complex with the need for more and faster information to manage these processes across boundaries – national, international, organizational. In the global economy, few firms do it all themselves from source to delivery, but they have to be able to manage a complex network of processes, often across great distances. Information technology (IT) provides the capability to speed up information collection and processing, enabling marketing to improve their understanding and responses to customer needs and to manage their supply processes, to move space, better and faster.

Information does more than support transactions, however. It is a product – an object of exchange – in its own right. The more information about customers, markets, channels and customers that is collected by the firm, the greater the need for an integration function to coordinate all the elements and analyse and interpret the mass data in order to build a complete picture. This is another key role that IT systems can perform that can help firms to better manage the functions required by the acquisition of mass information.

Marketers basically want to gather knowledge about consumers so they can make better marketing decisions in order to satisfy customers and meet company objectives. For managers to have *knowledge* of customers, however, requires judgement and expertise as well as information, in order to select and evaluate information in their decisions. Developments in IT enable the fusing of data, its sorting and evaluation with computer models. This is all the more important for marketers as consumers' behaviour keeps changing; therefore the most crucial pieces of information are about consumers' *actual* behaviour as opposed to generic segment characteristics such as their age, income or location. More crucial for distribution decisions, marketers need to know what consumers want to buy, how and when they want to purchase, and where they want to purchase.

It should be fairly clear to those readers who have experience of online purchasing that the internet has had an enormous effect on consumer buying behaviour and final market delivery. When shopping, looking or buying through company websites, the interaction between the buyer and seller is no longer dependent on the place or location of either party. The online transaction takes place in virtual cyberspace with no need for face-to-face interaction. This is not new, of course; this was always the case with shopping by TV, telephone or mail order. It is the retailing aspects online that have altered most significantly. Bricks and mortar features of shops, like physical space, architecture, layout, design, store atmospherics, colour schemes and displays, which have been found to affect customer responses, are all changed by internet shopping; where the marketplace is virtual, the customer can be anywhere and the 'shop' can be nowhere. So internet marketing has altered the marketing space in which exchange takes place.

Clarke and Purvis (1994) argued that the advent of this 'hyperspace', with its simulations and hyperreal shopping spaces, will have radical effects on the retailing system. While it is true that the internet has altered shopping space, many marketers also point out that 90 per cent of products and services are still exchanged in terrestrial markets and most internet purchases must still be delivered by the same transport and logistics processes. Not only do these physical distribution processes utilize new and faster means, but they are also themselves changing the use of spaces, turning more of them into retailing and shopping spaces such as gigantic retail malls with window displays, shopping arcades and galleries all utilizing glass constructions enabling shoppers to be in and see through both the public street and the shopping space simultaneously. This is what Benjamin (1955) described as the 'porosity' of the shopping arcades of Paris and Naples – apparently open spaces that are 'harnessed' to the needs of the market. These new physical sites of consumption bring consumers into spatial presence with other consumers, sellers, commodities, and a network of buildings and supporting artefacts which also alter spaces.

Another impact of advances in information technology and mobile communications is that companies can now track and trace materials as they travel from suppliers to their final destination. IT infrastructure and the internet has provided the framework to monitor the movement of materials instantaneously from anywhere in the world and that allows more effective management of the interwoven activities of the supply chain. Without these technological changes in the application and innovations of specialized electronics and communication systems, the effectiveness and speed of marketing channels and SCM would be greatly reduced.

The role of logistics

This section will discuss how logistics contributes to the 'moving' operations for marketing. Logistics includes the transportation and tracing of materials as they flow between the manufacturer and their customers. Logistics also includes the services of recording necessary production and shipping information that is beneficial to learning more about customers' needs. Logistics is also concerned with the steps involved in producing and moving materials. It is the role of logistics to document the processes involved in marketing. These processes include: production scheduling, determining the best method of delivering the materials, collecting customer feedback, managing the company's website.

Logistics *is the series of events required to move materials in a timely and cost-effective manner. It also includes the events or necessary steps in completing a project.*

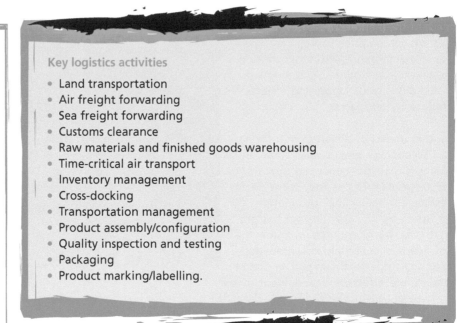

Key logistics activities

- Land transportation
- Air freight forwarding
- Sea freight forwarding
- Customs clearance
- Raw materials and finished goods warehousing
- Time-critical air transport
- Inventory management
- Cross-docking
- Transportation management
- Product assembly/configuration
- Quality inspection and testing
- Packaging
- Product marking/labelling.

The nineteenth century story of La Chaussee d'Antin (see margin) shows, on a grand scale, why logistics became a critical operation for ensuring the delivery of goods to customers in a timely and cost-effective manner. We can see that logistics now deals with more than the 'moving of materials', encompassing the organization, tracking and tracing of the shipments and movements involved, and the entire flow of materials into and out of the company. In the global economy, with multiple transportation modes and millions of such movements every day, logistics is a complex coordination and control function. It requires managing across national and company boundaries and balancing often conflicting objectives such as short lead times, small batch production, low inventories, speed and reliability of delivery, and immediate availability of many products.

Recently, many businesses have added logistical services to complement the products or services they provide their customers. An example of this is the services a travel agent provides. The travel agent not only sells airplane tickets but also provides a wide assortment of related travel services. These services may include car rental, hotel booking, sightseeing packages, etc. But in addition to these services, the travel agent offers logistical services. Some of the logistical services travel agents now offer are listed in Table 6.1.

These logistical services are considered essential for today's travelling customer and therefore they are now regarded as core competencies of a good travel

Table 6.1 Logistical services provided by travel agents

- Insurance
- Calculating the best flight connections
- Providing advice of which airline's service meets the travellers' expectations
- 'Watchdogs' for price savings and reducing travel costs
- Advising when the best time to travel is
- May have partner hotels, giving their customers better accommodation value

agent. By providing these logistical services, the travel agent is providing greater value to its customers, saving them time and money. In other words, the travel agent can become the customer's buying agent for the entire trip.

During the past decade, however, major airlines have lowered the commissions paid to travel agents and they have also persuaded the traveller to book online with various reward schemes. Indeed, many travellers now conduct these search and booking services for themselves on the internet. Where does this leave the travel agents: how can they survive? One solution could be for travel agents to expand their logistics services and shift their core business actions of booking travel tickets and hotels to become 'travel logistics consultants'.

Another logistics service that has changed drastically over the past 20 years is the overnight courier and the freight industry. There was a time when the customer was happy to receive the package/freight on time and in good condition. Today that is not good enough. Customers are demanding that their delivery company provide the following logistics:

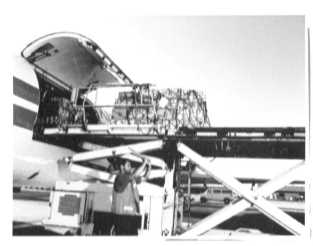

- Instantaneous tracking of their package/freight
- Confirmation of receipt of the package by the recipient within minutes of it being delivered
- Guaranteed delivery
- Guaranteeing the package will not be damaged
- Proper handling equipment.

This industry has spent millions of dollars to improve its fleet to be equipped to handle highly specialized containers and temperature controls. Also, many companies have now installed temperature-controlled holding areas on their premises to ensure goods are kept fresh (e.g. meats, flowers, fruits, chemicals). There has also been a dramatic shift in the type of goods the customer is shipping. In the past the majority of the items were overnight envelopes or small boxes. The freight being moved now is heavier, bulkier, going further distances and is much more time sensitive.

Simply moving the materials around the block or across the globe is no longer considered sufficient. To remain competitive freight and courier companies must also provide the logistical services that are required by the customer. Today's courier and trucking firms have become the customer's warehouse, shipper and logistics manager. Such logistical services are similar to the services listed above, including the following:

- *Daily* detailed *electronic* billing
- Real-time online tracking of the progress of freight
- Trucks displaying/advertising the *customer's* products
- Automatic compensation to the customer for delayed or damaged packages/ freight
- Detailed inventory records of incoming and outgoing shipments
- Custom brokerage
- Foreign currency exchange
- Storage (if needed)
- Ability to handle seasonal demands
- Advice for shipping items in the most efficient way.

It is the quality of provision of these added logistical services that differentiate leading companies in this industry. The customer's own business success is often dependent on the reliability, effectiveness and speed of the courier. As we have seen earlier, freight companies are not paid simply to move materials, they are providing 'peace of mind' for their customers, who know that the movement of their goods is now being safely handled by specialists. This enables customers to focus on their core competencies and contract out the delivery, pick-up, ware-housing, custom brokerage, etc. to their freight company that provides 'complete customized door-to-door logistics solutions' for each business customer.

The role of technology in logistics

As mentioned in the previous section, logistics now also involves the ability to track and trace the movement of materials. When a customer urgently needs to send a parcel to a foreign country as quickly as possible, they will likely choose an 'overnight courier'. The most critical factors for the courier in getting the parcel to its final destination are likely to include cost, timelines and en route tracking capabilities. The last factor, tracking, has become an essential component of the industry. Technology provides the latest equipment to enable companies to improve their logistical services. The logistical equipment for moving materials includes: mobile tracking devices, computers, wifi and internet connections, product code scanners, specialized material handling equipment and now delivery drones. Advances in information technology have dramatically improved companies' ability to track and trace materials as they travel from the senders to their final destinations (see Moving information – the role of IT).

But not all the technology required is 'hi-tech'. Take a simple example. A bicycle shop in London wants to start exporting bicycles to Morocco. The shop's expertise is selling bicycles, not shipping and exporting. By using an international courier, the bicycle shop will have the courier company handle all of the logistics such as packaging, customs, shipping, foreign exchange and local delivery services. The bicycle shop will contract out the logistical activities, since they are not part of its core competencies and be able to remain focused on its core competency – selling bicycles.

The role of logistics in marketing

Logistics has become an integral part of marketing. Marketers can even use logistics apps to instantly determine the appropriate price for various products by calculating and recording production schedules, shipping details and determining the most cost-efficient way of transporting the goods. Logistics are also used in marketing to collect and analyse consumer information. Logistics can gather marketing data such as how many materials are being produced, who is buying and where the customers are located. Logistics can also be helpful in recording historical marketing information that will assist in studying consumer decisions (see Moving information – the role of IT).

Other logistical data is gathered and analysed from a company's website and from the customers who log onto the company's website. Company websites are excellent marketing tools and can provide a variety of marketing information (see Table 6.2). It is the logistics of networking and sorting all of this 'big data' that enables the marketer to understand and manage the complexity of moving materials.

Table 6.2 The company website used as a logistical marketing tool

Subject areas	Benefits to the company
Determine where the customers are located	Websites are able to track where customers log in from; that is, able to determine geographical location
Determine how many customers are interested in which products	Logistics can calculate the number of people who view each component of the web page and for how long the customer views each page
Promotional tool; list and detail the company's materials available for sale; FAQs (frequently asked questions)	Allows the company to effectively promote and price their materials; feedback for customers
Convey logistical information, such as: production schedules, delivery timetables, product specifications, guarantees, accepted methods of payment	Customer is well informed, making the buying decision easier
Sales tool to accept orders, directly over the internet; 'e-tailing' (electronic sales)	Website will process the sales order; ensure all necessary information is obtained to complete the sale – logistically inform the sales department of the sale and begin the process of preparing the sales order

FURTHER READING

Christopher, M. (2000) The agile supply chain: competing in volatile markets. *Industrial Marketing Management*, **29** (1), 37–44.

Coyle, J., Bardl, E. & Lawley, C. (2003) *The Management of Business Logistics: A Supply Chain Perspective*, 7th edition. Thomson Learning/South-Western: Pennsylvania.

Shapiro, B., Rangan, V. & Sviokla, J. (1992) Staple yourself to an order. *Harvard Business Review*, July/August, 113–122.

Moving information – the role of IT

Mairead Brady

Information is the key to moving space in marketing. The organization and operation of supplying customers – channels of distribution, logistics, material flows, order processes, retailing outlets, offline and online – have become more complex, with the need for more and faster information to manage these processes across boundaries, national, international and organizational. In the global economy, few firms do it all themselves, from source to delivery, but they have to be able to manage a complex network of processes, often across great distances. Information technology (IT) provides the capability to speed up information collection and processing, enabling marketers to improve their understanding and responses to customer needs (see Creating Solutions).

Information does more than support transactions, however; it is an object of exchange in its own right. The more that information is broken up into bit-sized chunks, as it were, the more easily people can understand it, thus the greater its potential diffusion and use. The more it is broken up into discrete units for use, however, the greater the need for an integration function to coordinate all the elements and 'rebuild' a complete picture. IT can also assist firms to better manage these central functions associated with information space.

Take the example of Kleenex. The company knew that what it needed for the right information, at the right time, was an understanding of the purpose of the data and the focus and what is called 'sense making' from the data. How could they collect and connect the data so that it would be memorable and in a form that someone could see and understand what was needed and what could be done?

Kleenex have an online clip which shows how they use a software process they call 'Achoo' to find out where tissues are needed. They do this by aligning to the regions in the online world that are chatting online about having a cold or 'flu and where there are online searches for remedies for colds and 'flu. Previously this type of information was not available for companies to find in real time. It was also hard for companies to react quickly. But now due to technological advance, companies like Kleenex can target consumers on and offline to be where they are needed within hours. By correctly targeting the right consumers who need tissues and getting the tissues and their promotions to that area quickly, they take the guess work out of who to target and where they are. This greatly affects their returns on investment.

Collation of information

- How do marketers gather information?
- Why do marketers gather so much information?
- What do marketers use this information for?

This section discusses what sort of information marketers need, how it is packaged and exchanged/moved through space, and how IT helps them collect and analyse it.

Information – why is it crucial and where do marketers get it

Before we look at how marketers gather, move and analyse information, we need to consider what they use this information for. What marketers are always looking for is knowledge about consumers. They make all internal marketing decisions in order to satisfy customers while also being consistent with meeting company objectives. Perceived uncertainty in decision-making is reduced by the collection and use of information. For managers to have knowledge of customers (or anything else) requires not only information but also the ability to integrate and frame the information within the context of their experience, expertise and judgement (see Creating Solutions: Information technology and innovation). Managers utilize a mixture of intuition (suppressed expertise which resides in the subconscious), skills in classifying and reducing incoming information, and holistic analysis in order to sort out and evaluate information in the decision-making process. Modern developments in IT now enable the fusion of data and instinct with computer models.

What do consumers look like to marketers? Marketing data and analyses rarely deal with individuals; what marketers deal with are groups of people whom they call *target markets*. Target markets are groups of people who have similar needs and/or characteristics. Marketers divide consumers into groups by using segmentation variables (see Creating Solutions). This is the marketing term for saying that consumers are all different but not *that* different. So rather than mass marketing or using the same techniques for all consumers, what marketers do is take information from a variety of sources and analyse groups of consumers or even individual customers. Take Netflix – they use viewers' current viewing to suggest future viewing that aligns to their interests. Marketers use variables such as:

- demographics
- socio-economics
- lifestyle
- purchase-related usage and behaviour
- attitudes, interest and opinions.

> **Q.** Why is it that all too often business decisions are made by using gut instinct, based on limited information, when most companies are data rich?
>
> **A.** *Because there are major challenges in collecting, analysing, interpreting and utilizing information. There is also a need to develop this skill set.*

When marketers have grouped consumers into segments, they decide on which useful segments to target – which become their target markets. Marketers then design a marketing plan to satisfy these consumers. So in order to employ a segmentation methodology, a core information requirement is information about consumers' characteristics.

Information collection – a continuous challenge

Creating a picture of the customer is not a one-off task. The consumer cannot be considered as a static entity; consumers keep changing. The values and lifestyles, profiles and influences of consumers change over time. So marketers must keep researching consumers, gathering, analysing and interpreting information from a variety of sources – as in this Disney example.

Customer information at Disney World

The Walt Disney World team works hard at 'guestology', the study of the guests, who they are and what they want . . . A Research and Statistics Department conducts over 200 external surveys a year . . . Disney is constantly keeping track of guest information such as the following: demographics, evaluation of current marketing attraction evaluations, payment preferences, price sensitivity and the economy . . . To close the information loop and provide invaluable feedback to operations, guest comments reports, which condense the essence of all guest comments, are generated and distributed weekly to management. An Industrial Engineering Department continues the guestology process by constantly evaluating the resort's operating systems with daily inspections, show quality monitoring, wait-time studies, maintenance punch-lists and utilization studies . . . With the potential to generate so much data concerning its guests, Disney has learned to focus on what matters most. Through the process of guestology, guests are helping to design the future Disney World experience. While through understanding their customers and careful, thoughtful management of the 'cast' (people), settings, experiences and processes, a seamless and deeply impressive service experience is created and managed for consumers.

(Disney Institute & Kinni, 2011)

Marketers thrive on information and the most crucial pieces of information are about consumers' actual behaviour, as opposed to a common set of characteristics such as their age, income and location, which at best can only provide a rough, general guide to their purchase behaviour. Indeed, there is some evidence that as society has become more individualistic the emphasis on creating customer categories based on similarities between them, rather than differences, is much less appropriate. Traditional customer segments based on traditional economic and demographic characteristics are now an even-less-accurate guide to commonalities of purchases among members of each group. Yet marketers still want to, and need to, know what drives consumers to buy, what they purchase, how they purchase, when they purchase, whom they purchase for and where they purchase.

Inner space – the theatre of the mind

Marketers operate in what has been called the 'theatre of the mind' (Ingram, 2005). They wish to get inside consumers' heads. If you think of a movie like *Minority Report* with Tom Cruise, you can get some idea of how far developments in this area could go. By scanning the retina and working out his desires, the billboards change as Cruise walks down the street, thus 'narrowcasting' his personalized advertising. The technology for this future is not so far away and is already witnessed online when your search patterns show certain behaviours and your online adverts change to suit. So if you are browsing for clothes online then these clothes appear online each time you log on.

The mind is a wonderful information processor. Consider the range of choices and decisions that one person must go through just to carry out one shopping trip. In any supermarket visit a consumer may encounter up to 30,000 product lines within a 40-minute trip. Think of the agony of indecision if consumers could not process this mass of information and make decisions quickly. Marketers need to know how consumers make these decisions and what they can do to help make these decisions easier for consumers.

> *Once marketers have information about the drivers of consumer deci-sions they must design products and messages that speak to them on the subconscious level, for example the 'L'Oreal – because you're worth it' advertising campaign.*

Information collection – market research

Sometimes consumers will happily share information with companies. In other instances consumers are very protective of their information and preferences, and companies have to struggle to gather this information. According to Morey, Forbath and Schoop (2015), some consumers are happy for companies to know what is going on in their mind through their data use, and many consumers want companies to greet them, understand them, remember them and value them. Regardless of the orientation or desire of the consumer, companies must research consumers if they want to be able to react to their needs. Capturing information is a major challenge for marketers. Their credibility and power within the company is, in many ways, connected to their knowledge of the con-sumer, yet they have great difficulties in capturing and often using wisely the information available (see Creating Solutions, Market insights by research).

Information technology – a core requirement for market research, analysis and planning

The techniques by which companies store, manage, analyse and interpret infor-mation rely heavily on information technology. Table 4.1 in Creating Solutions: Information technology and innovation) shows the extent to which marketing practice has a dominant IT dimension (see also Brady *et al.*, 2002). Here we will concentrate on exploring the ITs that focus on information and decision-making, listed in Table 4.1 under the headings 'Analysis and planning', 'Databases' and 'Research'.

Database management

Most information collected by marketers nowadays resides in some form of data-base. A database is a computer system that holds aggregations of data records or files, such as sales transactions or product inventories; and customer databases hold customer profiles which can be analysed in various ways. Many softwares like salesforce.com provide easy to operate database templates. The database is often considered the most important asset within marketing. It is often called the customer relational database designed so that companies can explore and develop relationships with customers. As mentioned previously in this section, many consumers are aware that collecting database information is a critical operation for companies but are anxious to avoid any repercussions from the provision of this information.

Companies require centralized databases so that disparate elements of data can be collated to provide a very useful picture of customers and by extension a very useful picture of segments and markets. Every contact point and source of information between the company and the consumer can and often is tracked and traced. The reality is that companies have 'islands of data'. Every time an item is scanned at a checkout we assume that this information is being fed into a giant database and utilized for some marketing purpose. Every time we create a trail online we assume the same, and now more and more products and services have inbuilt tracking devices monitoring and tracking our every move (Porter & Heppelmann, 2015).

Data warehouses

The major task in database management is to generate *usable* information as the crucial ingredient in databases. A data warehouse simply holds the information. A data warehouse is an enterprise-level data repository that draws its contents from all critical operational systems and selected external data sources.

Two useful websites
- *A review of the top management database software products with product videos from a variety of companies – www.capterra.com/database-management-software/*
- *Best practice in data warehousing – www.computerweekly.com/tip/Data-warehousing-best-practices-Part-I*

Data mining

Once the information is collected, the marketer must look at ways of using this information. A data warehouse just stores data and a database only collects data in a centralized location – marketers must *do something* with this data.[1] What is needed is a search in the data for gems, for useful pieces of information, for links, connections, interesting observations – this is called data mining. Data mining enables companies to determine relationships among *internal* factors – such as price, product positioning or staff skills – and *external* factors – such as economic indicators, competition and customer demographics. And it enables them to predict the possible impact of any marketing strategy changes on sales, customer satisfaction and corporate profits, and to drill down and across information.

When Wal-Mart utilized data mining on their extensive database of consumer purchases, they found some interesting links. They noted a group of consumers who only brought two items – nappies and beer – between 7–9 pm on weekdays only. Can you guess the connection and the gender of the purchasers? What can Wal-Mart do with this information? They can look at a store plan and move the items further away to stimulate impulse purchase as the consumer walks between the two items. Or they can bring the items closer together to speed the purchase process and trigger connections between the two items. Once you think a little about the customer you would guess that this is a male in a hurry home from work and asked to get pampers. The choice is then obvious move the items as close to the door as possible to make the purchase easy.

The IT can supply the statistical analysis but gut instinct, education and knowledge are needed to analyse the findings.

[1]For a demonstration of the technology available within databases and how to utilize data-mining techniques within a database, you can take the tour on www.youtube.com/watch?v=Kz1zmyHw9G0 which is the Amazon relational database system (RDS), a cloud-based database.

Data mining *is 'the automated discovery of "interesting" non-obvious patterns hidden in a database that have a potential for contribution to the bottom line . . . it also encompasses the confirmation or testing or relationships through the discovery process' (Peacock, 1998).*

Q. What does data mining do?
A. *Once data has been acquired from internal and external sources, it allows marketers to do the following:*

- *Translate, clean and format the data.*
- *Analyse, validate and attach meaning to the data.*
- *Score the database for relationships and alignments to suggest correlations.*
- *Build and implement decision support tools and systems to make data mining results available to decision makers and other staff.*
- *Place filters on the data. The critical decision though is which filter.*

Data, information and knowledge

Data

Data are facts, numbers or text that can be processed by a computer and can include operational or transactional data such as sales, cost, inventory, payroll and accounting and/or non-operational data such as industry sales, forecast data and macro-economic data.

Information

The patterns, associations or relationships among all this data can provide information. For example, analysis of retail point-of-sale transaction data can yield information on which products are selling and when.

This type of static information as provided by the database software must be turned into usable information and creative strategies in order to work. There are also databases which track and monitor consumers online, like Radian 6. Online monitoring sites like the very popular www.socialmention.com, which tracks all conversations and then provides a review in real time, are invaluable.

From traditional surveys to scanning, monitoring and tracking

A core task of marketing is information gathering. In general, marketers will gather two types of data – qualitative and quantitative (see Creating Solutions: Information for innovative solutions, Market insight by research).

- *Qualitative data* – information which focuses on quality, emotions, feelings, perceptions and attitudes.
- *Quantitative data* – large quantities of descriptive data, analysed using statistical techniques.

Qualitative techniques

- *Personal interviews/focus groups – these can be held in person, on the telephone and online often using techniques like:*
  - *Projective techniques*
  - *Critical incident analysis*
  - *Cognitive mapping*
- *Observations*
- *Experimental research*
- *Eye cameras*
- *Mystery shopping*
- *Diaries.*

Quantitative techniques

- *Surveys, either in person, online or on the telephone:*
  - *Questionnaires and polls*
  - *Omnibus surveys*
  - *Manipulation of statistical data.*

Most of these traditional methods involve some level of collaboration and awareness between the consumer and the company. Some of these processes have been automated so that they can be carried out with the aid of IT applications. For example:

- *Video conferencing allows for focus group discussions to take place independent of location.*
- *Web surveys allow for online completion of surveys.*
  - *Email surveys are also increasingly popular with click through to surveys.*
  - *Qualtrics and SurveyMonkey are two online survey development tools that are very popular.*
  - *Cookies on sites allow for track and trace techniques which permit behavioural data to be tracked online and the information collated and analysed for use – remember the example of Kleenex discussed earlier.*

Tracking, scanning, surveillance – are you being watched?

Marketers often observe consumers without consumers being aware that they are being monitored, but now more than ever marketers are tracking consumers' behaviour through IT observation-based techniques. Marketers monitor, scan and track consumers on a regular basis. Hidden cameras are not that unusual. We are all being watched in shopping areas by ATM cameras for security purposes. Marketers can make valuable use of security footage of consumers.

In the retail trade, companies have placed tracking devices on shopping trolleys to monitor the store traffic. Web tracking has become very sophisticated, with more and more software applications available to track consumers' every move on the internet. Companies can now tell what site the consumer was on prior to their site and what site they go to on leaving their site. Google Analytics is a free web analytics service that tracks and reports website traffic. (For more information about Google Analytics, see Barden (2014) for a users' guide.) What Google Analytics and other web-traffic data-analysis softwares – whether off the shelf or developed in house – provide marketers with is the ability to trial, test and often to justify spending in the context of online activities.

Scanning techniques are now widespread. Every time a product is blipped through a checkout there is an information database entry. Marketers can then use this information to plan marketing campaigns.

Information technology – is this it?

As discussed earlier, IT is central to marketing practice. The use of information technology provides the marketers with something that they have always wanted – information. And not just information, but real-time, up-to-date information, readily accessible. All marketers' dreams come true – or is it? Information technology can supply marketers with loads of information, a proliferation of information, a magnitude of information. Information, information everywhere – but the reality is that many companies are drowning in a sea of useless data.

Technology – the information provider

Technology has been wonderful at automating applications, where it can repeat the same task over and over again without complaint and almost flawlessly. It is when much more is asked of technology that its limitations have become apparent.

There are a variety of systems (see Figure 6.3) that are utilized for information provision purposes. This subsection briefly introduces some of them. Many of these systems are looking at ways of capturing the information that flows around, into and out of companies. There needs to be a two-way information flow of materials, money and information all along the value chain, from the supplier right through to the final consumer.

Marketing information systems

A marketing information system (MIS) is 'a set of procedures and sources that manages use to obtain everyday information about developments in the marketing environments' (Kotler *et al.*, 2016: 171). MIS include three subsystems: the accounting information system, marketing research and marketing intelligence. The marketer must manage the information flows (see Figure 6.3) to aid in the decision-making process and aid the solutions to problems.

Yet never before have companies had such powerful technologies for interacting directly with customers, collecting and mining information about them, and tailoring their offerings accordingly. And never before have customers expected to interact so deeply with companies, and each other, to shape the products and services they use. To be sure, most companies use customer relationship management and other technologies to get a handle on customers, but no amount of technology can really improve the situation as long as companies are set up to market products rather than cultivate customers. To compete in this aggressively interactive environment, companies must shift their focus from driving transactions to maximizing customer lifetime value.
Rust et al., *2010*

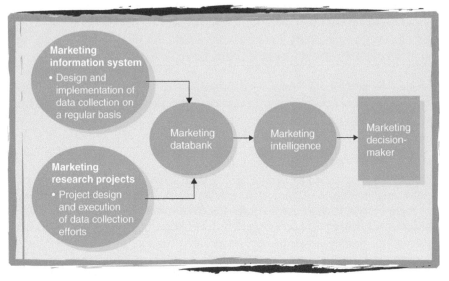

Figure 6.3 Information provision systems

Geographical information systems

We are intuitively aware that people in different parts of the world behave differently. We know that populations are not necessarily homogeneous, that cultural and regional preferences exist, and that there are large product-specific patterns within regions. Research can confirm or refute our instincts, with some geographic information running contrary to what would be expected. For example, research has shown that Californians drink less coke than Hungarians. Geographical information systems (GIS) are systems that can provide marketers with information from household figures upwards, and are very useful for companies. Most developed countries now have highly developed demographic information, with some countries being able to pinpoint individual households.

Marketing decision models

Consumers are rarely aware of the plethora of decision support applications that marketers use. These are internal IT applications which are used to analyse consumers and how they will react (predictive models) and how they did react (descriptive models) to certain marketing techniques. A well-designed decision support system should help marketers to make decisions optimally.

For example, the shelf displays in supermarkets: who decides on the contents and the display? Marketers now use sophisticated shelf-space maximization software in order to optimize the use and effectiveness of shelf space. There are a variety of software packages and customized software to aid the manufacturer and the retailer in maximum utilization of shelf space. One brand name is Shelf Logic, who supply 'planagram' software (www.shelflogic.com).

Summary

There have been many advances in information-gathering and research techniques. The major challenge is to make computers more human rather than to make humans more like computers. The data flood unleashed by advances in IT has only just begun and it is a challenge for marketers and business to understand and use all this data. Data analytics and data management are now core skills that marketers must have. A recent McKinsey study shows that companies that use data to make informed decisions increased their productivity by an average of 15–20 per cent and that that use of data distinguishes the leading brands (de Swaan *et al.*, 2014).

Until recently technology on its own has been a useless morass of boxes and cables which needs the intelligence of the human to operate it. The developing applications of artificial intelligence (AI), however, also enable the operational requirement for human intelligence to be replaced by machine. This opens up the vision of a future of business operations controlled by 'robots' – not in the form of anthropomorphized humanoid robots, but control through *inbuilt artificial intelligence technology.*

Questions marketers should ask

1 Why is big data is important to you and your organization?
2 What technology do you need to manage it?
3 How could big data change your job, your company and your industry?
4 How should you hire or develop the kinds of people who make big data work?
5 What are the key success factors in implementing any big data project?
6 How is big data leading to a new approach to managing analytics.

(Adapted from Davenport, 2014)

FURTHER READING

Uses and assimilation of IT

Brady, M., Saren, M. & Tzokas, N. (2002) Integrating information technology into marketing practice: the IT reality of contemporary marketing practice. *Journal of Marketing Management*, **18** (5/6, July), 555–578.

Davenport, T. (2014). *Big Data at Work: Dispelling the Myths, Uncovering the Opportunities*. Harvard Business Review Press: Cambridge, MA.

Disney Institute & Kinni, T. (2011) Be our guest: perfecting the art of customer service. 8 November, Disney Editions.

Joshi, A. & Giménez, E. (2014) Decision-driven marketing. *Harvard Business Review*, July–August, 55–63.

Kotler, P., Keller, K., Brady, M., Goodman, M. & Hansen, T. (2016) *Marketing Management*. Pearson: London.

Morey, T., Forbath, T. & Schoop, A. (2015) Customer data: designing for transparency and trust. *Harvard Business Review*, May.

Rust, R., Moorman, C. & Bhalla, G. (2010) Rethinking marketing. *Harvard Business Review*, January/February.

de Swaan, A.M., van den Driest, F. & Weed, K. (2014) The ultimate marketing machine. *Harvard Business Review*, July/August, 55–63.

Social media marketing

Annmarie Hanlon

Social media has existed since 1997 with the earliest social media network accepted as the now-defunct SixDegrees (Boyd & Ellison, 2007). The most dominant current social media network in the USA and Europe is recognized as Facebook, launched in 2004 and which today comprises over one billion active users.

This growth of social media networks has fundamentally changed the relationship between businesses and customers. In just over ten years, Facebook has become recognized as one of the world's most valuable brands (Badenhausen, 2013). Over 90 per cent of adults in the UK and the USA own a mobile phone, enabling them to tweet at any time. Fifty-one per cent of UK adults and 58 per cent of American adults own a smartphone, facilitating check-ins, posts and communication with brands at any time of the day (Ofcom, 2014; Pew Internet, 2014).

Scholars and practitioners agree that organizations are keen to use social media to engage with their customers. However, there is an issue about research and theory in this domain:

> Social media have been one of the biggest success stories on the internet, as sites like Facebook and Twitter have gone from zero users to more than 1 billion users in less than a decade. Yet the phenomenon of social media still lacks a coherent body of theory.
>
> (Kent, 2015: 1)

Because there is a lack of a body of knowledge, there is myth and misunderstanding, and there is no agreed definition of social media. To keep it simple, we define social media as *tools enabling personal and business processes*. This definition considers the evolving nature of technology as well as the ability to communicate on systems whether analogue or digital.

The connection between traditional and 'new media'

If you studied classical marketing you may remember the work of Igor Ansoff. Back in 1957, he wrote a seminal article in the *Harvard Business Review* entitled

'Strategies for diversification'. What we now call the 'Ansoff matrix' – which incorporates market penetration, market development, product development and diversification – features strongly within social media.

Market penetration aims to generate more sales from an existing customer group or market. While market penetration can be achieved via many traditional mechanisms, this strategy works well in an online environment. For example, the UK department store Marks & Spencer uses its Facebook page for market penetration, to promote offers to 'likers', who include customers.

Examples of *product development*, where companies promote new products or services to the existing customer base, include Marmite. The UK savoury spread, which is adored and disliked, hence the strap-line 'Love it or hate it' – like social media itself – uses Facebook to launch new packaged jars. There seems to be a jar for every season and an avid bunch of collectors waiting for the next edition.

The UK snack manufacturer, Walkers, uses Facebook for new product development. Walkers strategically uses social media, such as Facebook, to host competitions for product ideas, then encourages fans to vote for their preferred options; finally fans can see the winning products which are launched via the social media platform. This takes product development into a game-changing environment: faster development, faster to market, faster results.

The third aspect of the Ansoff matrix is *market development*, which considers taking the existing products or services into new markets. There are many examples of social media being the launchpad for new markets. A good example is GoPro, a camera that people wear on their head while cycling, surfing or skydiving. This business started 12 years ago with one employee but today has over 1,400 employees. It accessed new markets via social media as its customers shared their real-life experiences via YouTube.

Diversification is defined by Ansoff as 'a simultaneous departure from the present product line and the present market structure.' One example of this is the traditional UK newsagent WHSmith, which diversified online to offer personalized gifts and greetings cards via a new brand called Funky Pigeon, a new offer to new customers that was publicized with its goods being promoted across the social spaces.

How is social media used by organizations?

Companies seeking to build relationships are now keen to use social media to engage with their customers (Powers *et al.*, 2012; Sashittal *et al.*, 2012). There are challenges in this endeavour, however, because according to Kaplan and Haenlein (2010: 60) on social media 'firms have been relegated to the sidelines as mere observers' and, as Kietzmann *et al.* (2011: 242) put it, 'corporate communication has been democratized'. Additionally, there is evidence for these trends from Fournier and Avery's (2011) important empirical research into a concept known as 'the uninvited brand', looking at how brands are not always welcome in a user's personal social media space. As a result, some brands have failed in their attempts to capture audience attention whereas others have succeeded (Gallaugher & Ransbotham, 2010; Labrecque, 2014).

Specific aspects of business operations where companies are using social media to attract, convert and engage customers include:

- brand
- customer
- marketing
- operations
- sales.

Table 6.3 shows the detail of the different elements of business use of social media and, while several researchers have identified specific areas, many agreed that using social media to promote brand was a key business focus.

Table 6.3 Business use of social media by theme

Core theme	Typical example	Example authors
Brand	Mentions brand name or specific product name	Pletikosa-Cvijikj & Michahelles (2013)
Customer	Conversation with customer providing service, information (includes compliments, comments and complaints)	Dobele et al. (2015)
Marketing	Request for feedback, marketing activity (event invite)	Aladwani (2015) Ngai et al. (2015)
Operations	Redirects customer to automated system, website link or third party to save money or time	Järvinen et al. (2012)
Sales	Sales message; buy now, offer, prices	Tsimonis & Dimitriadis (2014)

Customer service and social media

Customer service is a critical part of social media. As customers realized they could contact companies online to gain a faster response, companies had to adjust to provide this service (Gregoire *et al.*, 2015). An analysis of nearly 20,000 tweets from a selection of travel brands (the UK airline, British Airways; another UK airline, Virgin Atlantic; the US airline, JetBlue; rail operators Eurostar and the UK's London Midland; and the taxi service Uber) shows the most frequently used words are 'sorry' and 'please' as shown in Figure 6.4.

Figure 6.4 Word cloud showing most frequently used words when responding to customers

Karen Jones (2014) is conducting research into what happens when things go wrong on social media. She has commented: 'Through social media consumers are exerting a progressively profound influence on business, with various industries transforming the way they communicate with customers.' An example of this transformation is British Airways, which joined Twitter in 2008. The following case example looks at its evolution.

British Airways – case example

When British Airways joined Twitter in 2008, the description used on its Twitter biography simply informed the online visitor that they had discovered the official Twitter page of British Airways in the UK. It signposted the online visitor to an alternate page if they were in the USA. This demonstrated that this micro-blogging platform was not considered part of the strategic marketing communi-cations, simply a statement of existence, as illustrated in Figure 6.5. This is an example of a lack of management change to adopt and embrace social media, little ongoing management in the social media page, little authenticity and a failure to adapt to social media flow.

> Bio The official Twitterstream of British Airways in the UK. If you're in North America follow us @British Airways

Figure 6.5 British Airways Twitter page, 2008

The page description had evolved by two years' later, shown in Figure 6.6, as British Airways started signposting online visitors to other sources of informa-tion. At this stage it did not consider the possibility that online customers might have used Twitter for assistance or information. Once again, this use of social media was not as part of an integrated communication plan; its role was a route to other communications. However, this demonstrated an element of ongoing management as the firm gave the customer a little more information.

> For flights, holidays and more visit ba.com
> For worldwide contact numbers, go to ba.com/contactus
>
> You can also find us at:
>
> 🅱 @BritishAirways for North America
>
> You Tube youtube.com/flybritishairways

Figure 6.6 British Airways Twitter page, 2010

This use of Twitter by British Airways altered in 2013, when a single customer forced management change as they demanded more from the company's use of the social media network. This customer (known as @HVSVN) was unhappy when his luggage was lost and he could not achieve the desired response from the company. To gain redress he publicly described the poor customer service and lack of response. In each tweet he referenced British Airways' Twitter name. When no formal acknowledgement from British Airways was forthcoming, he spent $1,000 to purchase Twitter advertising and promoted his comments across Twitter. The comments gained widespread attention and raised fundamental questions about the use and management of social media for businesses.

This is an example of a customer disseminating information on a peer-to-peer basis. It also demonstrated that if a customer has a limited network (as discussed by Peters *et al.*, 2013) they can simply buy a wider network through paid-for advertising. This customer action, as shown in Figure 6.7, displayed how customers could commandeer the firm's public messages. The power had moved from company to user.

°¿° @HVSVN · 3 Sep 2013
@BritishAirways @British_Airways is the worst airline ever. Lost my luggage & can't even track it down. Absolutely pathetic #britishairways

British Airways @British_Airways · 3 Sep 2013
@HVSVN Sorry for the delay in responding, our twitter feed is open 0900-1700 GMT. Please DM your baggage ref and we'll look into this.

°¿° @HVSVN · 3 Sep 2013
@British_Airways how does a billion dollar corp only have 9-5 social media support for a business that operates 24/7? DM me yourselves.

↩ Reply ⇄ Retweet ★ Favorite ≋ Buffer ••• More

Figure 6.7 British Airways tweets and response, 2013

Following this customer communication, British Airways today better uses Twitter to manage its customer services, to provide messages, respond to user-generated content and monitor its online reputation. The latest evolution of the British Airways Twitter home page explains to customers, 'We love reading your tweets & are here 24 hours a day, 7 days a week to help.'

How is social media used by consumers?

Different groups of consumers use social media in different ways. A useful framework was developed by Kietzmann *et al.* (2011) who created 'functional building blocks' of social media as shown in Figure 6.8. They argued that each block allowed researchers to explore aspects of the social media experience. Blocks may not all be visible at the same time.

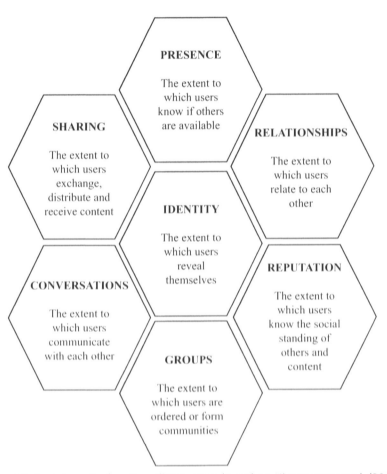

Figure 6.8 Social media functionality *Source*: based on Kietzmann *et al.* (2011)

- **Identity** may disclose information in professional platforms like LinkedIn and social platforms like Facebook, or anonymize details in secret social media platforms like YikYak.
- The **presence** element may not be a function of the platform; for example, within Twitter it is not possible to see if other users are present.
- **Relationships**, as connections, may be visible or invisible, depending on the platform as well as individual privacy settings. LinkedIn was constructed based

on the notion of sharing connections. Mark Granovetter (1973) discussed the concept of 'tie strength' based on our wider network. He suggested that weaker ties were often those that generated results in a job seeking environment. However, some users hide their connections within LinkedIn, which defeats the primary purpose of the platform.

- **Reputation** is another element which can be visible or hidden. LinkedIn is often a reputation sharing platform, disclosing qualifications and experience. This is less obvious on Twitter but can be ascertained by assessing a selection of content or exploring aspects of the brief biography. YouTube reputation is often based on the number of views and Instagram on the number of likes, even though likes and views can be bought, if not illegally, but through advertising on the sites to achieve the objective of 'more likes'.
- **Groups** is challenging as this is not a function available across all social media networks. For example, LinkedIn has many groups yet Twitter has not enabled this facility yet. To work around the lack of groups on Twitter, users group other users into 'lists' and several third-party applications have created group tools.
- **Sharing** and **conversations** depend on many factors. Lai and Chen (2014) have researched online communities and consider 'posters' – people who post content onto the site – and 'lurkers' – those visiting and viewing but not posting. Conversations between customer and company can include complaints, as we read in the British Airways example.

It is useful to understand how your audience is using social media platforms so that the content provided is appropriate and appreciated.

Research into social media

Unsurprisingly, social media has become an area of research for many scholars. Table 6.4 shows some examples of research into social media. There are many more researchers exploring different aspects of social media. As social media is a constantly evolving area, the easiest way to stay ahead is to attend relevant conferences and discover what's new.

The dark side of social media

While there are many benefits of social media, there is also a dark side. From trolls to stalking, from hacking to misuse of personal data, social media has demonstrated that bad things happen online too.

The sociologist Daniel Miller conducted a longitudinal research project over 15 months in different global locations with many researchers, to look at *How the world changed social media* (Miller *et al.*, 2016). He identified different aspects of troll behaviour and how and when this happens, as well as the use of

Table 6.4 Examples of research into social media

Research area	Exploring	Selected references
Identity	Facebook and identity	Hollenbeck & Kaikati (2012)
	Facebook fan types	Wallace *et al.* (2014)
	Consumer privacy	Venkatesh (2016)
Brand	Managing brands online	Gensler *et al.* (2013)
	Use of Twitter by brands	Watne, Cheong & Turner (2014)
Selling	Social commerce	Yadav *et al.* (2013)
	Firm generated content and sales	Kumar *et al.* (2016)
Engagement	Use of Twitter with students	Barn (2016)
	Content type and impact	Pletikosa-Cvijikj & Michahelles (2013)
Strategy	Framework to evaluate social media strategies	Effing & Spill (2016)

social media for negative purposes, such as where young people share indecent images of themselves among a group but this can be subsequently shared, outside the group, in a practice known as 'revenge porn'. This misuse of personal data (considering that a personal image is a piece of data) has grown with the 'self-destruct' platforms such as Snapchat, where an image appears and is said to be erased automatically within 10 seconds. There appears to be some security in the knowledge that an inappropriate image will disappear and therefore has less of an effect in the long term.

At the same time, while a negative impact of social media occurs, researchers are working to offer a counter-balance. For example, researchers at Stanford and Cornell are developing 'troll identification' software (Cheng *et al.*, 2015). This could be used by online community managers to identify at an early stage potential troll behaviour and to subsequently monitor and take action as needed.

The future of social media

Since the first social media network was established in 1996, we have seen several networks come and go or become consumed by other platforms. This will continue. Those platforms that have evolved into behemothic structures with external shareholders, such as Facebook and Twitter, will carry on. However, they will need to adapt to meet the ever-changing needs of the consumer. This means Facebook and Twitter work in an environment of constant change, often driven by a combination of access to technology and the behaviour of their newer competitors. Snapchat offered its advertisers 'vertical video views' and Facebook met this with the ability for its advertisers to create Facebook Canvas, a vertical story about their brand. The challenge for business is staying ahead in a fast-moving environment and ensuring they continue to meet the needs of their users.

FURTHER READING

Boyd, D. M. & Ellison, N. B. (2007) Social network sites: definition, history and scholarship. *Journal of Computer-Mediated Communication*, **13** (1), 210–230.

Effing, R. & Spill, A. M. T. (2016) The social strategy cone: towards a framework for evaluating social media strategies. *International Journal of Information Management*, **36** (1), 1–8.

Fournier, S. & Avery, J. (2011) The uninvited brand. *Business Horizons*, **54** (3), 193–207.

Miller, D., Costa, E., Haynes, N., McDonald, T., Nicolescu, R., Sinanan, J., Spyer, J., Wang, X., Venkatraman, S. & Wang, X. (2016) *How The World Changed Social Media*. UCL Press: London. www.ucl.ac.uk/ucl-press/browse-books/how-world-changed-social-media, accessed 20 May 2017.

Resources to stay ahead in social media

Facebook:

- www.insidefacebook.com
- www.facebook.com/business/resources
- http://newsroom.fb.com

Twitter:

- https://business.twitter.com

Instagram:

- https://help.instagram.com

References

Aladwani, A.M. (2015) Facilitators, characteristics and impacts of Twitter use: theoretical analysis and empirical illustration. *International Journal of Information Management*, **35** (1), 15–25.

Ansoff, H. (1957) Strategies for diversification. *Harvard Business Review*, **35** (5), September/October, 113–124. http://shr.receptidocs.ru/docs/1/509/conv_1/file1.pdf, accessed 18 October 2014.

Badenhausen, K. (2013) The world's most valuable brands. www.forbes.com/powerful-brands/#page:5_sort:0_direction:asc_search:, accessed 20 October 2014.

Barden, B. (2014) *A Beginner's Guide to Google Analytics*. Available at www.benbarden.com/downloads/Ben_Barden_-_A_Beginners_Guide_to_Google_Analytics.pdf, accessed 19 May 2017.

Barn, S. S. (2016) 'Tweet dreams are made of this, who are we to disagree?' Adventures in a #Brave New World of #tweets, #Twitter, #student engagement and #excitement with #learning. *Journal of Marketing Management*, **1376** (May), 1–22.

Baudrillard, J. (1983) *Simulations*. Semiotext(e): New York.

Benjamin, W. (1955/2004) *The Arcades Project* (H. Eiland & K. McLaughlin, trans.). Belknap Press: Cambridge, MA.

Boyd, D. M. & Ellison, N. B. (2007) Social network sites: definition, history and scholarship. *Journal of Computer-Mediated Communication*, **13** (1), 210–230.

Brady, M., Saren, M. & Tzokas, N. (2002) Integrating information technology into marketing practice: the IT reality of contemporary marketing practice. *Journal of Marketing Management*, **18** (5/6, July), 555–578.

Brennan, R. (2006) Evolutionary economics and the markets-as-networks approach. *Industrial Marketing Management*, **35** (7), 829–838.

Cheng, J., Danescu-Niculescu-Mizil, C. & Leskovec, J. (2015) Antisocial behavior in online discussion communities. In: *Ninth International AAAI Conference on Web and Social Media*. Oxford, UK, 61–70.

Christopher, M. (1997) *Marketing Logistics*. Butterworth-Heinemann: Oxford.

Christopher, M. (2000) The agile supply chain: competing in volatile markets. *Industrial Marketing Management*, **29** (1), 37–44.

Chung, C. J., Inaba, J. & Koolhaas, R. (2001) *Harvard Design School Guide to Shopping*. Taschen: New York.

Clarke, D. & Purvis, M. (1994) Dialectics, difference and the geographies of consumption. *Environment and Planning A*, **26**, 1091–1109.

Davenport, T. (2014). *Big Data at Work: Dispelling the Myths, Uncovering the Opportunities*. Harvard Business Review Press: Cambridge, MA.

Disney Institute & Kinni, T. (2011) Be our guest: perfecting the art of customer service. 8 November, Disney Editions.

Dobele, A., Steel, M. & Cooper, T. (2015) Sailing the seven Cs of blog marketing: understanding social media and business impact. *Marketing Intelligence & Planning*, **33** (7).

Effing, R. & Spill, A. M. T. (2016) The social strategy cone: towards a framework for evaluating social media strategies. *International Journal of Information Management*, **36** (1), 1–8.

Fournier, S. & Avery, J. (2011) The uninvited brand. *Business Horizons*, **54** (3), 193–207.

Gallaugher, J. & Ransbotham, S. (2010) Social media and customer dialog management at Starbucks. *MIS Quarterly Executive*, **9** (4), 197–212.

Gensler, S., Völckner, F., Liu-Thompkins, Y. & Wiertz, C. (2013) Managing brands in the social media environment. *Journal of Interactive Marketing*, **27** (4), 242–256.

Giddens, A. (1990) *The Consequences of Modernity*. Polity: Cambridge.

Granovetter, M. S. (1973) The strength of weak ties. *American Journal of Sociology*, **78** (6), 1360–1380.

Gregoire, Y., Salle, A. & Tripp, T. M. (2015) Managing social media crises with your customers: the good, the bad and the ugly. *Business Horizons*, **58** (2), 173–182.

Grönroos, C. (1989) Defining marketing: a market-oriented approach. *European Journal of Marketing*, **23** (1), 52–60.

Hollenbeck, C. R. & Kaikati, A. M. (2012) Consumers' use of brands to reflect their actual and ideal selves on Facebook. *International Journal of Research in Marketing*, **29** (4), 395–405.

Ingram, J. (2005) *Theatre of the Mind*. Harper Collins: Canada.

Järvinen, J., Tollinen, A., Karjaluoto, H. & Jayawardhena, C. (2012) Digital and social media marketing usage in B2B industrial section. *Marketing Management Journal*, **22** (2), 102–117.

Jones, K. (2014) Social media enabled service failure identification and recovery: in the UK and Irish retail sector. In: *47th Academy of Marketing Conference*. Bournemouth, 7–10 July: Academy of Marketing.

Kaplan, A.M. & Haenlein, M. (2010) Users of the world, unite! The challenges and opportunities of social media. *Business Horizons*, **53** (1), 59–68.

Kent, M. L. (2015) Social media circa 2035: directions in social media theory. *Atlantic Journal of Communication*, **23** (1), 1–4.

Kietzmann, J. H., Hermkens, K., McCarthy, I. P. & Silvestre, B. S. (2011) Social media? Get serious! Understanding the functional building blocks of social media. *Business Horizons*, **54** (3), 241–251.

Kotler, P., Keller, K., Brady, M., Goodman, M. & Hansen, T. (2016) *Marketing Management*. Pearson: London.

Kumar, A., Bezawada, R., Rishika, R., Janakiraman, R. & Kannan, P. K. (2016) From social to sale: the Effects of firm-generated content in social media on customer behavior. *Journal of Marketing*, **80** (1), 7–25.

Labrecque, L. I. (2014) Fostering consumer–brand relationships in social media environments: the role of parasocial interaction. *Journal of Interactive Marketing*, **28** (2), 134–148.

Lai, H. M. & Chen, T. T. (2014) Knowledge sharing in interest online communities: a comparison of posters and lurkers. *Computers in Human Behavior*, **35**, 295–306.

Mafessoli, M. (1996) *The Time of the Tribes: The Decline of Individualism in Mass Society* (D. Smith, trans.). Sage: London.

Massumi, B. (1992) *A User's Guide to Capitalism and Schizophrenia: Deviations from Deleauze & Guattari*. Swerve: London.

Miller, D., Costa, E., Haynes, N., McDonald, T., Nicolescu, R., Sinanan, J., Spyer, J., Wang, X., Venkatraman, S. & Wang, X. (2016) *How The World Changed Social Media*. UCL Press: London. www.ucl.ac.uk/ucl-press/browse-books/how-world-changed-social-media, accessed 20 May 2017.

Morey, T., Forbath, T. & Schoop, A. (2015) Customer data: designing for transparency and trust. *Harvard Business Review*, May.

Ngai, E. W. T., Moon, K. L. K., Lam, S. S., Chin, E. S. K. & Tao, S. S. C. (2015) Social media models, technologies and applications: an academic review and case study. *Industrial Management and Data Systems*, **115** (5), 769–802.

Ofcom (2014) Cost and value of communications services in the UK. http://stake holders.ofcom.org.uk/binaries/research/consumer-experience/tce-13/cost_value_final.pdf

Peacock, P. (1998) Data mining in marketing: part 1. *Marketing Management*, **6** (4), 8–18.

Peters, K., Chen, Y., Kaplan, A.M., Ognibeni, B. & Pauwels, K. (2013) Social media metrics: a framework and guidelines for managing social media. *Journal of Interactive Marketing*, **27** (4), 281–298.

Pew Internet (2014) Mobile technology fact sheet. www.pewinternet.org/fact-sheets/mobile-technology-fact-sheet/, accessed 20 October 2014.

Pletikosa-Cvijikj, I. & Michahelles, F. (2013) Online engagement factors on Facebook brand pages. *Social Network Analysis and Mining*, **3** (4), 843–861.

Porter, M. & Heppelmann, E. (2015) How smart connected products are transforming companies. *Harvard Business Review*, October, 97–114.

Powers, T., Advincula, D., Austin, M. S., Graiko, S. & Snyder, J. (2012) Digital and social media in the purchase-decision process: a special report from the advertising research foundation. *Journal of Advertising Research*, **52** (4), 479–490.

Reilly, W. J. (1931) *The Law of Retail Gravitation*. University of Texas: Austin, TX.

Rust, R., Moorman, C. & Bhalla, G. (2010) Rethinking marketing. *Harvard Business Review*, January/February.

Sashittal, H. C., Sriramachandramurthy, R. & Hodis, M. (2012) Targeting college students on Facebook? How to stop wasting your money. *Business Horizons*, **55** (5), 495–507.

Storbacka, K. & Nenonen, S. (2011) Scripting markets: from value propositions to market propositions. *Industrial Marketing Management*, **40**, 255–266.

de Swaan, A.M., van den Driest, F. & Weed, K. (2014) The ultimate marketing machine. *Harvard Business Review*, July/August, 55–63.

Tsimonis, G. & Dimitriadis, S. (2014) Brand strategies in social media. *Marketing Intelligence & Planning*, **32**, 328–344.

Venkatesh, A. (2016) Social media, digital self and privacy: a socio-analytical perspective of the consumer as the digital avatar. *Journal of the Association for Consumer Research*, **1** (3).

Wallace, E., Buil, I., de Chernatony, L. & Hogan, M. (2014) Who 'likes' you . . . and why? A typology of facebook fans: from 'fan'-atics and self-expressives to utilitarians and authentics. *Journal of Advertising Research*, **54** (1), 92–109.

Watne, T. A., Cheong, M. & Turner, W. (2014) #Brand or @user ? How Australian 'mass brewers' and 'craft brewers' communicate with consumers through Twitter. In: *47th Academy of Marketing Conference*. Bournemouth, 7–10 July: Academy of Marketing.

Yadav, M. S., de Valck, K., Hennig-Thurau, T., Hoffman, D. L. & Spann, M. (2013) Social commerce: a contingency framework for assessing marketing potential. *Journal of Interactive Marketing*, **27**, 3.

Note: Page numbers in **bold** type refer to **figures**
Page number in *italic* type refer to *tables*
Page numbers followed by 'n' refer to notes